Money, Finance and Capitalist Development

Money, Finance and Capitalist Development

Edited by

Philip Arestis

Professor of Economics, South Bank University London, UK

Malcolm Sawyer

Professor of Economics, University of Leeds, UK

Edward Elgar

Cheltenham, UK • Northampton, MA, USA

Published by
Edward Elgar Publishing Limited
Glensanda House
Montpellier Parade
Cheltenham
Glos GL50 1UA
UK

Edward Elgar Publishing, Inc.
136 West Street
Suite 202
Northampton
Massachusetts 01060
USA

A catalogue record for this book is available from the British Library

Library of Congress Cataloguing in Publication Data

Money, finance and capitalist development / edited by Philip Arestis, Malcolm
C. Sawyer.
    p. cm.
  Includes bibliographical references and index.
  1. Finance. 2. Money. 3. Keynesian economics. 4. Capitalism. I. Arestis, Philip,
  1941– II. Sawyer, Malcolm C.
HG173.M6355 2001
332—dc21   2001023729

ISBN 1 84064 598 9

Printed and bound in Great Britain by MPG Books Ltd, Bodmin, Cornwall

Contents

Figures and tables

FIGURES

TABLES

Contributors

Philip Arestis, South Bank University London, UK
John Cornwall, Department of Economics, Dalhousie University, Halifax, Canada
Wendy Cornwall, Department of Economics, Mount Saint Vincent University, Halifax, Canada
Jim Crotty, University of Massachusetts, Amherst, USA
Gary Dymski, Department of Economics, University of California, Riverside, USA
Peter Howells, Department of Economics, University of East London, UK
Costas Lapavitsas, Department of Economics, School of Oriental and African Studies, London, UK
Malcolm Sawyer, University of Leeds, UK
Jan Toporowski, South Bank University London, UK

Preface

This book of essays, based on contributions which have already appeared (but revised and updated) in the *International Papers in Political Economy*, seeks to contribute a critical analysis of the financial sector in view of its economic and political importance. We wish to thank all the contributors to this volume and to the issues of *International Papers in Political Economy*. Without their support this and other volumes, based on the *International Papers in Political Economy*, would never see the light of the day. Edward Elgar and Dymphna Evans have been excellent publishers. We wish to thank them for their continuous encouragement and close collaboration on this and, of course, on many other projects. As always we are grateful to both of them and their staff.

1. Money, finance and capitalist development

Philip Arestis and Malcolm Sawyer

INTRODUCTION

There can be little doubt that the financial sector is much more important now than it was even 20 or 30 years ago. This is not to deny that the financial sector has always been central to capitalism, but rather to point to its increased importance over the period. This importance may be seen in the growth of financial services through to the rapidly increasing flows across the foreign exchanges. The statistics on this account are staggering,

> no other good or service has witnessed similar rates of growth in the period 1980–97. The value of financial service exports has increased almost fivefold; over the same period, growth in trading manufactured goods has only tripled. Interestingly, financial services are ahead even compared with major areas of growth in international trade, such as telecommunications/information technology (IT) and travel. (Seifert et al., 2000, p. 51)

Employment in the financial sector has also generally increased substantially. This era has also been outstanding in terms of increased financial flows across the foreign exchanges (with increases of the order of 50 per cent each three years: see Arestis and Sawyer, 1997), with the inevitable feature that a much decreased proportion of the exchange of one currency for another is linked to trade or to long-term direct investment, and a much increased proportion has been short-term financial movements seeking out higher financial returns or seeking to gain from movements in the exchange rates. In the past three decades, during the period of rapid growth of the importance of finance (going alongside the liberalization and deregulation of the financial sector), there has been much slower economic growth across the globe as compared with the quarter of a century ending in 1973 (the 'golden age of capitalism'). There have also been dramatic financial crises, which have impacted on living standards and employment.

Chapter 2 by Cornwall and Cornwall addresses the issue of the broad determinants of capitalist development, whilst Crotty and Dymski in Chapter 3 review the causes of the East Asian financial and economic crisis of 1997–98. Toporowski focuses on the (increasing) role of financial derivatives in Chapter 4, conventionally seen as a way of offsetting risk. In contrast, Toporowski sees them as uncertainty increasing rather than risk decreasing. There has been an increasing trend across the world for both an increased emphasis on monetary policy (at the expense of fiscal policy) operated by an 'independent' (of democratic influence) Central Bank in pursuit of the objective of low inflation. The next three chapters that follow relate to this phenomenon.

CAPITALIST DEVELOPMENT AND FINANCE

Chapter 2 by John Cornwall and Wendy Cornwall provides a general framework for the analysis of the long-run macrodynamics of capitalist economies. Their framework has many aspects but two central elements, as suggested in the title of their chapter, namely the role of aggregate demand and the role of institutions. Aggregate demand does not only determine the rate of unemployment, but also its rate of growth strongly influences the growth of output and productivity. Further, the growth of aggregate demand impacts on the distribution of income and output (for example between sectors) and induces structural changes on the supply side. Structural change includes changes to institutions, which are defined as 'the beliefs, customs, laws, rules and conventions that govern the behaviour of individuals and groups within society' (p. 15 of this volume). The authors apply their framework to the broad sweep of postwar economic history tracing through the origins and nature of the 'golden age' (the quarter century or so ending in the early 1970s), the move from the golden age to 'the age of decline'. The high levels of unemployment generally experienced since the early 1970s (despite declines in some countries during the 1990s) is seen as reinforced by 'institutional changes which have reinforced the already depressed economic conditions' (p. 42 of this volume). Two institutional changes stand out, both of which have increased the use of restrictive aggregate demand policies. The first is the new forms of hysteresis in labour markets, which the authors view as increasing the rate of inflation under low unemployment conditions. The second is the breakdown of the Bretton Woods agreement, the move to a flexible exchange rate system and the increasing deregulation of international capital movements. The authors argue that 'under this new regime the inflation costs are increased in any economy that depreciates its currency as part of a stimulative, aggregate demand package' (p. 43 of this volume).

The end of the Bretton Woods regime of fixed exchange rates in 1971/72 gave way to a regime of largely floating (market determined) exchange rates, overlaid with attempts to operate quasi-fixed exchange rates (for example within the European Exchange Rate Mechanism with fixed parities amongst member currencies subject to relatively wide bands). The volatility of exchange rates in this era is well known. Movements of exchange rates of the order of 25 per cent within a single year are commonplace. The post-Bretton Woods period has seen many substantial financial crises which have often imposed large costs on the people in the economies suffering the crisis with rising unemployment and poverty and falling real incomes. The crises in Mexico of 1982 and then in 1994 are amongst the best-known examples. The most recent major ones have been the East Asian crisis of 1997, and the Russian and Brazilian crises of 1998/99. Numerous explanations were advanced for the crisis and its rapid spread between the economies of East Asia.

One group of explanations can be described as focusing on a 'flawed microfoundational mechanism of the "Asian model"' (Crotty and Dymski, p. 54 of this volume). These included charges of 'crony capitalism', or the results of implicit government guarantees on loans which led to risky lending (see, for example, McKinnon and Pill, 1997).[1] Another group of explanations focused on national and international macroeconomic and financial conditions. These included a focus on the effects of foreign loans denominated in dollars on the local economies when the local currency was forced to devalue against the dollar. James Crotty and Gary Dymski argue that whilst these explanations have merit, the crisis did not arise from any of these explanations acting by itself. Instead they see the crisis as arising 'simultaneously as a conflict between international and national forces, on the one hand, and as localized struggles between capital and labour, on the other' (p. 54 of this volume). They also explore the shift from the golden age to a post-early 1970s era, which they describe as the 'global neoliberal regime'. They also consider the 'myths and reality' of the East Asian model. But their analysis places considerable emphasis on the large flows of short-term foreign capital that flooded into the Korean economy as it was liberalized in the mid 1990s. However, the authors attempt to investigate the deeper structures which lie underneath the unstable cross-border financial flows. They point to the structure of the global economic regime within which these financial flows occur. They argue that 'a complete understanding of the causes and consequences of the Asian crisis, encompassing ultimate as well as proximate causes, requires an investigation of the basic contradictions of the global Neoliberal regime' (p. 87 of this volume).[2]

The financial markets necessarily operate in an uncertain environment, where uncertainty is distinguished from risk and refers to the essential unknowability of the future. Yet the literature on finance is dominated by the view that the future is risky rather than uncertain, that is there is a frequency distribution which governs the returns from each financial investment (of which the mean and the variance are taken to be the important parameters). Further, the development of financial futures including derivatives appear 'as a spontaneous and ardently competitive set of markets' projecting a web of certain prices into an uncertain future, banishing the uncertainty that is the black hole in inter-temporal general equilibrium' (Toporowski, p. 102 of this volume). Jan Toporowski in Chapter 4 argues that the operation of financial futures can operate to increase the degree of uncertainty, rather than the more conventional perception that financial futures help to reduce risk. Toporowski argues that the conventional analysis of financial futures instruments, which is based on perfect competition, is not consistent with the rationale for these markets in terms of projecting values which are certain onto an uncertain future. The emergence of different types of agents (industrial and commercial companies, banks or brokers, and investment funds) along with financial stability and large capital inflows into financial markets help to account for the rapid expansion of financial futures. The chapter seeks to advance a simple way of regulating the trading of derivatives, and examines the financial fragility associated with the derivatives markets. Toporowski argues that the ultimate challenge to financial derivatives is presented by instability in financial markets. The conventional view would be that growing financial instability would lead to increasing use of financial derivatives to hedge against instability. In contrast, Toporowski argues that there should be pessimism on the prospects for financial futures. He concludes that in time 'financial futures [will be seen] less as a class of financial innovations that secures us all against financial instability, and more as peripheral, speculative markets that flourished in the era of finance at the end of the twentieth century' (p. 131 of this volume).

MONEY AND THE CLASSICAL DICHOTOMY

The financial system, notably in the form of banks, provides loans and bank credit, which enables the expansion of expenditure to be financed. The expansion of expenditure and thereby of the economy depends crucially on the granting of bank credit. The banks are then at the heart of the credit and monetary system. This simple, and rather obvious, statement is closely linked to the nature of money. The monetarist 'story' has long been that an expansion of the money stock (rather misleadingly labelled money supply) leads to 'excess' money (there being more money than people wish to hold) which in turn leads to spending which bids up output and then prices. With the addition of the assumption that output will tend to be at a 'natural' (equilibrium) level set by the supply potential of the economy, it follows that the expansion of the stock of money leads to rising prices. The 'natural' level of output corresponds to the 'natural rate of unemployment' (Friedman, 1968).

The separation between the real side of the economy and the monetary/financial side of the economy has often been referred to as the 'classical dichotomy'. This permits the idea that the supply-side forces (interaction of the demand and supply for goods and services) determine the level of output and employment (and indeed the allocation of output and employment between different sectors of the economy). The level of aggregate demand is portrayed as sufficient to ensure that the available supply is demanded and bought (Say's Law). The monetary side (which is also identified with the demand side in that the level of demand is dependent on the real value of the money stock) is instrumental in the determination of the level of prices, and hence changes in the stock of money lead to changes in prices (inflation).

The 'natural rate of unemployment' (the NRU) is a terminology still in use (especially on the American side of the Atlantic), though many would now draw on the concept of the non-accelerating inflation rate of unemployment (NAIRU) as the supply-side equilibrium. The NRU and the NAIRU share many common features, notably that both are supply-side equilibrium concepts with departure of unemployment from those levels involving accelerating inflation (if unemployment is below the NRU or the NAIRU) or accelerating deflation (if unemployment is above the NRU or the NAIRU).

Friedman (1958) used the 'story' of dollar bills being dropped from a helicopter, picked up by individuals who now feel better off. These lucky individuals then proceeded to spend these dollar bills, bidding up output and then prices. The term 'helicopter money' has often been used to sum up this story. It is a useful story in so far as it vividly illustrates the nature of money as envisaged in the monetarist thesis. It comes into existence in an exogenous manner in that individuals finding the dollar bills may be glad, but had not sought them out or expected them to come into existence. The individuals did not have to give up anything to procure these dollar bills nor did they have to make promises to repay in the future.

In the world in which most of us live, money is not at all like this. The vast majority of trade is not financed by dollar bills, pound notes, euro notes (or whatever cash is), but rather by the transfer from one bank account to another (whether through the writing of a cheque, electronic transfer or other means). A deposit is moved from one bank account to another. Money is largely or entirely credit money. Money is simultaneously an asset (deposit held by non-bank public) and a liability (of the bank). Money comes into existence when a bank grants a loan and the loan is spent and arises as a deposit in the bank account of the recipient. Money goes out of existence when a loan is repaid and the corresponding deposit destroyed. Loans are usually taken out because the lender wishes to spend the loan and are made by banks because the banks judge them to be profitable. Banks can make more or less loans depending on their perception of the rewards and risks involved: individuals can take out more or less loans depending on their plans to spend (including acquiring assets) and their ability to repay the loan.

The differences between the monetarist approach and the one that has just been sketched can be described in terms of exogenous versus endogenous money – whether the money is created outside of the private sector or created within the private sector (through the actions of banks and the public). Debates over these issues can be traced back to at least the early nineteenth century with the debates between the bullionists and the anti-bullionists, and later with the currency school and the banking school. However, as Chick (1992) argued, the banking system changes over time and can be viewed as proceeding through a number of stages. The analysis of this paper is based on the view that the banking system in industrialized countries has reached stage 5 in Chick's terminology, where (changes in) the demand for loans leads to changes in the amount of loans, which generates (changes in) deposits, which in turn cause (changes in) reserves. In recent years, the analysis of endogenous money has become particularly associated with post Keynesian economics where there has been considerable debate on the specific nature of endogenous money (Moore, 1988; Cottrell, 1994: Arestis and Howell, 1996; and drawing on the circuitist approach, Graziani, 1989).

In Chapter 5 Peter Howells reviews the present state of the thesis that money is endogenous. The central idea of the endogeneity thesis is 'that the money supply is determined by the demand for bank lending' (Howells, p. 134 of this volume) which in turn depends on the 'state of trade'. The endogeneity of money provides a direct refutation of the Quantity Theory of Money by reversing the direction of causation between the stock of money and the level of nominal income, and the endogeneity approach views causation running from nominal income to money stock, and specifically views inflation as the cause of expansion of money stock (rather than the reverse).

There have been, though, many debates and differences of analysis and of emphasis amongst those who broadly adopt the endogenous money approach. In his chapter, Howells pays particular attention to the more contentious aspects of the endogeneity thesis. He draws a contrast between endogeneity and exogeneity before proceeding to review the question as to whether the endogeneity of money is a feature of particular stages in the evolution of the banking system (or whether money has, in some sense, always been endogenous) The chapter then moves on to look at the question of why reserves (from the Central Bank) appear to be always available to validate whatever growth of loans and deposits occurs to 'meet the needs of trade'.

It is generally observed that the Central Bank sets the key discount rate (which may go under a number of names, for example Bank Rate, 'repo' rate) and that other interest rates generally move in sympathy with that key discount rate. How exactly the mark-up of, for example, the rate of interest on loans over the discount rate and the mark-down of the rate of interest on deposits is set, is not so obvious. The notion that money is endogenous has been given the simple representation of a horizontal supply curve, in contrast to the vertical supply curve of the exogenous money (in both cases the supply curve is drawn in the quantity of money, interest rate plane). Howells questions whether what has been drawn as a horizontal supply curve is really a supply curve at all. The chapter concludes by reviewing the debates over the mechanisms which bring decisions to lend money (reflected in loans) and decisions to hold deposits (demand for money) into reconciliation. Loans and deposits are the major items on the two sides of bank balance sheets. Loans bring money into existence, but money remains in existence only if someone willingly holds it (rather than uses it to repay loans). A variety of mechanisms have been proposed for bringing loans and deposits into equality with one another.

The 'monetarist experiment' in the form of controlling or targeting the growth of the stock of money to control the rate of inflation ended in failure and was relatively quickly abandoned. For example, monetary targeting was adopted in the UK in the mid 1970s and dropped in the mid 1980s: in the US it was adopted in 1979 only to be dropped in August 1981. The chosen stock of money proved difficult or impossible to control, targets were often missed, and the supposed empirical links between growth of money and growth of prices went awry. For the believer in exogenous money, this failure may have been failure of will by the Central Bank or monetary authorities to impose monetary discipline (or may have been due to treachery by Central Bankers: see, for example, Friedman, 1980). For those who could see that money is endogenous, there was no surprise. The stock of money will grow at any target rate if the demand for money grows at that rate, which depends on what is happening to prices, real incomes and the propensity to hold money.

Two significant shifts in monetary policy have occurred in a wide range of countries in the past two decades. The first was a general shift to the more explicit use of the Central Bank discount rate as the major (or sole) form of monetary policy. The second was making the Central Bank independent – that is independent of political control. Alongside this 'independence', the Central Bank (or a part of, such as the Monetary Policy Committee of the Bank of England in the case of the UK) was given the single objective of low inflation or price stability. These two are combined to give the view that the discount rate (which then influences the general spectrum of interest rates) is the instrument to be used in pursuit of the objective of low inflation. One instrument, one objective. The justification for this is that monetary policy is appropriate for the control of inflation, and the level of unemployment is determined on the real side of the economy in line with the classical dichotomy at the NAIRU. We return to a discussion of the NAIRU below.

This approach is predicated on a series of dubious premises. The first is the idea that the single objective of monetary policy should be the rate of inflation, without regard to the consequences for employment, investment, foreign trade (via the exchange rate), or any other real variable. The second is that the rate of interest is an appropriate and effective instrument for influencing the rate of inflation. The argument appears to be that the rate of interest will influence the level of aggregate demand (consumer expenditure, investment and so on) which in turn influences the rate of inflation. Each of those links is, at most, a weak one, and high interest rates can readily have long-lasting adverse effects. If high interest rates are effective in reducing investment, then there are long-lasting consequences on productive capacity and future possibilities for non-inflationary high levels of employment (Sawyer, 2000). If high interest rates put upward pressure on the exchange rate, there will be effects on export demand.

The third is that an 'independent' Central Bank will establish greater credibility in the eyes of the financial markets that the objective of low inflation will be pursued. It is argued that bankers have a reputation for being 'conservative' in the sense of placing greater weight on low inflation and less weight on high levels of employment than most politicians and others. Inflationary expectations are lower (than otherwise) enabling low inflation to be more readily realized (see, Forder, 2000, for a fuller discussion).

Costas Lapavitsas in Chapter 6 analyses the political economy of central banks and asks whether these banks are agents of stability or sources of instability. He argues that 'the recent theoretical emphasis on the role of the central bank in the financial system orchestrates its significance' (p. 179 of this volume) as there are narrow limits constraining the effectiveness of central bank operations which are placed by the demands and requirements of capital accumulation. The capitalist economy involves financial and economic instability, which cannot be abolished by the central bank, no matter what objectives the central bankers pursue (or are instructed to pursue), their experience or the economic thinking which influences their decisions.

Lapavitsas concludes that central bank independence is a 'deeply problematic notion in theory and practice' (p. 000 of this volume). The credit system has a central bank to underpin credit money through the provision of reserves for the banking system. The central bank is forced to supervise the credit system and to lend reserves in times of financial distress. But there are limits to what the central bank can do as the provision of credit is linked with seeking to foresee an unknowable and uncertain future, occurring within the anarchy of the underlying process of capital accumulation. A central bank holds 'an organic position in the financial system' (p. 200 of this volume), and cannot be independent of either the state or of the private sector. The present trend towards Central Bank 'independence' is seen as a response to the monetary instability of the post-Bretton Woods world. However, financial innovation in the generation of credit money set limits to the ability of the central bank to pursue price stability.

The other part of the 'monetarist' story has been the NRU (and the NAIRU) as mentioned above. In Chapter 7 Malcolm Sawyer presents a detailed critique of the concept of the NAIRU. He points out that there are many different formulations of price and wage determination which go to form an economic model for which the NAIRU is an equilibrium solution. Nevertheless, these models have sufficient similarity to be able to discuss their common features. The focus of the chapter is on the question of whether there is a level of unemployment for which inflation would be constant and, if so, what are the determinants of that level of unemployment. In particular, is any such level of unemployment to be regarded as capable of being shifted through changes in the capital stock, measures to arrive at a consensus over the distribution of income and so on. There is little consideration of aggregate demand in connection with the NAIRU. Aggregate demand has to be considered in deriving relationships between the real wage and employment, and in underpinning any level of employment (equilibrium or not) which could be achieved. Further, aggregate demand enters into the determination of the level of unemployment in two further respects, namely through its effect on capacity and in a range of cases where the relationship between price and wage is settled at the enterprise level. The basic arguments pursued in the chapter are that there are a series of theoretical weaknesses with the approach to the NAIRU, and in particular there has been a rather cavalier dismissal of the role of aggregate demand. Specifically, if the notion is that for some given set of institutional and other arrangements there is a level of unemployment which would be consistent with constant unemployment, then it is necessary to explore the determinants of that level of unemployment, and the degree to which it can be shifted over time with appropriate aggregate demand, income distributional and supply-side policies.

NOTES

1. See Chang (1999) for a detailed critique of this approach.
2. See Robinson Group (1999) for proposals for the reform of the world financial system.

REFERENCES

Arestis, P. and Howells, P. (1996), 'Theoretical reflections on endogenous money: the problem with "convenience lending"', *Cambridge Journal of Economics,* **20** (5).
Arestis, P. and Sawyer, M. (1997), 'How many cheers for the Tobin financial transactions tax?', *Cambridge Journal of Economics*, **21** (6), 753–68.
Chang, H.-J. (1999), 'The over-borrowing syndrome: structural reforms, institutional failure and exuberant expectations: a critique of McKinnon and Pill'. *World Development,* **27**.
Chick, V. (1992), 'The Evolution of the Banking System and the Theory of Saving, Investment and Interest', in P. Arestis and S. Dow (eds), *On Money Method and Keynes: Essays of Victoria Chick*, London: Macmillan.
Cottrell, A. (1994), 'Post-Keynesian monetary economics, *Cambridge Journal of Economics*, **18** (6), 587–606.
Forder, J. (2000), 'The theory of credibility: confusions, limitations, and dangers', *International Papers in Political Economy*, **7** (2).
Friedman, M. (1958), 'The Supply of Money and Changes in Prices and Output', in Joint Economic Committee, *The Relationship of Prices to Economic Activity and Growth*, Washington, DC: US Government Printing Office. Reprinted in M. Friedman (1969), *The Optimum Quantity of Money, and Other Essays*, London: Macmillan.
Friedman, M. (1968), 'The Role of Monetary Policy', *American Economic Review*, **58** (1).
Friedman, M. (1980), *Memorandum to the House of Commons Select Committee on the Treasury and Civil Service: Monetary Policy*, HC720, London: HMSO.
Graziani, A. (1989), 'The theory of the monetary circuit', *Thames Papers in Political Economy*, Spring 1989.
McKinnon. R.I. and Pill, H. (1997), 'Credible economic liberalisations and over-borrowing', *American Economic Review, Papers and Proceedings*, May, 189–203.
Moore, B. (1988), *Horizontalists and Verticalists, the Macroeconomics of Credit Money*, Cambridge: Cambridge University Press.
Robinson Group (1999), 'An agenda for a new Bretton Woods', *International Papers in Political Economy*, **6** (1).
Sawyer, M. (2000), 'The NAIRU, aggregate demand, and investment', University of Leeds, mimeo.
Seifert, W.G., Achleitner, A.-K., Mattern, F., Streit, C.C. and Voth, H.-J. (2000), *European Capital Markets*, Basingstoke: Macmillan Press Ltd.

2. An evolutionary–Keynesian analysis of capitalist performance

John Cornwall and Wendy Cornwall[1]

2.1. ALTERNATIVE FRAMEWORKS

Over the course of this century, the records of the currently advanced capitalist economies reveal two outstanding characteristics of macroeconomic development. First, economic growth has been accompanied by radical transformation of economic structures; and second, as Table 2.1 shows, lengthy periods of rapid growth and near full employment have alternated with equally long episodes of stagnation and high unemployment.[2] Our objective is to develop a framework that explains both good and poor macroeconomic performance as outcomes of a dynamic process that emphasises the changing structure of capitalist economies as they develop. Of central interest is the interaction between economic performance and economic structure that generates endogenous changes in each.

Development is not mere expansion of output. History shows that growth and structural change are inseparable in real economies. As industrialization and modernization proceed, the structure of the economy changes; and structure includes not only tastes and technologies, but also the institutions that govern economic activity. While some change may be traced to exogenous causes, much of it is endogenous, the result of routine economic activities. Endogenous changes in structure link the past with the future, demonstrating that development is an evolutionary process, not simply a sequence of disjointed phases. We argue that the most significant structural change of the post-World War II era occurred in institutions.[3] Consequently, the framework introduced here concentrates on institutions, on how they influence performance, and on the endogenous process of institutional change as the link between episodes of good and poor macroeconomic performance. This does not deny the importance of exogenously caused change, which is also included in our explanation; but emphasizing endogenous change allows us to analyse capitalist development as an evolutionary process.

Table 2.1 Unemployment rates (U), growth rates of real per capita income (y) and real GDP growth rates (Q̇): selected periods for 16 OECD countries

Country	1922–29 U	1922–29 ẏ	1922–29 Q̇	1930–37 U	1930–37 ẏ	1930–37 Q̇	1955–73 U	1955–73 ẏ	1955–73 Q̇	1974–98 U	1974–98 ẏ	1974–98 Q̇
Australia	5.7	−0.7	1.2	14.1	2.5	3.3	2.0	2.7	4.9	9.0	1.7	3.1
Austria	6.0[a]	3.7	4.0	13.4	−1.8	−1.7	2.1	4.5	5.1	3.2[f]	2.1	2.4
Belgium	0.9	1.8	2.8	8.8	−0.1	0.4	2.4	3.7	4.3	8.7	1.8	2.0
Canada	3.2	4.1	5.9	13.6	−1.0	0.1	5.1	3.1	5.0	9.9	1.5	2.7
Denmark	8.4	2.9	3.7	11.0	0.9	1.7	2.1	3.6	4.3	7.5	1.9	2.1
Finland	1.6	4.0	5.0	4.2	3.7	4.5	2.0	4.3	4.9	12.1	2.0	2.5
France	1.7[b]	3.9	4.5	3.4[e]	−0.1	0.0	1.9	4.1	5.2	11.2	1.7	2.1
Germany	4.4	2.8	3.5	9.7	3.0	3.6	1.4	4.0	5.0	6.3	1.9[h]	2.0
Italy	1.7[c]	2.3	3.2	4.8	1.9	2.7	5.2	4.7	5.4	10.8	2.0	2.2
Japan	n.a.	1.5	2.9	n.a.	3.3	4.8	1.5	8.1	9.3	2.9	2.3	3.0
Netherlands	2.4	6.8	4.6	8.5	−0.4	0.8	1.8	3.3	4.6	6.0	1.7	2.4
Norway	5.6	3.2	3.7	8.4	2.0	2.5	2.0	3.3	4.1	5.1	3.0	3.5
Sweden	3.0	4.2	4.5	5.6	2.5	2.8	1.8	3.6	4.2	7.3	1.3	1.6
Switzerland	0.4[c]	4.6[d]	5.2[d]	3.0	−0.2	0.3	0.0	2.9	4.4	1.4[g]	0.7	1.0
United Kingdom	7.8	2.5	2.9	11.8	1.9	2.4	2.8	2.5	3.0	8.5	1.7	1.9
United States	4.1	3.2	4.7	18.2	0.5	1.2	4.8	2.0	3.4	5.9	1.7	2.6
Unweighted average	3.8	3.2	3.9	9.2	1.2	1.8	2.4	3.8	4.8	7.4	1.8	2.3

Notes
[a] Average for 1924–29. [b] Average for 1921, 1926 and 1929. [c] Unemployment rate in 1929. [d] Interpolations for the years 1922 and 1923. [e] Average for 1931 and 1936. [f] Average for 1974–89 and 1993–98. [g] Average for 1974–89 and 1991–97. [h] Break in 1991.
Sources: Maddison (1991) Tables A.8, B.2 and C.6; OECD *Economic Outlook 66*, December 1999, Annex Tables 1 and 22; OECD *Historical Statistics 1960–67*, Tables 1.1, 3.1 and 3.2; OECD *Labour Force Statistics 1978–1998*.

Change cannot be analysed within the mainstream equilibrium framework. Rooted in mechanics, the neoclassical growth model describes only the response of the system to changes that occur outside the model, that is, in the structural variables. When a structural variable changes, the model's sole response is to restore equilibrium, the original one if the change is temporary, a new one if it is permanent. The cause of all long-run economic change is to be found outside the economy.

There are additional difficulties with modelling development within an equilibrium framework. According to the conventional wisdom of neoclassical economics, capitalism is a self-regulating system. If it is not actually moving along a full employment steady state growth path, it is converging toward one. The implicit assumption is that the speed of adjustment to equilibrium is rapid relative to the frequency of exogenous disturbances. If this cannot be assumed, the concept of equilibrium loses much of its usefulness as an organizing concept for analysis. And indeed the record shows clearly that during the approximately 80 years for which data are available there have been two prolonged episodes of widespread high unemployment in the OECD economies. If we exclude the World War I and World War II years, these two episodes account for half of the period, yet they are regarded as simple disturbances followed by convergence to equilibrium.

The neoclassical model is ahysteretic, that is, the equilibrium is uniquely determined by values of exogenous structural variables. This equilibrium is assumed to be stable, so that any temporary shock, no matter how large or small, or when it occurs, or which of the state variables is affected, has no long-run effect; the economy returns to the previous equilibrium. If the change is permanent, the economy moves toward the new equilibrium; the previous equilibrium or behaviour of the economy has no impact on the new one. It is as though history did not exist. There is no independent role for aggregate demand in the neoclassical model; it simply adjusts passively to aggregate supply. The weakness of the proposed adjustment mechanism is taken up elsewhere (Cornwall and Cornwall, 1997). Here, we simply point out that the occurrence of lengthy periods of high unemployment is evidence of this weakness. Lastly, in the neoclassical model institutions appear solely as 'market imperfections' which cause deviations from the equilibrium path of the economy. They are obstructions to be removed by policy, so that the self-regulating mechanisms of the economy can operate unhindered.

Our evolutionary–Keynesian framework draws upon three traditions: that associated with Schumpeter (1961) and Svennilson (1954), with its emphasis on structural change and transformation as an integral part of the economic evolutionary process; institutional economics with its stress on rules, laws, customs and beliefs as structural determinants of economic and political behaviour; and Keynesian economics with its emphasis on aggregate demand as a key determinant of economic performance and outcomes.

Sections 2.2 and 2.3 outline our approach, which is designed to analyse the causes of change. Sections 2.4 to 2.7 discuss other theories to provide the context for our approach. Sections 2.8 to 2.12 and 2.13 to 2.17 apply the approach to explain the two post-World War II episodes, the golden age and the subsequent age of high unemployment, respectively. We investigate the underlying changes that allowed the golden age to follow the depression of the 1930s, and the changes that caused it to come to an end, leading to the current period of high unemployment and low productivity growth rates. Sections 2.18 to 2.20 discuss the advantages of using an evolutionary–Keynesian approach, both to diagnose the causes of malfunction and to establish appropriate remedies, followed by the conclusion. In covering the development of many OECD economies over half a century, this chapter provides highlights of a very broad study, rather than presenting a compact single topic.[4]

2.2.   AN EVOLUTIONARY–KEYNESIAN FRAMEWORK

2.2.1.   An Extended Keynesian Approach

In a study of macroeconomic performance and the evolving structure of the economy, a decision must be taken on which dimensions of performance to emphasize. We focus on aggregate demand and its rate of growth, and use the unemployment rate to indicate the strength or weakness of aggregate demand conditions. The focus on aggregate demand reflects both its direct impact on other economic variables and its indirect impact on the structure of the economy. In a world devoid of invisible hands, full employment even in the long run is not guaranteed; the unemployment record will reflect the state of aggregate demand. As well as the unemployment rate, the level and growth of aggregate demand directly influence the behaviour of other economic variables such as the levels and growth of output, productivity and per capita incomes. Less obvious but of great importance, the rising levels of per capita incomes and affluence generated by growing aggregate demand and output alter the distribution of sectoral output and employment, the result of differences in sectoral productivity growth rates and income elasticities of demand. Growing aggregate demand also alters the distribution of output between public and private sectors, as rising per capita incomes permit the expansion of government's taxing and spending.

In contrast, stagnant per capita incomes and high unemployment bring these aspects of transformation to a halt, as illustrated by the Great Depression.

Clearly in our analysis (as in the real world), there are no steady-state balanced growth equilibrium outcomes. Nor are there any long-run outcomes determined entirely exogenously, because the total impact of aggregate demand is more profound than the distributional effects just cited. These effects in turn induce structural changes on the supply side. For example, aggregate demand and its growth influence the choice of production techniques and the growth of the labour force through induced effects on participation rates and immigration. Finally, growing incomes and rising affluence induce institutional changes, for example, by shifting the distribution of power from capital to labour and by raising the aspirations and expectations of ordinary workers (Kalecki, 1943). Directly and indirectly, Keynesian forces initiate dynamic processes that play a pivotal role in economic development by changing several dimensions of the economic structure. The influence of aggregate demand on aggregate supply even at full employment, but especially its role in changing the structure of the economy extends Keynes's analysis.

2.2.2. The Role of Institutions

Institutions can be defined as the beliefs, customs, laws, rules and conventions that govern the behaviour of individuals and groups within society. They define what is acceptable behaviour, the rights and responsibilities of individuals and groups, and the penalties for noncompliance. Institutions are the rules of the game, individuals and organizations are the players (North, 1990). They are intrinsically collective in nature, reflecting the culture and values of the society and a desire for orderliness in social relations. In the broadest sense, they 'legitimize' actions, including the assertion of power by individuals and groups, and reconcile conflict. Clearly, we limit our study to institutions that influence economic behaviour; as an integral part of the economic structure they are among the determinants of economic performance. However, like tastes and technologies they are subject to change. Indeed, as will be apparent, institutional change has been the overriding structural change leading both to the golden age and to its eventual end.

Although we regard the inclusion of institutions as essential to a clear understanding of these events, they cannot be simply added to the economic variables. Institutions provide structure to social and economic interchange, a function that requires stability. Their collective nature promotes this stability, since change requires general consent. In stable societies, and especially in democracies, significant institutional change is infrequent, the culmination of a slow process as collective support is established, or as the relative power of groups within the society shifts. Change is also actively resisted when vested interests exert the power they derive from existing institutions to protect the *status quo*. The main point here is that significant change to the institutional structure is slow compared to the rate at which economic variables change. Consequently, we are able to make a distinction between the short run, when the institutional structure is regarded as effectively fixed, and the long run when it undergoes change. In each short run, the prevailing institutions affect performance by structuring behaviour, either enabling or hindering the achievement of economic goals.

The choice of institutions to study flows from the decision to emphasize aggregate demand as a prime determinant of economic performance. Relevant institutions are those that determine whether high and growing aggregate demand will prevail, or whether it is weak or stagnant; a law forbidding fiscal deficits is an obvious example. Of equal note are institutions that enable or thwart the realization of other desirable goals under full employment conditions. For example, if labour market institutions that reduce or eliminate inflation at full employment are weak or absent, full employment will not be achieved, as governments have consistently given priority to a low inflation target. Using the unemployment rate to indicate the strength of aggregate demand, we divide the postwar years under study into two episodes, shown in Table 2.1. An episode is defined as a period during which the institutional structure exerts an unchanging influence on aggregate demand, determining whether unemployment performance is good or poor. Using Marshall's view of equilibrium as a state of rest, this is a state of institutional rest.

2.2.3.   Path Dependence: Institutional Hysteresis

That institutions matter was the central point of the last section. Here, we stress that history also matters, that events and trends of the past influence the present and future and that institutional change is prominent among the manifestations of this influence. In general terms, a hysteretic system differs from the ahysteretic system of neoclassical analysis in that its long-run path is dependent upon its history. '[The] distinguishing feature of a system in which hysteresis is postulated to be present is that the behaviour of the system cannot, *ex hypothesi*, be explained by reference to state variables alone: instead the past history of the system has to be invoked, as well as state variables, in order to explain the behaviour of the system' (Cross and Allen, 1988, p. 26).

Consider a simple example, couched in terms familiar to mainstream analysis. Suppose there is a one-off exogenous shock to an economic system initially on a full employment growth path, that causes unemployment to rise. In mainstream equilibrium analysis, it does not matter what caused the shock, or whether unemployment rises to 10 per cent or 50 per cent; nor does it matter how long the system is out of equilibrium. As long as there is no change to the structural variables, the economy will return to its original growth path. In a hysteretic system, we expect the disequilibrium to cause further changes which will differ, depending upon the type and severity of the shock and on the path of the economy as it responds to the disturbance. Most importantly, these changes can alter the structural variables or the parameters of the system (Setterfield, 1997, ch. 5), so that the economy will not return to its former growth path.

Institutions are part of the economic structure, and path dependence shows that even a one-off shock can alter them, whether directly or indirectly, and is capable of radically changing future performance. Therefore the kind of economic shock that will have no permanent effect in the neoclassical model may well have a lasting effect in our model if it causes institutions to change. However, it is the institutional change itself (from whatever source) that influences the future path of the economy, via the new set of institutional structures it imposes on aggregate demand. We use the term institutional hysteresis to describe this path dependence.

2.2.4. Institutional Change: the Long Run

Some institutional change might reinforce current performance or have no effect, but our interest lies in explaining the causal process underlying the alternating historical periods of high and low unemployment and related macroeconomic measures. Therefore, we concentrate on institutional change that alters aggregate demand conditions, leading to radically different economic performance; that is, resulting in the advent of a new episode. Furthermore, while the source of institutional change may be either exogenous or endogenous, we argue that in the post-World War II era endogenously generated institutional change has provided the evolutionary mechanism in the OECD economies.

Endogenous change in institutions is induced by the performance of the economy. For example, prolonged periods of either good or poor performance shift the distribution of power between capital and labour, and alter the institutions of the labour market; these changes may be embodied in law or established as new behavioural norms, as one group or the other exerts its growing power. This process of change demonstrates path dependence, because it is the institutions in one episode that determine the state of aggregate demand, which in turn determines the performance that induces institutional change, thus establishing the new institutions that will operate in the next episode, influencing its performance. It is also an evolutionary process, with change initiated endogenously, not brought about by exogenous events, providing a mechanism by which capitalism transforms itself. The central role of aggregate demand in this process is reflected in the term 'evolutionary–Keynesian' used in the title.

However, in real economies exogenous events are a second source of institutional change, which they cause in either of two ways. The first is an exogenous shock that directly changes one or more of the institutions that determine the state of aggregate demand and unemployment. For example, if the majority of countries in a trade agreement decide to change the rules, the others must abide by the changes or cease to be members of the group. Either way, their rules are changed, a direct effect of external forces. Besides discrete events of this sort, there are also exogenous trends such as the extension of the franchise, the spread of literacy and increasing urbanization, all of which change behaviour and beliefs and contribute to institutional change. The second possibility is that instead of directly causing institutional change, an exogenous shock has an indirect effect by first affecting economic performance, and only subsequently, via the feedback from performance to institutions, inducing institutional change. In this case, an external shock sets an evolutionary process in motion.

Here, we have isolated three distinct routes by which institutional change can occur and produce a new episode. Two of them are evolutionary processes, one purely endogenous, induced by existing performance within an episode, the other induced by a change in performance initiated by an exogenous shock. Both provide the link between episodes essential to an evolutionary process. The third is not evolutionary, institutional change being the direct result of exogenous forces. It is only in the new episode brought about by the institutional change that it caused, that the effects of this external shock become part of the evolutionary process; in the new episode, these changed institutions determine the economic performance that will induce further change. The distinction between the three routes of institutional change is useful in applications, where the historical record shows that there is usually some combination of them at work simultaneously and that their influences are often mutually reinforcing. It allows us to clarify the individual contributions of events and processes that lead to a new unemployment episode.

2.3.   A VISUAL REPRESENTATION OF THE SOURCES OF CHANGE

Figure 2.1 provides a simple picture of these processes of change. The left-most box depicts the economic structure in place for episode A. Then, given the specific Keynesian endogenous mechanism describing the aggregate demand side of the model, the *detailed* macroeconomic performance of episode A is determined; this is represented by the left-most of the horizontal arrows. However, of most interest is the initial configuration of institutions that determines the *general* characteristics of macroeconomic performance of the episode. These institutions govern economic behaviour, determining whether or not a high level of aggregate demand will obtain. This will decide whether unemployment is low and macroeconomic performance good, or if episode A has poor performance. The three routes of institutional change are also shown. First, the performance determined by the structural variables can induce institutional change, a process shown by the sequence of horizontal arrows. Second, exogenous factors affect performance, shown by the vertical arrow, and this changed performance induces institutional change. These are the two types of evolutionary process.

In both cases the performance-induced changes in institutions alter performance in the next period, that is, they generate a negative feedback, allowing us to model alternating historical episodes of high and low unemployment (and related measures of macroeconomic performance). For example, assume episode A is a period of low unemployment and that performance eventfully induces changes in institutions which lead to an episode of high unemployment. Moving further from left to right across the diagram, developments from one episode to the next are portrayed by the two middle horizontal arrow segments ending at the right-hand-side box. The new box depicts the set of structural variables of episode B and the beginning of a period of poor performance.

Finally, exogenous events can directly alter institutions, shown by the diagonal arrow. The result in each of the three cases is to establish a new set of institutions, initiating a new episode. However the third case illustrates institutional hysteresis but not evolutionary change; it is not linked to past performance, but it will influence future performance and in doing so may become part of a future evolutionary process.

It should also be emphasized that all arrows in the diagram refer only to events or trends that either directly or indirectly led to changes in institutions, as these were the linkages in the post-World War II era. Changes in tastes and technologies, whether induced by performance or exogenous, are of interest only to the extent that they directly or indirectly alter institutions in ways that affect the unemployment record. Hence the horizontal and

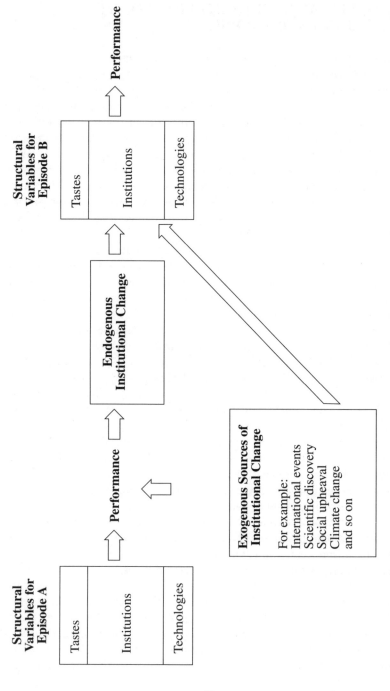

Figure 2.1   Three routes for institutional change

diagonal arrow segments end at the institution panel of the right-hand-side box. We do not preclude the possibility of positive feedbacks affecting dynamic processes in real world situations. These occur within an episode, contributing to its persistence. But it is negative feedback that causes change, allowing us to model the historical record of alternating episodes of high and low unemployment.

2.4. ALTERNATIVE THEORIES OF CAPITALIST DYNAMICS

The objective of this section is to provide some context for our framework of analysis and its explanation of twentieth-century economic develop-ment. We do this by first examining new growth theory, which has two branches. The first, endogenous growth theory, is in the neoclassical growth theory tradition with its neglect of institutions. The second branch includes institutions in its analysis but does not attempt to integrate them into any kind of dynamic process. We then turn to examples of theories in the 'polit-ical economy tradition' in which structural change, especially institutional change, is an integral feature of the development process.

2.4.1. New Growth Theory

Endogenous new growth theory suffers from most of the shortcomings of neoclassical growth theory, particularly its lack of concern with structural change, including institutional change and the implicit assumption of con-tinuous full employment. As in neoclassical growth theory, the centrepiece of the model is an aggregate production function, distinguished from the former by an important modification. In place of the neoclassical assump-tions of diminishing returns to capital and constant returns to scale, it assumes constant returns to capital (Romer, 1986, 1990; Lucas, 1988). The main impact of this change is that the long-run rates of growth of output and productivity are no longer independent of the savings (and investment) ratio. However, this 'correction' is bought at great cost; the model lacks robustness. The *slightest* deviation from the assumption of constant returns to capital leads to either ever-accelerating rates of growth or zero growth.

The second branch of new growth theory, quite distinct from the first, is comprised of international cross-section regressions with average growth rates of productivity of the different economies as the dependent variables, and with income levels and a set of institutional-economic variables repre-senting influences such as religion, educational levels and the development of democratic institutions as independent variables (for example, Barro,

1991). This branch of new growth theory resembles the work of Olson (1982), who stressed the favourable effect of disruptions of institutions on the growth process and growth rates in developed capitalist economies. Such studies constitute only the first stage in a framework for modelling structural change over time. No attempt is made to incorporate feedback from growth to the structural influences assumed to determine growth as in our study.

2.4.2. The Political Economy Tradition

New growth theory models in the neoclassical aggregate production function tradition describe the interactions of purely economic variables, ignoring structural change even while professing to model long-run outcomes. These theories demonstrate the marked contrast between current mainstream macrodynamics and those treatments of the subject that fall under the heading of the political economy tradition. For the most part, political economy theories have developed independently of the trend toward formal modelling, and while broader in scope have too often been content to rely on rather loose generalizations. As in our study, a common theme is that periods of economic malfunction are inherent to capitalist development, a fundamental difference from conventional macrodynamics, which either ignores malfunction completely or treats it as a temporary aberration, attributable to correctable market imperfections or to exogenous shocks.

Marx must be counted among the most influential of the early political economists. Whether they accepted Marx's views or opposed them, later writers have benefited from his insights. What is of interest here is not whether Marx correctly predicted the fate of capitalism, or even whether he provided a complete theory, but that he recognized capitalist development as a process of both economic and structural (including institutional) change, brought about by periods of serious malfunction generated within the system itself. This conception of capitalist development as structural change is discernable in many other theories of long-run economic development. Most of these have stressed technological change as the source of transformation, others highlight institutional change. They fall into three groups. The first group includes theories that focus on technology as the driving force behind economic development, with only a passing interest in institutions. Theories in the other two groups include institutional change as an integral part of the analysis. In the first of these, institutional change and economic performance are essentially responses to exogenous forces. These theories incorporate dynamic processes that are hysteretic but not evolutionary. In the third group, technology plays an important but largely exogenous role; these stress evolutionary mechanisms of the type discussed in Sections 2.2 and 2.3.

2.5.   TECHNOLOGY AS THE ENGINE OF DEVELOPMENT: THE LONG CYCLE SCHOOL

The first group includes various versions of long cycle theory (Kondratiev, 1925; Mandel, 1964; Van Duijn, 1983). The existence of long cycles is controversial, but our interest lies in the methodology used by its proponents. Their objective is to explain what they see as fairly regular long-run swings in economic activity with special emphasis on rates of growth of GDP. These swings are claimed to be driven by the pattern of investment which is governed by technological change. Technological change is treated as exogenous.

In these theories good times alternate with bad, as the initial expansionary phase of the cycle comes to a close when overexpansion of capacity, market saturation and reduced profitability lead to the downturn. While each proposes an endogenous process of decay, there is no agreement among them about how the upturn originates, and none provides a convincing explanation. In earlier work, explanations of the upturn relied upon the *ad hoc* introduction of exogenous events, whether scientific discovery or discovery of new territories, which are met with a burst of entrepreneurial activity. More recent versions assume there is an underlying steady growth in demand that eventually eliminates over-supply. In each case, this marks the beginning of a new long phase of growth, which ends with the next downturn as the pattern inevitably repeats itself. The reliance on exogenous events seriously weakens the claimed regularity of the cycles, and reduces them to a series of disjointed phases. This lack of connection between cycles is the greatest obstacle to any claim that these are coherent theories of capitalist development.

The explanation we offer differs from long cycle theory in several respects. First, ours is not a theory of cycles. There is no *a priori* reason to claim that an episode will be of any particular length. Second, the shift from good to poor performance in long cycle theory is a simple exhaustion of the current boom; in our approach the shift is the result of structural change, as is the reverse shift. Lastly, the engine of change is not constant from one episode to the next; each has its own unique combination of forces effecting change. In tracing the linkages between episodes to structural change, we include technological change, but open up other components of structure, institutions in particular, as potential causes of changed performance. Institutions are given no place in long cycle theory.

It is precisely this expansion of structure beyond merely technology that permits explanation of both upturns and downturns, providing the linkages between episodes of good and poor performance that long cycle theory fails to provide.

2.6.   THEORIES WITH VARIABLE INSTITUTIONAL STRUCTURES

This section considers models that include institutions as part of the changing structure that typifies capitalist development. While the processes of change they propose exhibit path dependence, they are not evolutionary. Evolutionary theories are left for the next section.

2.6.1.   Early Schumpeter

Schumpeter's early work (1912) had much in common with long cycle theory, in particular its reliance on long-run exogenous forces, for example, new technologies such as the development of the railway system in the nineteenth century. Long-run cyclical growth was very much dependent upon the result of a periodic bunching of technological innovations, which together with induced effects on investment in older, less innovative industries, generated long-run investment and growth cycles. Schumpeter's long cycles eventually came to an end for the same reasons advanced by long cycle theorists. Put simply, they were the natural consequences of the cycle itself and hardly qualified as the beginning of a crisis. Indeed Schumpeter assumed labour was fully employed throughout the long cycle. The forces reversing the downswing were not well developed and thus the timing of a bunching of innovations was poorly explained. Certainly inventions, the necessary scientific basis of innovations, were considered exogenous to the economy's performance. In these features Schumpeter's earlier work is virtually indistinguishable from long cycle theory. But Schumpeter also placed great emphasis on capitalist development as a sequence of phases, defined rather generally by their institutions.

His particular interest was to explain the phase before capitalism had become 'trustified' and 'laboristic', with the different phases dominated by long-run exogenous components. In this way institutional change was recognized as an important historical element, but there was little in the way of an endogenous theory of either technological or institutional change in this part of his work.

2.6.2. The Regulation School

The notion that the 'wrong' political and social institutions impede economic progress, and that the right ones must be found to allow economic progress to proceed smoothly and yield its benefits to society, is found in the ideas proposed by the Regulation School (for example, Aglietta, 1979; Boyer, 1986). Based in Marxian economics, regulation theory also draws upon Keynes and Kalecki to develop an institutionalist analysis of capitalist transformation in the twentieth century. In this theory, demand is an important component, determining the balance between consumption and investment spending. Regulationists view capitalism as a series of episodes, each with a different technological base, which determines the internal organization of firms, including work itself.[5] A central theme is that periods of severe malfunction are caused by a mismatch between the technological base and the institutional 'superstructure'. While they emphasize the role of technological change, the regulationists differ from long cycle theorists in their Marxian perspective. Technological change alters the way production and investment are carried out, and requires compatible institutional change if malfunction is to be avoided and the potential of the new technology realized. Whenever there is a mismatch between the technology and the institutional superstructure, crisis follows and persists until appropriate institutions are established. Like us, the regulationists stress the importance of institutions. They trace out an endogenous process of breakdown as a cumulative process in which technological change and institutional failure to change reach a critical point and instability, crisis and poor economic performance follow. But there is no comparable process inducing the institutional change needed to resolve the crisis.

2.7. EVOLUTIONARY MODELS: 'MATURE' SCHUMPETER AND NORTH

Theories of variable institutional structures, rather than assume institutions to be exogenous, have in effect simply introduced an alternative exogenous force, technology, to 'explain' institutional change and performance. The key idea of evolutionary theories is that macroeconomic development must be modelled as transformation resulting from endogenously generated change. In such models, economic performance induces changes in the economic (and social) structure, and the new structure influences the path of future performance, generating a long-run interaction between them. A comparison with the later works of both Schumpeter (1942) and North (1990) to our hysteretic evolutionary approach is illustrative. In these works, both economists model development to a large degree as an evolutionary–hysteretic process arising from a joint interaction of economic variables and the structure of the economy. They do, however, allow exogenous variables to act as important determinants of long-run development. Thus their theories combine elements of the variable structures models with the evolutionary approach, as does ours.

2.7.1. Late Schumpeter

In his later work these induced changes appear as the inherent tendency of capitalism to sow the seeds of its own destruction. In the very process of growth and accumulation and rising living standards, institutional changes are induced that lead to capitalism's downfall. More exactly, rising incomes and technological maturity lead to increased worker discontent, the atrophy of entrepreneurship and eventually to socialism. Thus in some historical long run a period of successful economic performance of capitalism induces institutional changes which eventually lead to a negative feedback in the form of macroeconomic malfunction.

This process of endogenous change is entirely consistent with our approach. However, Schumpeter's heavy reliance on the behaviour of the entrepreneur as the endogenous initiator of change stems from the Marshallian roots of his work, and its implied full employment tendencies. We have emphasized demand conditions, which provide the environment conducive or not, for entrepreneurial activity, and which influence and are influenced by the economic and political power relationships of capital and labour. The inclusion of aggregate demand conditions broadens the avenues for institutional and other structural change.

2.7.2. North

Like Schumpeter, throughout his work North highlights the entrepreneur as the agent of change, with exogenous changes in 'relative prices' the originator of institutional change (1990, ch. 10). The causes of relative price shifts include changes in relative factor supplies, in the costs of information, that is, transaction costs, and in technologies. Whatever the cause, the changed relative prices give rise to unexploited gains. Institutional adaptations occur as entrepreneurs act to exploit these gains. Consider the following sequence. Allow some initial exogenous change in relative prices, for example, an unexplained increase in the rates of growth of population and the labour force or a technological innovation, and assume this gives rise to unexploited gains from trade. Within this framework the response of entrepreneurs is to alter institutional arrangements in an effort to reduce transaction costs and thereby increase profits. However, because of radical uncertainty and limited ability to learn by doing and adaptation, efforts to optimize and to adapt institutions become continuous learning processes, shaped by both past and existing institutions and their interactions with past and current performance. The evolving institutions need never be optimal, nor in the aggregate need the institutional framework at any point in time be 'socially efficient'. In this work, we have an evolutionary process that, while initiated by an exogenous event, sets in motion a sequence of institutional adaptations that influence performance, with changed performance inducing further institutional adaptation and further changes in performance, and so on.

Our distinction between long-run and short-run treatment of institutions is missing in North's analysis, except to the extent that he envisages the emergence of inefficient (that is, growth inhibiting) institutions. However, as long as the prevailing institutional framework ensures that markets are competitive, there will be no permanent deviation from the long-run efficient growth path of the economy (North, 1990, p. 95). Information feedback and the ongoing maximization activities of entrepreneurs (both economic and political) will induce further institutional change to resolve the problem. In North's terms, we are investigating these deviations, although in our view there is no *a priori* reason why an economy must return eventually to a particular growth path. Indeed our view of the 'deviations' is that they are a normal part of capitalism, no more deviant than periods of good performance. Finally, while the process of change North develops is both path-dependent and evolutionary, the mechanism of change is confined to entrepreneurial activity. We have introduced ideology and power relationships as well as economic performance itself to explain institutional change.

2.8. ORIGINS OF THE GOLDEN AGE

The second task of this chapter is to specify the institutional changes that explain the two post-World War II episodes and the sources of these changes. To do so we venture into the complex realms of history and politics, to highlight the trends and events of greatest significance. Inevitably this and the next sections tend towards description. We begin with the golden age.

The upper left-hand box in Figure 2.2 depicts the economic structure at the beginning of the high unemployment Great Depression episode. Figure 2.2 also summarizes the many influences at work, acting through the three routes discussed above, which link the golden age to the depression of the

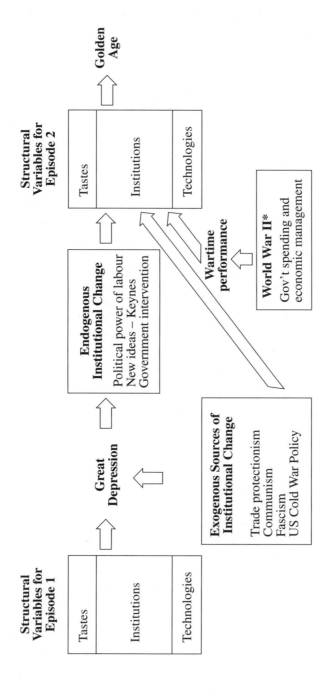

Note: *World war II is treated separately from other exogenous shocks, because the change in economic performance it caused cannot be regarded as part of normal capitalist development. Wartime performance induced institutional change, by demonstrating the effectiveness of government intervention. At the same time as convincing other segments of society of the value of intervention, it reinforced labour's previously established beliefs, but this self-reinforcing effect cannot be shown in the figure.

Figure 2.2   From the Great Depression to the golden age

1930s. However, the golden age did not emerge directly from the 1930s. Over ten years of war and reconstruction intervened, administering exogenous shocks and trends of such magnitude and duration that they introduced a fourth route for institutional change. This is depicted by the vertical arrow from the lower right-hand box to 'wartime performance' and then the diagonal arrow to the 'Institutions' panel in the upper right-hand box. To these, we must add the advent of the Cold War and the US policy response, exogenous events that directly changed institutions, shown by the diagonal arrow from the lower left-hand box. The events of this ten-year interlude are treated separately from other exogenous factors in the next two sections. Here we consider events of the 1930s that contributed to institutional change via the routes identified in our framework.

The institutional changes induced by the prolonged period of poor economic performance of the 1930s centred on rejection of the view that unemployment was a temporary and unavoidable phenomenon that would right itself. Labour had already come to believe that government was responsible for its welfare in times of adverse economic conditions; but the new belief was that government could and should undertake measures to improve those conditions. As mass unemployment took hold in the early 1930s, unions in the UK and Germany called for expansionist policies, but neither the British Labour Party nor the German Social Democrats could be persuaded to break with the economic orthodoxy of balanced budgets; in the mid-1930s the French Popular Front government's attempts to meet similar demands were quickly reversed. Also induced by the economic performance of the time was the revolution in economic thought formalized in *The General Theory*; Keynes and his ideas were to have a pervasive influence in the postwar world. As the depression lengthened, union membership and power declined, forcing labour to seek a solution in the political arena.

Political ideas were the strongest exogenous influences of the time.[6] As capitalism faltered, other ideologies gathered strength. Communist and other left-wing parties gained membership, but now fascism presented another alternative, adding to governments' fears of social unrest.[7] Efforts were made to bring some order to labour relations. Draconian measures in Italy and Germany imposed contracts upon labour and capital. Elsewhere, new legislation amounted to a formal recognition of labour as a legitimate player in economic affairs, and although high unemployment limited its immediate practical value, such recognition became an essential component of the institutions of the golden age. Fears of social unrest also led to some improvement of the rudimentary social benefits of the time, and many governments embarked on public works programmes, made cheap credit available to private firms in key industries, and introduced massive agricultural support programmes. Governments had begun to accept an interventionist role.

An example of an exogenous force acting first on economic performance, and through this effect inducing institutional change, were the beggar-thy-neighbour international trade policies of the 1930s.[8] While the effects of these policies induced governments to agree to the multilateral trade and payments system negotiated at Bretton Woods, its implementation was secured by another exogenous development, the advent of the Cold War.

2.9.   WORLD WAR II AND RECONSTRUCTION

The public works and other relief measures undertaken by governments in the 1930s are evidence that they had come to accept responsibility for the welfare of their citizens, but World War II demonstrated their power over economic performance itself. The war effort extended the role of government in the European and North American economies, providing evidence of the effectiveness of government spending to create and sustain high levels of employment. Viewed in isolation, wartime full employment can be seen as a simple response to national emergency, but it reinforced ideas that had developed earlier. It demonstrated the effectiveness of ideas that Keynes had propounded in *The General Theory* for sound management of a peacetime economy. In all segments of society, unemployment ceased to be regarded as an unavoidable fact of life; rather it was the responsibility of government to use economic policy to maintain full employment. In the UK this view was accorded official status when all political parties espoused the goals laid out in the second Beveridge Report (1944). Expanding acceptance of this wider role for government is shown in the lower right-hand box of the figure as institutional change induced by wartime economic performance. However, in this case, performance was the result of an exogenous event as the requirements of war dictated government policy.

The demonstration that government spending could solve the unemployment problem was only one facet of the massive intervention required by the conduct of total war. Governments used a series of controls to ensure that resources were allocated to the necessary output, gaining both experience and confidence as economic managers. Such direct intervention was to become an essential component of postwar reconstruction outside of North America. There was great variation among countries in the form that intervention took, from the British approach of continuing wartime controls, to the far more elaborate French Monnet Plan. But whatever route was chosen, success would depend on the cooperation of labour, and on capital resuming its essential function of organizing production.

In Western Europe, labour emerged from the war more radical than at any time in its history. The resistance movements had been manned largely by the working class, among whom communists and socialists were the majority. This wartime activity gave moral force to labour's claims for social justice, and to its new demands for state ownership in key sectors and state management of the economy. Similar demands were made by labour in the UK, where union membership had increased during wartime full employment. Across Western Europe, labour exerted its political power at the ballot box, electing governments favourable to its cause.[9] The task of these governments was to reconcile the competing demands of labour and capital, so that reconstruction could proceed.

Faced with the large investments that would be required and the inevitable risk that this entailed, capital's greatest practical concerns centred upon financing these expenditures, and reducing costly disruptions threatened by industrial unrest. In addition, the fear of social upheaval that prevailed between the wars was not forgotten, increasing capital's willingness to compromise. The compromises that governments negotiated would not only permit recovery, but would prove to be central to the period of rapid growth that ultimately followed. Although differing in detail and emphasis from one country to another, they had features in common that would meet the priorities of all parties. First, most governments in industrialized countries accepted full employment as a goal.[10] They also took steps to ensure that union rights were clear, that collective bargaining was an orderly process, and that conditions of employment and procedures for lay-offs were fair to labour. Social safety nets were improved, both regarding the numbers covered and the benefits that could be claimed. In return labour agreed to wage restraint, with raises lagging productivity to generate higher profits for investment during the recovery period. Tax breaks, government loans and subsidies encouraged firms to distribute only a small proportion of profits, and to invest the rest. That labour agreed to wage restraint is an indication of the relative preference for security that prevailed among workers who remembered the Depression all too clearly (Phelps Brown, 1975). Labour had gained a political presence that yielded many of the economic benefits it had long sought, and more were promised as productivity and incomes rose. Capital had reason to expect economic stability and orderly industrial relations, reducing the risk for the large investments to be made. These were the elements of the postwar compromise that laid the groundwork for recovery and growth. In many OECD economies, this compromise was also the basis for new industrial relations systems that were designed to resolve potential problems arising from the competing demands of capital and labour.[11]

2.10. THE COLD WAR AND US POLICY

Although recovery proceeded rapidly at first, its dependence upon imported inputs soon created a shortage of dollar reserves that threatened to stall it. This coincided with the start of the Cold War, which resulted in a sharp change in US policy. European security became a prime goal, with political and economic stability its essential components. Through the European Recovery Program (the Marshall Plan) the US recycled its trade surpluses, making credit available that removed supply constraints on foodstuffs and capital goods, and allowed recovery to continue. Two other outcomes of US involvement were of particular moment. One stemmed from the technical assistance component of the Marshall Plan, which supported the US view that social conflict could be resolved by rising living standards. Its aim was to modernize, rather than simply rebuild, European industry. It was to have a large impact on productivity growth in the golden age. The second was the leverage provided by the Marshall Plan to induce the European economies to move more rapidly towards the multilateral trade and payments system that were a US policy priority. The rapid expansion of trade that followed, together with rising productivity, were key elements in securing the prosperity of the golden age.

2.11. AGGREGATE DEMAND: THE ABSENT CONSTRAINTS

2.11.1. Supply Constraints

Section 2.2 presented our extension of Keynesian analysis, emphasizing the dynamic effects of full employment on productivity and income growth rates, the case of demand creating its own supply, although within some limits. Technology limits are reached when the supplies of labour, raw materials or capital goods cannot keep pace with growing demand. The main purpose of this section is to summarize how the institutions of the golden age removed other constraints on aggregate demand. But potential supply constraints require a brief assessment. At the end of the war labour was plentiful in Western Europe and Japan as armies were demobilized and refugees further increased their labour forces. Over time, immigration and the reallocation of labour from agriculture continued to increase supply. Raw materials production had increased during the war, a response to demand, and both European and US investment in the Third World was increased in the postwar period to assure continued supply increases. Capital goods production had also increased in the US, but once the Cold War had made

European recovery a priority, there were fears that US production could not meet domestic and European demand simultaneously. This was resolved by a change in US policy that established West Germany as a major capital goods exporter. Lastly, it must be noted that the institutional changes that encouraged technology transfer from the US to its Cold War allies removed another potential supply constraint.

2.11.2. The Inflation Constraint and Social Bargains

Achievement of the government goals of full employment and growth was essential to the maintenance of the postwar compromise, but carried a serious hazard in the form of an inflationary bias.[12] In combination with the social safety net, full employment strengthens the economic power of labour relative to capital. Rising incomes and expanding safety nets increase the ability of individuals and unions to withstand the costs of strikes, again increasing their economic power. If labour believes it is treated unfairly, and decides to exercise its market power, money wage inflation at full employment is likely, creating a strong inflationary bias. It is an outstanding feature of the golden age that in most countries rising affluence and full employment rates of unemployment did not lead to high rates of inflation. These were the countries where the postwar compromise had been embodied and preserved in their industrial relations systems to create a social bargain. The critical feature of the bargain was labour's willingness to restrain money wage demands in exchange for full employment and growth in real wages. The latter would be justified by rapid productivity growth, stemming from strong investment growth induced by booming aggregate demand. Others were not so successful; they failed to develop a social bargain and higher rates of unemployment to keep down money wage demands were the result (Cornwall, 1994, ch. 5). Section 2.15 below provides further discussion of the social bargains.

2.11.3. The Balance of Payments Constraint

Even if there is no inflationary bias, a second difficulty presents itself. As employment and aggregate demand increase in an economy, so does the demand for imports, introducing the possibility of a deterioration of the payments balance. Payments problems threaten to bring recovery and growth to an end as governments are forced to adopt restrictive policies. This problem was avoided in the early postwar period by the US recycling its trade surpluses, providing the needed international liquidity, at first through the European Recovery Program and the European Payments Union and later by military spending under the Mutual Security Act. In the

1950s and 1960s, trade within Europe and between Europe and the rest of the world expanded rapidly. Although some of the smaller countries ran payments deficits, they were able to avoid a payments constraint. Their deficits were small relative to output, and in most cases, export growth significantly outpaced GDP growth, so that under reasonable assumptions rising import demand was unlikely to generate fears of permanent large or increasing imbalances. Consequently, foreign lenders were willing to finance them, and their governments willing to accumulate foreign debt. Later in the golden age, the apparent preference of West Germany and Japan to continue as large surplus countries forced them to tolerate deficits elsewhere.

2.11.4.   Other Political Constraints

Political constraints such as the fear of 'big government', budget deficits and rising debt-to-GDP ratios were largely absent in the golden age. Big government was viewed as necessary to the new order, in which government intervention was an essential component if economic stability was to be maintained. Governments had not abandoned the eventual goal of balanced budgets, but in the Cold War environment priorities had shifted and deficits were tolerated. As prosperity increased, in most countries the deficits that occurred tended to be small, relative to GDP. Lastly, massive debts accumulated during war had created very large debt-to-GDP ratios but with high rates of output growth, these were falling rapidly, even in countries with budget deficits.

2.12.   FROM THE GOLDEN AGE TO THE AGE OF HIGH UNEMPLOYMENT

The golden age was made possible by the absence of these critical constraints on aggregate demand. This allowed rapid growth of incomes and full employment in most of the advanced OECD economies. During this period institutions existed that relieved these economies of any desire or need to restrict aggregate demand below full employment levels by permitting the simultaneous achievement of other desirable goals, for example, politically and economically acceptable rates of inflation, external balance. The lifting of constraints was the direct outcome of institutional changes, some induced by the economic performance of the 1930s, some the result of exogenous trends of that period, and others traceable to the massive exogenous shocks of World War II and the Cold War. Thus to a large extent the golden age institutions were causally linked to economic performance in the 1930s and the 1940s, illustrating the importance of evolutionary and hysteretic processes connecting the pre- and post-World War II eras. What emerged was a new form of capitalism, as beliefs about social justice and the economic role of government changed, and became the basis for policies in the golden age. The 'new order' was secured by US international leadership. The tools forged by the new institutions were state intervention and international economic management. Thus it was favourable institutions at the national and international levels that led to the golden age, not the invisible hand. Hobsbawm summarizes the new order that arose:

> For thirty years or so there was a consensus among 'western' thinkers and decision-makers, notably in the USA, which determined what other countries on the non-communist side could do, or rather what they could not do. All wanted a world of rising production, growing foreign trade, full employment, industrialization and modernization, and all were prepared to achieve it, if need be, through systematic government control and the management of mixed economies, and by cooperating with organized labour movements so long as they were not communist. The Golden Age of capitalism would have been impossible without this consensus that the economy of private enterprise . . . needed to be saved from itself to survive. (1994, p. 273)

Unfortunately this solution to the unemployment problem was to last only a quarter of a century. What followed was an episode linked to the golden age much as the golden age was linked to events of the 1930s and 1940s. What differed was the latter linkage led to the high point of capitalism's economic development; the former linkage ushered in an episode of high unemployment, low growth and rising rates of poverty.

Most of the remainder of the chapter will utilize the evolutionary–Keynesian framework to explain the poor performance in the episode since the golden age. Emphasis is given to institutions that permitted the simultaneous achievement of several macroeconomic goals and their replacement by a collection of institutions which no longer did so. The result was the sacrifice of the full employment goal. Besides the impact of institutions on performance, we also focus on examples of the impact of performance on institutions, the mechanism that provides causal linkages between the golden age and the present episode. In this manner, the high and upward trend in unemployment and the general deterioration in performance in the current episode of high unemployment is traced to a marked change in institutions, largely induced by the performance of the previous episode.

2.13.   THE AGE OF HIGH UNEMPLOYMENT

The golden age is generally agreed to have reached its end in the early to mid 1970s. In hindsight, it is clear that by this time the process of transition from an episode of growth and full employment to another of stagnation and high unemployment was firmly established. Early signs of future events are identifiable in the accelerating inflation of the late 1960s observed in the majority of OECD countries, the initial phase of the 'Great Inflation'. Continued rising inflation in the 1970s, coupled with payments problems in many economies in 1973–74, were met by the implementation of restrictive policies. These policies achieved a modest reduction in inflation rates, but failed to reduce them to golden age rates. The strongest effect was on unemployment, which rose quickly to rates twice as high as those of the 1960s. A pattern had been established which was to recur throughout the 1980s and into the 1990s. In 1979–80, a second oil price shock compounded the problems faced by governments, as inflation rates began to accelerate once more. The policies they introduced in the early 1980s were even more restrictive, and by 1986 inflation had fallen to golden age rates, accompanied by further severe increases in unemployment. Success with inflation proved to be only temporary. By the late 1980s, inflation rose again as many economies began to recover, even though average unemployment rates were about three times as high as in the golden age. Recovery brought a drop in unemployment rates but this ended in the early 1990s, when recession caused them to rise once more to the high rates experienced in the early 1980s. In this recession, inflation finally fell to rates comparable with those of the early 1960s. Whether the aim of policy was to reduce inflation, to reduce labour's power, or to correct payments difficulties, the results have been purchased at high cost in terms of the continuing high unemployment throughout the OECD.

2.14.   THE MAINSTREAM VIEW

The mainstream explanation of the inability of capitalist economies to live up to expectations since the golden age comes in two versions. One was influential in the period following the end of the golden age; the other gained acceptance more recently. The first version is well illustrated by the 'McCracken Report' sponsored by the OECD (1978). In the immediate aftermath of the decline in GDP growth and rise in unemployment that began in 1974, this interpretation of events emphasized shocks, including policy errors, as the culprits.[13] These were held responsible for the accelerating rates of inflation beginning in the second half of the 1960s, which necessitated the initiation of restrictive policies and rising unemployment rates. The difficulties were attributed to 'an unusual bunching of unfortunate events unlikely to be repeated on the same scale, the impact of which was compounded by some avoidable errors in economic policy' (p. 98). Recovery required 'a sustained expansion, initially less rapid than would otherwise be desirable during which memories of recent inflation should fade, and confidence in rising sales and employment be restored' (p. 274). It was claimed that by 1980 recovery would return conditions similar to those of the golden age if the Report's recommendations were followed. Clearly the optimism of the McCracken Report was unfounded.

The more recent explanation focuses on 'market imperfections', with the term 'Eurosclerosis' often used in academic journals and the media to denote this view. This more pessimistic version, benefiting from hindsight, sees the now prolonged difficulties as due to structural change, stressing the negative impact of a wide range of institutional developments over the postwar era that led real economies to deviate from the competitive textbook model, for example, centralized trade union movements and regulated work conditions. These institutional developments allegedly created barriers that, if they did not make it impossible to reduce unemployment by Keynesian methods, made it impossible to do so without creating ever accelerating rates of inflation. Recovery would follow policy-induced changes in institutions on the 'supply' side, for example, reducing the power of the trade unions, greater 'flexibility' in the labour market. Clearly, these two versions of the mainstream view show a continuing implicit affirmation of capitalism as a self-regulating system.

Our explanation of the end of the golden age and its replacement by a high unemployment episode has one thing in common with the 'market imperfections' view of the malfunction; persistent high unemployment is rooted in institutional causes and will persist until policy-induced institutional changes occur. We differ, and the differences are fundamental, about what caused the Great Inflation and how it ended the golden age, about the impact on institutions of the restrictive policy responses to inflation and about the nature of the policy-induced institutional changes required for recovery.

2.15. AN ALTERNATIVE EXPLANATION OF THE GREAT INFLATION[14]

While a bunching of exogenous shocks certainly had a significant short-run impact on inflation, they played a much smaller role than usually claimed, and are not among what we consider to be the basic causes of the Great

Inflation. The shocks in oil and other commodity markets, so often cited in the literature, came later and while they lasted amplified the already entrenched wage and price inflation. Following the imposition of restrictive policies in the mid 1970s, inflation rates in international commodity markets fell sharply. This brought down the overall rate of inflation, which nevertheless remained appreciably higher than before the wage explosion, in spite of a substantial increase in unemployment rates. This suggests that the Great Inflation and its inflationary after-effects were generated by something other than transient shocks.

We maintain that the lasting effect of the Great Inflation can be traced to institutional changes in the labour market. It is because these changes are still embedded in the institutional framework of the economies that the Great Inflation plays a critical role in ending the golden age. The overall stance of policy has remained restrictive long after the Great Inflation ended. Thus the persistent high unemployment since the mid-1970s can be traced in the first instance to policy responses to inflation. These include the response to an increasingly serious inflation problem during the late 1960s and early 1970s, and subsequently to the response of governments and monetary authorities concerned that capitalist economies had developed a strong inflationary bias. Simply put, institutional changes had led to a situation in which the downward sloping Phillips curve had shifted outward to such an extent that the full employment rate of unemployment was associated with politically unacceptable rates of inflation.[15]

We do not rule out the possibility that payments problems caused by oil shocks may have influenced aggregate demand policy or that subsequent institutional changes other than those affecting the inflationary bias have also operated to restrain aggregate demand, for example, balanced budget regulations, Maastricht criteria, a desire to reduce the power of labour. However, we argue that the institutional changes that led to the inflationary bias were also the initiating and sustaining causes of restrictive policies and the consequent deterioration in macroeconomic performance. To show more clearly the nature of these institutional changes, we begin with a brief examination of the labour market institutions that existed during the golden age.

At the beginning of the golden age, the advanced OECD economies fell into two groups, distinguished by their strategies for wage determination. In the larger group, labour and capital had agreed to a social bargain strategy; in the second group a market power strategy prevailed. The social bargains were sets of institutions that allowed full employment without serious inflationary pressure. These were the embodiments of the postwar compromise in the industrial relations systems of most OECD economies. In the market power group, this compromise was absent or inadequately developed, resulting in uncooperative industrial relations systems. The unemployment rates in these economies were higher and their growth generally slower than in the social bargain group, a consequence of the inflationary bias which governments controlled by restrictive policy measures. For either type of economy, the initial structure is depicted in Figure 2.3 by the left-hand box.

From the beginning of the golden age, the modernization of industry and rapidly expanding exports yielded productivity gains and growing incomes throughout the OECD. In most economies, this growth also supported expansion of social safety nets, further increasing the economic power of labour. But even during this great expansion, the differences between the two groups of countries were plain. The greatest difference lay in the unemployment rates, and resulted from the strategy used by labour to secure a fair distribution of the growing real income.

In many economies, for example Austria and Sweden, labour entered into a social bargain in which money wage demands were restrained and wage settlements coordinated with the national goals of wage and price stability in return for benefits such as guaranteed full employment, rising real wages and a generous welfare state. The result was that even in economies with strong centralized trade union movements, the social bargain restrained inflationary pressures at full employment for most of the golden age. In the 'market power' group, for example Canada and the United States, labour sought its real income goal by maximizing the rate of money wage increase, given the degree of tightness of the labour market. Since labour's market power increased when unemployment rates fell, this strategy generated a negative relationship between rates of unemployment and wage inflation. In these economies, even during the golden age inflation rose to politically unacceptable rates before full employment was reached, that is, an inflationary bias existed. Inflation was met by restrictive policies. As a result inflation rates differed little between the two groups of economies, but unemployment was substantially higher in the market power group. A large part of this variation in unemployment rates (and in aggregate demand policies) can be explained ultimately in terms of differences in the labour market institutions of the two groups (Cornwall, 1994, ch. 5).

2.16.   THE END OF THE GOLDEN AGE

For both groups of countries, the end of the golden age can be traced to the late 1960s, but the initiating causes differ. Many of the social bargain countries experienced wage explosions in the second half of the 1960s, which passed through to prices and accelerated the rate of price inflation,

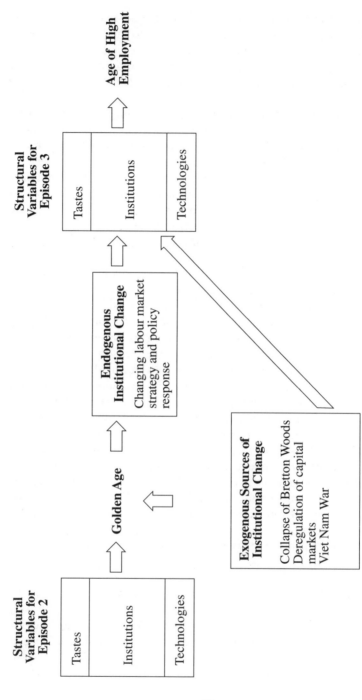

Figure 2.3   From the golden age to high unemployment

a trend which was to continue into the mid 1970s. This outcome, as well as the rising unemployment rates that followed, arose from an evolutionary process induced by the economic performance of the golden age (Cornwall, 1994, Chapters 8 and 9; Flanagan et al., 1983; Phelps Brown, 1971; Perry, 1975; and Soskice, 1978). Even in the economies that had adopted a social bargain strategy during the golden age, the prolonged and increasing prosperity of this period generated growing aspirations and rising expectations. In addition, the distribution of income had shifted towards profits, undermining the distributional fairness characteristic that was a keystone of social bargains (Goldthorpe, 1978). By the second half of the 1960s and into the early 1970s labour, especially the rank and file, dissatisfied with recent trends in real wages and other aspects of employment, was unwilling to restrain money wage demands as in the past. The chosen remedy was to push for higher rates of growth of money wages. The resulting wage explosions and higher strike volume in many Western European economies in the late 1960s and early 1970s indicated the collapse of social bargains and a shift to a market power strategy. To put the argument in its simplest terms, the success of capitalism in the golden age induced a profound change in institutions throughout most of the OECD economies and these changed institutions still persist. This endogenous process, induced by economic performance, is shown in Figure 2.3 by the two middle horizontal arrows.

In economies which had never adopted a social bargain strategy, economic events of the late 1960s–early 1970s also led to increased labour militancy. The escalation of the Viet Nam war exerted a strong inflationary effect in the United States, which failed to raise taxes to support the expanded military spending. The effect spread to her trading partners, especially Canada, where export demand for both military and civilian goods rose. In both countries these strong aggregate demand pressures pushed unemployment rates to low levels by North American standards, accelerating wage and price inflation. In Figure 2.3, this is represented by the vertical arrow from the 'exogenous sources' box to performance.

Initiated by different causes, inflation was accelerating in both sets of countries. The view of the authorities was that the employment performance enjoyed before 1974 could be restored only if the goals of price and wage stability were sacrificed; this was unacceptable politically, and restrictive policies were used to fight inflation by increasing unemployment.[16] It was the breakdown of social bargains, leading to inflation and the restrictive policy response, that ended the golden age in most economies. In the market strategy group, where restrictive policies had previously been used intermittently, they now became persistent. For both groups, the policy response to the Great Inflation established the new institutions for the current episode of high unemployment, shown in Figure 2.3 by the right-most horizontal arrow leading to the structural variables for episode 3. These two groups of countries exhibit evolutionary institutional change, that is change induced by economic performance. In one case, change is endogenously initiated by performance leading to the removal of labour market institutions that fostered social bargains. In the other, exogenously generated change in economic performance led to institutional change.

In addition to these two evolutionary routes for institutional change there is a third. It is not evolutionary, but results from the direct effects of exogenous events. The breakdown of the Bretton Woods system falls into this category for any individual country except the United States. While efforts to rejuvenate Bretton Woods continued for several years, these ultimately failed, and its collapse in the early 1970s changed international institutions dramatically. This is shown in Figure 2.3 by the diagonal arrow from the 'exogenous sources' box to the institutions of episode 3. The implications of this change for economic performance are taken up in the next section.

2.17. REINFORCING DECLINE

In spite of some decline in unemployment in the later 1980s and in officially measured rates in the 1990s, unemployment in the OECD has shown a strong upward trend for the past three decades,[17] reflecting the response of the authorities to perceived increases in the inflationary bias. During the current episode further institutional changes have reinforced the already depressed economic conditions. Some have been laws explicitly constraining aggregate demand policies, for example, budget deficit restrictions, Maastricht criteria. Others have worsened the trade-off between inflation and unemployment, causing a higher rate of inflation at full employment by the 1990s, in almost all OECD economies. Two institutional changes deserve special attention, one induced by the deteriorating unemployment performance, the other exogenous to all economies with the possible exception of the United States. Both have increased the use of restrictive aggregate demand policies, reinforcing the adverse unemployment effects of the end of social bargains.

First, the prolonged period of policy-induced high unemployment since the mid-1970s has generated new forms of hysteresis in labour markets. By the 1990s labour believed that *when labour market conditions improve,* money wage demands must be sufficient to generate a 'catch-up' in real wages which had stagnated or declined in the 1980s. Also, labour's view that it has borne an unfairly high share of the cost of fighting inflation will further increase its militancy in pursuit of money-wage increases when unemployment falls. These hysteretic effects operate with special force under low unemployment conditions, increasing the associated rates of inflation (Cornwall, *op. cit.*, p. 169). The resulting increased inflationary bias has only strengthened the resolve of the authorities to push unemployment rates even higher in order to control inflation.[18]

Second, the breakdown of the Bretton Woods Agreement initiated radical changes in the international monetary system. As well as the move to a relatively flexible exchange rate system, the 1970s ushered in a period of increasing deregulation of international capital movements. Under the new regime the inflation costs are increased in any economy that depreciates its currency *as part of a stimulative aggregate demand package*. In this case, the response of managers of large, mobile capital funds to unilateral reflationary policies acts to worsen the inflation–unemployment trade-off both directly and by interacting with the hysteretic effects just discussed. This introduces an additional constraint on the use of stimulative aggregate demand policies. Together with the end of social bargains, these two institutional changes guaranteed high unemployment almost everywhere in the OECD. Even without including the purely political constraints on aggregate demand, such as balanced budget rules or the Maastricht criteria, the conditions that have developed are best described as a high unemployment equilibrium trap.

2.18.   CONCEPTS

The discussion has so far ignored some rather obvious practical problems involved in modelling historical processes. Chief among these is the need to establish which institutions matter in determining performance. Conceptually the short-run exogeneity and long-run endogeneity treatment of institutions is easily stated. As the short-run episode is defined, the evolutionary and hysteretic properties of the long-run model are deliberately and temporarily suppressed in order to isolate the impact of a given institutional structure on macroeconomic tendencies (Setterfield, 1997, pp. 39–43). Obviously an institutional structure is composed of a large number of institutions; not all of them are relevant when considering the impact of institutions on macroeconomic performance and the changes in institutions that move the system to a new episode. Therefore we focus only on those institutions that permit or preclude the continuous high levels of aggregate demand that are a necessary prerequisite of a full employment level of unemployment. In order to better appraise the internal structure of our analysis and the benefits it provides in explaining historical developments,

the procedure for selecting the relevant institutions, that is, those that ultimately determine unemployment performance, must be formulated.

We need to spend little time discussing the obvious examples of laws or
rules explicitly limiting stimulative aggregate demand policies such as balanced budget rules or Maastricht criteria. More complex are those situations in which there are trade-offs between full employment and other
macroeconomic goals, with terms of the trade-off being set by the presence
or absence of certain institutions. In these cases, the procedure to identify
relevant institutions is as follows. First, a macroeconomic goal of special
interest is specified, in our study full employment. Next we determine other
desirable goals whose attainment may be jeopardized by strong aggregate
demand pressures and full employment conditions, such as politically
acceptable rates of inflation or external balance. Finally we determine the
institutions that allow or prevent the simultaneous achievement of these
other goals. These are the relevant institutions.

Sections 2.15 and 2.16 provide an example. They relate differences in
unemployment and inflation records in the golden age to differences in
institutions, for example, labour market strategies. For ease of exposition,
it is useful to simply assume that inflation below some maximum rate is the
only goal that might be jeopardized by full employment, and that the
labour market strategy alone allows or prevents the simultaneous achievement of acceptable rates of inflation. Under this assumption the chosen
labour market strategy becomes the relevant institution in determining the
inflation costs associated with the full employment rate of unemployment.
As discussed in Section 2.15, there were two possible labour market strategies, a social bargain and a market power strategy. Following the argument
of that section, economies in which labour adopts a social bargain strategy
experience aggregate demand levels consistent with full employment
because this institution restrains inflationary pressures at full employment.
As long as a social bargain strategy prevails, low rates of unemployment
and inflation are realized simultaneously.

Superior macroeconomic performance is a manifestation of the presence of an institution, in this example a social bargain strategy, which
allowed full employment levels of aggregate demand. Since our efforts are
directed towards explaining as well as identifying unemployment episodes, we therefore characterize episodes not merely in terms of some low
average unemployment rate. We also describe such episodes in terms of
the institutions whose presence permits the simultaneous realization of
low unemployment *and* low rates of inflation. The low inflationary implications of the social bargain strategy allow full employment levels of
aggregate demand.[19] In contrast, in those economies in which labour
adopted a market power strategy, the inflationary consequences of pre-

vailing labour market institutions are unacceptable and the full employment goal abandoned.

2.19.   INTERTEMPORAL ANALYSIS

A maintained hypothesis in this study is that just as differences in certain institutions account for unemployment and inflation rate differences among countries, changes in these institutions are responsible for changing macroeconomic performance within a country. For example, a shift within an economy from a social bargain to a market power strategy will initiate a new short-run episode. An institutional change of this particular kind is historically relevant, since it leads to an episode of high unemployment, as the authorities respond to the new inflationary tendencies by a reduction in aggregate demand.

In keeping with the earlier analysis, the institutional change within the economy could be induced by the performance of the economy or it could be the direct effect of an exogenous change. In either case the economy is moved to a new episode characterized by new institutions that lead to poorer macroeconomic performance. Consider again a shift from a social bargain to a market power strategy induced by the performance of the economy. This describes an evolutionary process with negative feedback; the previous episode of superior performance is causally linked through induced institutional change and policy response to a succeeding episode of poor performance. There the system remains as long as the new labour market strategy prevails. To escape this high unemployment trap, the precondition is that institutions must change so as to allow full employment without generating unacceptable inflation. Only a well designed policy is likely to achieve the needed change in a timely manner, and only when this is accomplished can stimulative aggregate demand policies be used to secure full employment. In this example the required policy-induced institutional change is the creation of inducements to capital and labour to adopt a new social bargain strategy,

2.20.   APPLICATION

2.20.1.   Interpreting Changes in Performance

The predictive powers of our approach are as limited as those of mainstream approaches, and neither can predict institutional change. Even so, we claim superior *ex post* explanatory powers for our approach, and greater ability to formulate the appropriate remedial measures. In explaining historical processes the central and difficult practical issue is how to interpret whether a change in performance is due to shocks, with no permanent effect on institutions, or to a change in institutions; and if it is the latter, to identify the institutions that are involved. The question is which theoretical framework is the most likely to interpret events correctly and it is here that our approach, by emphasizing institutions, proves superior.

A central hypothesis of this study is that while an economy is at all times subject to exogenous disturbances that temporarily affect performance within any episode, alternating episodes of poor as well as superior macroeconomic performance are normal outcomes of capitalist development. Capitalism is not self-regulating nor does it self-destruct, but institutions may emerge that lead to unacceptably high rates of inflation at full employment. In contrast, believers in capitalism's self-regulating properties argue that any search for causes of a significant deterioration in performance, such as a marked acceleration in inflation rates, should focus on outside disturbances, including policy errors, or on market imperfections. If the cause is attributed to temporary disturbances, conditions will soon improve, if not automatically, then with the introduction of available conventional policies to counter the influence of disturbances. If attributed to market imperfections, on *a priori* grounds malfunction is the effect of bad institutions, those that have led to a further deviation of the system from the competitive model, for example, the recent introduction of a minimum wage law.

The case in support of our approach as the more likely to provide an accurate interpretation of events rests on its predisposition to study the institutional prerequisites for successful performance as well as for macro malfunction, in other words a continuous engagement in a research agenda relating economic performance to institutions. Thus, when performance deteriorates in some economy, an inspection of institutional arrangements prevailing before the deterioration in performance, or in economies currently not experiencing the malfunction, is of immediate assistance. For example, when inflation rates accelerate in an economy previously experiencing low rates of inflation at full employment, an early diagnosis of the causes may be possible by examining events in the labour market before and after the change in the inflation record. Absence of evidence of increased labour discontent in the form, say, of wildcat strikes, of rank and file challenges to union leadership and of excessive money wage demands would suggest that the acceleration of inflation rates was due to shocks, for example increased oil prices. If so, conventional policy measures to offset the impact of shocks would likely be sufficient to restore the previously favourable economic conditions.

On the other hand, sharp increases in strike volume, in challenges to union leadership and in money wage demands, followed by an acceleration in the rate of wage inflation, would be evidence of increased worker discontent and militancy, indicating a shift from a social bargain to a market power strategy by labour (Soskice, 1978). Driving the associated rise in rates of price inflation is a change in labour market institutions. However, accurate diagnosis requires information on institutions and such an inventory of information is not likely to be available or to be considered of value to believers in self-regulating capitalism. In contrast to the mainstream equilibrium approach, we find much to gain from studying an economy's institutions and its history. An awareness of the role institutions play in determining performance reduces both the likelihood of failing to intervene to alter institutions when such policies are appropriate, and the propensity to intervene when no intervention is called for.

2.20.2.   Institutional Change and Policy

This raises a related point and an additional gain from adopting an evolutionary–Keynesian approach. Not only is a continuous focus on institutions as determinants of macroeconomic performance more likely to lead to an early and accurate analysis of the causes of malfunction, in those cases in which institutional change has been properly diagnosed as the basic cause of malfunction, the necessary remedial polices are more clearly recognized. Assume that it is generally accepted by economists and policymakers that institutional change has been responsible for an acceleration in inflation rates. To those who perceive capitalism as subject to periodic malfunction, having diagnosed the cause of malfunction as a shift in labour market institutions from a social bargain to a market power strategy, the obvious remedial measure is to use policies to effect changes in institutions. The analysis of Sections 2.15 and 2.16 indicates the reintroduction of a social bargain strategy, hardly a move towards more competitive conditions, improves performance.[20] In contrast, when malfunction is attributed on *a priori* grounds to some form of deviation from the competitive model, policy measures advocated will be of a quite different sort, for example, elimination of minimum wage laws, reduction in union powers.

2.21.   CONCLUSIONS

Among the assumptions of our analysis, the most important is the view that capitalism is not self-regulating but is subject to lengthy episodes of malfunction, particularly high unemployment. The inability of neoclassical equilibrium theory to analyse the unemployment issue satisfactorily has been a major reason for our rejection of this framework and for our desire to formulate an alternative. Basic to the development of our framework is a view that severe malfunction can only be understood in terms of structural change, and then only when structural change is understood to include institutional change. The same case can be made for understanding the forces leading to superior macroeconomic performance. Specifically, we have outlined a framework that distinguishes between and encompasses evolutionary and hysteretic mechanisms, both of which we believe are necessary to model historical processes. Even the concept of an equilibrium, when properly interpreted as a state of institutional rest rather than a steady state balanced growth condition, can be encompassed in our framework.

The objective of this chapter has been to present an analytical framework for the study of long-run macroeconomic dynamics, and to demonstrate how it can be used to model historical processes. The applications we have included emphasize the role of institutions and institutional change in economic development and performance. In these applications, we have attempted to underscore two points central to our thesis. The first is that institutions are as fully a part of the economic structure as are tastes and technologies, and that institutional change produces effects as profound and persistent as technological change. The second is that mainstream macrodynamics either neglects institutions entirely or misrepresents them as hindrances to the automatic and continuous full employment promised by mainstream growth models, whether the Solow–Swan or new growth theory versions; consequently these models assume away the characteristics of capitalist development, rather than explaining them.

The narrative of the chapter has been predominantly historical, in order to present the approach in broad outline. A more analytical account would include a detailed explanation of the extended Keynesian mechanism that drives the system within each episode and induces the institutional change that links successive episodes. This would have clarified the strong Keynesian roots of our evolutionary–Keynesian approach, and our intention to offer a long-run complement to the traditional Keynesian short-run theory of aggregate demand (see Cornwall and Cornwall, 1997). A more comprehensive account would have extended the analysis further back in time to include a structural explanation of the Great Depression. As argued elsewhere, the link between the industrialization episode of American development and the Great Depression was developments in technology (Cornwall and Cornwall, 2001)

While acknowledging that the predictive capacity of our approach is no greater than that of mainstream models, we are convinced of its superior explanatory power. Once the belief in invisible hands is abandoned, a concern with the structural features of the economy comes to the fore. It is in the examination of structure, and especially of institutional change and its causes, that our approach expands analysis beyond the mere response to exogenous shocks. Understanding of the role of institutions and institutional change requires a research agenda that can identify the institutional characteristics that support successful economic performance or produce economic malfunction. This understanding provides a clearer diagnosis of the causes of any deterioration in performance.

The issues raised here are not merely part of a debate within the economics profession. Economists promoting the self-regulating view of capitalism have led the movement for institutional change toward more competitive markets and deregulation, and they have profoundly influenced political debate for over two decades. An example is the 'Eurosclerosis' programme for a return to full employment *and* acceptable inflation rates. Unfortunately, their policy prescription is counterproductive, as the unfair distribution of the costs of fighting inflation through high unemployment increases social divisions, impeding efforts to introduce a second generation of social bargains. Sections 2.15 and 2.16 discussed the weak empirical basis of policies that flow from a belief in Eurosclerosis. We examine the historical record, and assesses the role of institutions, revealing that these same institutions viewed in the Eurosclerosis account as market imperfections actually fostered the golden age, and their collapse led to its end. The remedy is then clearly to establish new institutions that will perform the same function.

NOTES

1. This is a joint paper. The work was supported by grants from the Mount Saint Vincent Internal Research Fund and the Department of Economics at Dalhousie. We wish to thank Geoff Hodgson, Geoff Harcourt, Shaun Hargreaves Heap, Steve Pressman, Kurt Rothschild, Mark Setterfield, and Peter Skott for their useful remarks and criticisms.
2. Full employment is defined as the absence of involuntary unemployment. Although the 2.4 per cent average for 1955–73 probably includes some involuntary unemployment, no great error results from assuming this to be the full employment rate, since our main concern is with *changes* in unemployment rates between episodes.
3. Technological change played this role in the Great Depression (Cornwall, 1992).
4. The chapter focuses on long-standing members of the OECD; the less developed and some very small economies are excluded. Included are the 16 economies of Table 2.1 plus Ireland and New Zealand.
5. We note that the regulationist 'episode' is defined by the prevailing technology, while we define episodes according to performance.
6. The spread and adoption of political ideas, when triggered or accelerated by economic conditions, are endogenous in our terms. The ideas themselves usually encompass broader social issues, making them exogenous.
7. Keynes takes up problem of compatibility of capitalism and democracy in Chapter 24 of *The General Theory*, a reflection of these concerns.

8. These are exogenous to any single country, because it is the response of the others that worsens the problems that protectionist measures are expected to remedy.
9. In contrast, no political party in the United States took up labour's cause to the same degree. Wages became the primary issue, and strikes in 1946 were followed by a series of anti-union measures culminating in the Taft–Hartley Act (1947).
10. This commitment varied widely in its practical aspects. For example, it was an integral part of the British Labour Party's platform, to be achieved by fiscal measures as Keynes had prescribed, and was enshrined in the French Constitution; in the US it was reduced to a responsibility of the President, who had no power to achieve it.
11. The case of Japan was quite different. The US originally imposed unions modelled on their own, but the widespread demonstrations, workplace occupations and strikes that followed led them, with the support of the Japanese government and employers, to replace these with new unions which promised harmonious industrial relations.
12. An inflationary bias does not necessarily imply that inflation increases; it means that the position of the Phillips curve results in unacceptably high inflation at full employment.
13. The Report also mentioned labour's rising expectations and aspirations as influences on events but these were ignored in the policy prescriptions.
14. For a fuller treatment of the main ideas in this and the next two sections see Cornwall (1996) and Cornwall and Cornwall (1996).
15. For an argument in support of a downward sloping long-run Phillips curve and a rejection of vertical long-run curves see Cornwall and Cornwall (1997).
16. Exceptions were Austria, which maintained full employment until the late 1980s, and Japan, Norway, Sweden and Switzerland which did so until the early 1990s (OECD, 1997, Annex Tables 21 and 22).
17. See OECD, *Labour Force Statistics*, various issues and *Economic Outlook* June, 1997, Annex Table 23, OECD, Paris, 1997.
18. The induced effect on labour attitudes just described illustrates a process of positive feedback or one with reinforcing properties. It is neglected in the diagram purely for pedagogical reasons.
19. In Tinbergen's terms, the two goals of full employment and politically acceptable rates of inflation can be achieved simultaneously because there are two instruments available for achieving these goals, aggregate demand policies and a social bargain.
20. Assuming the goals of policy are still only full employment and low inflation.

REFERENCES

Aglietta, M. (1979), *A Theory of Capitalist Regulation*, London: New Left Books.
Armstrong, P., Glyn, A. and Harrison, J. (1984), *Capitalism since World War II*, London: Fontana Paperbacks.
Barro, R. (1991), 'Economic growth in a cross section of countries', *Quarterly Journal of Economics*, May.
Beveridge, W.H. (1944), *Full Employment in a Free Society. A report*, London: George Allen and Unwin.
Boyer, R. (1986), *Théorie de la régulation, une analyse critique*, Paris: La Découverte.
Cornwall, J. (1992), 'Stabilization of mature economies: what did we learn from the collapse of the 1930s?', in K. Villupilai (ed.), *Nonlinearities, Disequilibrium and Simulation: Quantitative Method in the Social Sciences*, London: Macmillan.
Cornwall, J. (1994), *Economic Breakdown and Recovery: Theory and Policy*, Armonk, New York: M.E. Sharpe.
Cornwall, J. (1996), 'Notes on the trade cycle and social philosophy in a post-

Keynesian world', in G. Harcourt and P. Riach (eds), *A Second Edition of the General Theory*, London: Routledge.

Cornwall, J. and Cornwall, W. (1996), 'Two views of macroeconomic malfunction: the "Great Inflation" and its aftermath', in P. Arestis (ed.), *Employment, Economic Growth and the Tyranny of the Market*, Cheltenham, UK: Edward Elgar.

Cornwall, J. and Cornwall, W. (1997), 'The unemployment problem and the legacy of Keynes', *Journal of Post Keynesian Economics*, **19** (4), 525–42.

Cornwall, J. and Cornwall, W. (2001), *Capitalist Development in the Twentieth Century: An Evolutionary–Keynesian Analysis*, Cambridge, UK: Cambridge University Press.

Crafts, N. and Toniolo, G. (1996), 'Post-war growth: an overview', in N. Crafts and G. Toniolo (eds), *Economic Growth in Europe since 1945*, Cambridge: Cambridge University Press, pp. 1–37.

Cross, R. and Allen, A. (1988), 'On the history of hysteresis', in R. Cross (ed.), *Unemployment, Hysteresis and the Natural Rate Hypothesis*, Oxford: Basil Blackwell.

Eichengreen, B. (1995), 'Mainsprings of economic recovery in post-war Europe', in B. Eichengreen (ed.), *Europe's Post-War Recovery*, Cambridge: Cambridge University Press, pp. 3–35.

Flanagan, R., Soskice, D. and Ulman, L. (1983), *Unionism, Economic Stabilization and Incomes Policies, European Experience*, Washington, DC: Brookings Institution.

Glyn, A., Hughes, A., Lipietz, A. and Singh, A. (1990), 'The Rise and Fall of the Golden Age', Chapter 2 in S.A. Margin and J.B. Schor (eds), *The Golden Age of Capitalism*, Oxford: Clarendon Press, pp. 39–125.

Goldthorpe. J. (1978), 'The current inflation: towards a sociological account', in F. Hirsch and J. Goldthorpe (eds), *The Political Economy of Inflation*, Cambridge, Mass.: Harvard University Press.

Hobsbawm, E. (1994), *Age of Extremes. The Short Twentieth Century, 1914–1991*, London, Michael Joseph.

Kalecki, M. (1943), 'Political aspects of full employment', *Political Quarterly*, **14**, 322–31. Reprinted as chapter 12 in M. Kalecki (1971), *Selected Essays on the Dynamics of the Capitalist Economy, 1933–1970*, Cambridge: Cambridge University Press.

Kondratiev, Nikolai D. (1925), 'The Long Wave in Economic Life', translation in *The Review of Economics and Statistics*, **17**, November 1935, 105–15.

Lindbeck, A. and Snower D. (1987), 'Union activity, unemployment persistence and wage employment ratchets', *European Economic Review*, **31**, Feb–Mar.

Lucas, R. (1988), 'On the mechanics of economic development', *Journal of Monetary Economics*, **22** (1), 3–42.

Maddison, A. (1991), *Dynamic Forces in Capitalist Development*, Oxford: Oxford University Press.

Maier, C. (1987), 'The Politics of Productivity: foundations of American international economic policy after the war', in *In Search of Stability*, Cambridge: Cambridge University Press, 121–152.

Mandel, E. (1964), 'The economics of neo-capitalism', *Socialist Register*, 56–67.

Marglin, S.A. (1990), 'Lessons of the Golden Age: an Overview', Chapter I in S.A. Marglin and J.B. Schor (eds), *The Golden Age of Capitalism*, Oxford: Clarendon Press, 1–38.

North, D. (1990), *Institutions, Institutional Change and Economic Performance*, Cambridge: Cambridge University Press.

OECD (1978), *Towards Full Employment and Price Stability*, Paris: OECD.

OECD (1997), *Economic Outlook* Paris: OECD, June.

OECD (1999a), *Historical Statistics 1960–97*, Paris: OECD.

OECD (1999b), *Economic Outlook 1966*, Paris: OECD.

OECD, *Labour Force Statistics*, Paris: OECD, various issues.

Olson, M. (1982), *The Rise and Decline of Nations. Economic Growth, Stagflation and Social Rigidities*, New Haven: Yale University Press.

Perry, G. (1975), 'Determinants of wage inflation around the world', *Brookings Papers on Economic Activity*, 2.

Phelps Brown, H. (1971), 'The analysis of wage movements under full employment', *Scottish Journal of Political Economy*, November.

Phelps Brown, H. (1975), 'A non-monetarist view of the pay explosion', *Three Banks Review*, March.

Romer, P. (1986), 'Increasing returns and long-run growth', *Journal of Political Economy*, **94** (5), 1002–37.

Romer, P. (1990), 'Endogenous technological change', *Journal of Political Economy*, **98**, S71–102.

Schumpeter, J. (1912) *The Theory of Economic Development*, Leipzig: Duncker and Humblot. Translated by R. Opie, Cambridge, MA: Harvard University Press, 1934. Reprinted, New York: Oxford University Press, 1961.

Schumpeter, J. (1939), *Business Cycles. A Theoretical, Historical and Statistical Analysis of the Capitalist Process*, 2 vols, New York: McGraw-Hill.

Schumpeter, J. (1942), *Capitalism, Socialism and Democracy*, New York: Harper.

Setterfield, M. (1997), *Rapid Growth and Relative Decline*, London: Macmillan Press Ltd.

Shonfield, A. (1965), *Modern Capitalism. The Changing Balance of Public and Private Power*, Oxford: Oxford University Press.

Soskice, D. (1978), 'Strike waves and wage explosions, 1968–1970: an economic interpretation', in C. Crouch and A. Pizzarno (eds), *The Resurgence of Class Conflict in Western Europe Since 1969, Vol. 2*, New York: Holmes and Meir.

Svennilson, I. (1954), *Growth and Stagnation in the European Economy*, Geneva: Economic Commission for Europe.

Van Duijn, J.J. (1983), *The Long Wave in Economic Life*, London: Allen and Unwin.

3. Can the global neoliberal regime survive victory in Asia? The political economy of the Asian crisis

Jim Crotty and Gary Dymski*

> The Crisis consists precisely in the fact that old is dying and the new cannot be born; in this interregnum, morbid phenomena of the most varied kind come to pass. (Antonio Gramsci, *Prison Notebooks*, 1996)

3.1. INTRODUCTION

The sequence of events that is still denoted the 'Asian' financial crisis has now produced a global economic crisis. It began with the destabilization of several Southeastern Asian currencies in summer 1997. By summer 1998, Wall Street had lost momentum. The IMF's inability to stop Russia's mid-summer crisis then turned the cracks in Wall Street's dizzy consensus concerning the end of history into gaping holes. Traders worldwide ran for safety, leading to spasmodic new rounds of currency and equity-market collapses in Latin America and Asia.

Merely documenting what has happened will fill volumes. We focus here first on the architecture of the crisis as a whole, and then on one case: South Korea. There are several reasons for choosing Korea. First, it occupies the pivotal place in the sequence of events: the tsunami that built up in Southeast Asia hit the Republic of Korea with full force in autumn 1997, and lingered there through the spring before assaulting New York, Russia and Latin America in summer 1998. Second, Korea is perhaps the prototype for the Asian developmental model. Third, we have observed the Korean situation firsthand. In effect, Korea provides us with a lens for viewing the innumerable layers of crisis in the current situation.

Our central point is that the essence of the current crisis is its inherent structural complexity; it cannot be reduced to a single mechanism operating at a single behavioural level, but involves instead a series of interlinked

53

conflicts operating at several levels simultaneously. Understandably, most analysts have focused on one or the other contributing causes in this crisis. Some have tried to identify a flawed microfoundational mechanism of the 'Asian model' – for example, Krugman's (1998) model of perverse borrower–lender relations due to unwise government guarantees. Others have emphasized national policy mistakes – for example, Grabel's (1998) argument that over-reliance on hard-currency foreign loans without controls over portfolio investment flows triggered many recent financial crises. Still others have emphasized flaws in the structure of international markets – for example, Paul Davidson's (1998) view that the Asian crisis reflects liquidity-shortage chickens coming home to roost in the post-Bretton Woods world.

We find much to agree with in these works. But we do not think the crisis in its current form could have resulted only from problematic microeconomic design, flawed national strategy, or a perverse international environment. Rather, the current crisis has arisen simultaneously as a conflict between international and national forces, on one hand, and as localized struggles between capital and labour, on the other.

The crisis is thus inherently international, national and class-based all at once. In our view, no single behavioural cause or design flow can be identified as having nudged the End-of-History ship toward the iceberg. Instead, this crisis has arisen due to long-term contradictions embedded in the structures and policies of the global neoliberal regime, political and economic contradictions internal to affected Asian nations, and the destructive short-term dynamics of liberalized global financial markets. The system is broken at so many levels that serious study of the structured complexity of global conflict must precede proposals for institutional and policy change designed to solve the many problems created by the crisis.

The sections that follow first discuss the transition from the golden age system to the global neoliberal regime, and then the myths and reality of the East Asian economic model. We then provide an overview of the Asian crisis, emphasizing the fundamental structural incompatibility between this model and the neoliberal regime. After critically evaluating the use of mainstream equilibrium-based models to understand the Asian crisis, we provide a more detailed discussion of the crisis in Korea. We end with some reflections on policy.

3.2.   FROM THE GOLDEN AGE TO THE GLOBAL NEOLIBERAL REGIME

The so-called golden age of modern capitalism, lasting from World War II through the early 1970s, was built on the foundation of state regulation of the economy.[1] In the international financial system, exchange rates were fixed relative to the dollar, which in turn was pegged to gold. Significant barriers to capital mobility were in place. Domestically, governments in the North operated managed capitalist systems. They controlled aggregate demand to meet unemployment and inflation targets; they regulated business and finance, established rights for workers, redistributed income via the tax/transfer system and underwrote a social safety net. In the workplace, a period of relative labour–capital peace was achieved through widespread adoption of what has been termed the Fordist production model. Economic output was centred on capital-intensive goods manufactured in large-scale facilities by largely unionized workforces. Many workers obtained higher real wages and gains in job security and workplace safety. Admittedly, experience in the countries of the South was extremely varied, in large part because many nations were emerging from neo-colonial domination by European powers. Fuelled by high Northern growth rates, much of the South did achieve sustained expansion.

The golden age's increasing prosperity did not, however, create capitalism without conflict. The struggle within each nation among firms and workers over wages, relative prices and working conditions continued unabated. And economic conflict among nations did not cease. During the golden age, the capital–labour class conflict was mediated by gains-sharing contracts that raised real wages; and national–capital conflicts were obviated by the Pax Americana within which the Bretton Woods system operated. These resolutions were, to some extent, mutually reinforcing. The top portion of Figure 3.1 demonstrates this point, using arrows to indicate causal influence. That is, the fixed-exchange rate regime facilitated the pursuit of Keynesian demand management built on redistribution and high employment; this created a political environment in which the public supported these policies, ensuring their continued implementation. Firms meanwhile engaged in co-respective competition based on (and thus expanding) the use of high-wage, high-productivity labour.

But eventually this solution came undone. The balance of power between domestic governments and real and financial capital seeking international mobility swung decisively toward the latter in the 1970s. This in turn legitimized a free-market revolution in economic policy, pursued most successfully by conservative politicians and economists in the US and the UK in the early 1980s. With the golden age in ruins, the Reagan and Thatcher administrations put the neoliberal regime into place.

The defining elements of the neoliberal regime are deregulation, privatization and liberalization – that is, a contraction of the state's role in an increasingly integrated global economic system. The hallmark of neoliberalism is the pursuit of unregulated markets almost everywhere for almost

The Golden Age period, 1946–71

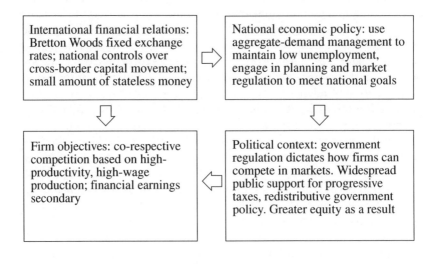

The neoliberal regime, 1980–present

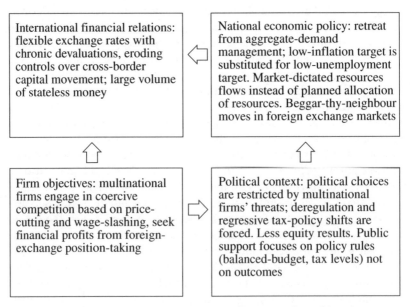

Figure 3.1 Systemic interactions in the golden age and neo liberal regimes

everything. These economic relations are supported in the ideological realm by the dominance of neoliberal economic and political theory – even within economics departments in Asian countries.

Guiding the emergence of this order are the G7 nations, especially the United States, together with the multinational corporations and banks of the North (and, increasingly, of the South). Supporting these agents are domestic elites, North and South, and a set of four multilateral institutions – the International Monetary Fund (IMF), the World Bank, the World Trade Organization and the Bank for International Settlements (BIS). The United States has stood at the apex of global economic power both in the golden age and in the neoliberal regime. The hallmark of the neoliberal order, however, is the power of global rentiers. The past two decades have seen the construction of a globe-girdling network of financial centres and off-shore financial havens. These centres and firms provide an infrastructure for financial speculation; the instability of exchange rates and interest rates in the neoliberal regime provide the requisite motivation.

The threat of nearly instantaneous cross-border capital movements triggered by speculative motives in turn has imposed severe constraints on state economic policies. Indeed, managed capitalism has been moving in the direction of laissez-faire capitalism. Monetary policy now aims at lowering inflation, not unemployment; safety-net and social-welfare programmes have been cut; the countercyclical role of government expenditure in sustaining aggregate demand has been virtually eliminated; business has been deregulated; and workers' rights have been restricted. The nations of the South are expected to follow suit if they expect to continue to trade with the North.

Economic conflict in the workplace is also resolved differently than in the golden age. The Fordist production model has been largely replaced by the 'post-Fordist' model, featuring substantial use of subcontracting, often with bid-price competition, just-in-time inventory methods and outsourcing. Together with the erosion of income-transfer programmes and state protection for workers, this has led to less gain-sharing by firms; regressive redistribution from labour to capital thus has helped sustain profits just as they were being eroded by increased interest payments. Many firms have taken advantage of the ease of capital mobility to adopt the global factory model, in which components are manufactured and assembled in multiple off-shore locations.

Advocates of neoliberal policies have argued that they would yield better national and global economic performance than in the golden age – higher GDP, employment and productivity growth. Technology transfers from the North would let less developed nations converge to the developed nations' level of economic performance. Such projections have proven to be wide of the mark. Neoliberal policies have generated higher profits for some multinational firms and banks, and much higher returns for rentiers throughout the world. But for most people, neoliberalism's promised benefits have not materialized. In the North, economic growth rates have been well below historical trends. European unemployment has hovered near depression levels for a decade, while in the US, median real wages have substantially declined and inequality has risen dramatically since the late 1970s. In much of the South, the situation is even worse. Latin America had its 'lost decade' after the Mexican debt default of August 1982. Eastern Europe's economies have stumbled badly after a widely heralded start.

The most recent *Trade and Development Report* of UNCTAD (1998) points out that global economic growth averaged just 1.9 per cent between 1990 and 1995; it rose to 3.0 per cent in 1996 and further to 3.2 per cent in 1997 – largely because the effects of the Asian crisis were not yet felt. But it is projected to fall to 2.0 per cent in 1998, perhaps to fall further in 1999. In the entire 1990–97 period, the economies of the developed nations have grown more slowly, on average, than the global economy as a whole – an average of 1.7 per cent in the 1990–95 period, 2.5 per cent in 1996, 2.7 per cent in 1997 and 1.8 per cent in 1998 (projected). East and Southeast Asia and the US are the only areas of the globe to have generated consistently high growth rates in the neoliberal era.

Why is Global Growth Stagnant?

Weak global growth rates in the neoliberal regime can be traced to two mutually reinforcing, fundamental problems: (1) chronically insufficient growth in aggregate demand; and its flip-side, (2) chronic excess aggregate supply. The structural tendency of the neoliberal regime to generate chronically inadequate aggregate demand growth provides the context within which the outbreak of the Asian crisis can be best understood.

Here we identify five interconnected roots of weak global aggregate demand deeply embedded in the structures of the neoliberal regime. First are a series of forces holding down wages and mass consumption. These include the threat of capital mobility (which, in the case of FDI, is underestimated by the measured volume of capital mobility),[2] rising import competition and chronic job 'churning', which can be traced both to technical change and to new corporate strategies of downsizing and re-engineering. In effect, changes in laws and technology made it feasible for multinational corporations to substitute low-wage Southern labour for equally-skilled but higher-paid Northern labour.[3] It bears emphasis that these anti-worker corporate policies were made possible by two prior shifts in government policy: the erosion of support for unions and regulated labour–capital bargaining; and the slow deconstruction of social safety nets, which made workers' exit option less attractive.

The second factor depressing global growth rates is the high real interest rate regime created by independent central banks and reinforced by global rentiers. This monetary-policy shift coincided with the elections of Reagan and Thatcher, who helped create a secular increase in the reserve army of the unemployed and thus forced the costs of the global crisis of the 1970s and early 1980s onto workers. This shift in monetary policy was reinforced by the rising power of global rentiers in the 1980s in the wake of financial deregulation. The rentiers were able to punish countries that used policy to pursue growth and employment rather than low inflation.

A third factor was the emergence of restrictive fiscal policy. The high interest-rate regime played a role: rising interest payments eat up larger shares of public spending, all else being equal. But more importantly, lower taxes and a shrinking social safety net have been the political order of the day. The importance given to austere fiscal policy was recognized explicitly in the criteria established under the Maastricht treaty. Further, rentiers and independent central banks together punished countries that ran excessive deficits.

A fourth factor was the level and character of global investment. Investment spending in the neoliberal regime has been, on average, low, due to high real interest rates and sluggish aggregate-demand growth. But beyond this, much investment was labour-saving rather than capacity-expanding: thus, the increased aggregate demand created by investment spending has often been counteracted by cuts in worker consumption caused by the job and wage losses associated with this investment.

The final factor explaining low aggregate demand is the role of the IMF. As more developing countries experienced national insolvency, the IMF has increasingly played a new role – lender of last resort to countries with inadequate foreign exchange reserves. The IMF has invariably mandated austerity macroeconomic policies plus neoliberal restructuring in return for its money. The growth of IMF austerity programmes around the developing world (not to mention the self-imposed macroeconomic austerity programmes adopted by countries like Brazil to avoid falling under the control of the IMF) has left global aggregate demand even more constrained.

Why hasn't supply adapted to reduced demand growth? In the neoliberal regime, demand problems have generated destructive competitive processes which, in turn, have aggravated demand deficiencies. The neoliberal regime has replaced the 'co-respective competition' (to use Schumpeter's phrase) among large firms in the golden age – characterized by long-term planning horizons, restrained capital–labour conflict and avoidance of those dimensions of competition that undercut industry-wide profitability, with 'coercive

competition' based on predatory pricing, overinvestment, waves of technological innovation that render recently constructed capital goods obsolete
(and the debt used to finance them potentially unpayable) and aggressive
regimes of labour policy.[4] The key is to understand why the neoliberal regime
has forced competition into a coercive and destructive mode.

The modern global economy has a discrete number of key manufacturing, service and financial industries that dominate international trade and
investment – such as banking, insurance, autos, airplanes, computers, semiconductors, electric appliances, steel and machine tools. Mature industrialized countries have large multinational corporations that desire to maintain
their traditional domination of these key industries. In addition, however,
developing countries moving up the technology/productivity/value-added
ladder – such as Japan, Korea and Taiwan – must establish footholds, followed by strongholds, in many of these same industries. So each new wave
of entrants, like the countries of South East Asia in recent decades, further
crowds these global markets. If global and Northern aggregate-demand
growth was strong, this problem would be contained to some degree. But,
as we have seen, it is not; the neoliberal regime severely constrains the
growth of demand. In the absence of exit by established players, waves of
new entrants leads to chronic overcapacity, low profits for many firms
(except at cyclical peaks), fierce competition and a deflationary bias in
global commodity markets.

Given the centrality of these markets and the sunk costs required to enter
them, most competitors try to stay in the game even as competition mounts,
hoping to survive current struggles so they can reap the high profits
expected to emerge when the losers are eventually forced out. Consequently, they tend to overinvest, building plants in areas with cheaper
labour and/or adding cutting-edge technology. In markets such as semiconductors and airplanes, best-practice technology requires huge investment.
Ironically, investment aimed at insuring competitive strength simultaneously generates risk. Overinvestment in a period of low profit rates and high
interest commitments requires many firms to use high leverage. While high
leverage is a well-known feature of Asia's economies, rising leverage occurs
in any system with high investment levels, falling profits and high interest
burdens.

In neoclassical textbook models, the downward pressure on profits,
capacity utilization and prices is soon eliminated by the exit of firms to
industries with higher profits. But in the neoliberal regime it is reproduced,
because entry is not matched by exit. The more these pressures develop, the
more they force firms to cut wages, smash unions, move to areas of cheaper
labour, and push for tax cuts and other government policies which restrict
aggregate demand – one of the major causes of the excessive competitive

pressures in the first place. The elements causing slow aggregate-demand growth and excess aggregate supply thus reinforce one another in a vicious circle.

The pattern of excess supply leading to coercive competition in the real sector is repeated in the financial sector. In the wake of continuing financial deregulation, removal of capital controls and technical change, large banks are forced to compete globally for up-scale customers.[5] Accompanying this trend is a shift in these banks' revenue generation from traditional intermediation (lending to hold) to fee-based income (lending to sell). This shift reflects both the premium placed on liquidity in the uncertain economic climate of the neoliberal order, and also banks' reluctance to absorb default and other risks in this climate. However, in shifting away from intermediation and toward fee-based activities, banks are moving into heightened competition both with investment and brokerage firms and with one another. Increasingly, high profits can be obtained in the financial sector only in two ways: by opening up new lending venues and enjoying a scarcity rent on funds lent; or by taking on highly-leveraged excessive risks. Events in recent months have made it clear that the bets these players take can jeopardize the stability of the entire global financial system.

In sum, the step-by-step dismantling of Keynesian policies from the mid 1970s onward and the freeing of capital movement have pushed the world's economies deeper into a neoliberal economic trap which increasingly shuts in on itself. As the bottom portion of Figure 3.1 illustrates, Pax Americana and the fixed exchange-rate regime no longer set the tone for global economic policy, as in the golden age; multinational firms and mobile capital do. Restrictions on state action reduce the scope for redistributive policies and hence erode mass support for lift-all-boats efforts. This in turn eliminates Keynesian employment-based demand management and leaves states with price stability targets, contributing to a global deflationary bias.[6] The golden age political consensus in favour of Keynesian demand management, market regulation and income redistribution now appears to be an exercise in hopeless utopianism; replacing this consensus is a global sense of pessimism on the part of national electorates, whose erstwhile leaders have conditioned them to expect nothing and hope for nothing.

3.3. THE EAST ASIAN MODEL: MYTHS AND REALITY

This brings us to the East Asian model itself. The shock-waves emanating from this region's current crisis should not cause us to forget East Asia's immense long-term achievements. The prototype was Japan in the 1950s' 'income doubling' period, while from 1961 through 1996, South Korea's average annual rate of growth of real per capita GDP and real wages averaged about 7 per cent per year. Though East and South East Asia constitute about 25 per cent of global GDP, in the 1990s about half of the growth of world GDP has originated in this area. Ajit Singh recently observed that: 'It is no exaggeration to say that the post-World War II development of East Asia (including Japan) is the most successful story of sustained economic expansion in the history of mankind' (Singh, 1996, p.1).

This economic success has been achieved through a structure of state-led growth originated in Japan, refined in the four 'Tigers' (South Korea, Taiwan, Singapore and Hong Kong), and subsequently adapted for use in South East Asia, China and elsewhere. The beginning of wisdom about the East Asian model is the recognition that it has differed substantially from one country to another and within countries from one period to another.[7] This variability has allowed analysts to explain the elements behind East Asia's brilliant economic performance very differently. Marcus Noland has remarked in private correspondence that East Asia has been a mirror, in which many analysts have seen the reflections of their own preconceived ideas. For example, some economists have attempted to attribute the success of Taiwan, and East Asian economies more generally, to their pursuit of policies that a market-oriented economic approach would have dictated anyway – despite voluminous evidence to the contrary (Wade, 1990).

It is thus important to be clear on the essential features of the Asian model – what this model is and is not. A common misimpression regards the Asian model as controlled by a giant predatory state which monopolizes national output and builds wealth by running aggressive trade surpluses, and devalues its currency aggressively to maintain its edge in global markets. Reality is far more complex. First, the government accounts for no larger a share of output in East Asia than elsewhere. Further, East Asian countries do not uniformly run trade surpluses. Figure 3.2 shows that Korea and Thailand have more often run trade deficits than surpluses. In the 1990s Korea has consistently had trade deficits with both the US and Japan. As for chronic currency devaluations, Figure 3.3 shows that throughout the 1980s and 1990s, two East Asian currencies (the Japanese yen and Taiwanese dollar) have risen substantially against the US dollar, while three others held their value against the dollar until the 1997 crisis period.

What then are the points of commonality in the East Asian model? First is the shared structural circumstances and historical legacy of nations in this portion of the world. Of special importance is the relative paucity of mineral resources and oil, which helps explain the centrality of trade

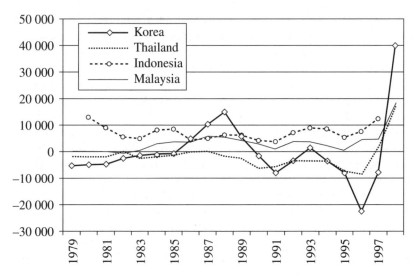

Source: Asian Development Bank

Figure 3.2   Trade balance for three East Asian countries, in millions of dollars, 1979–98

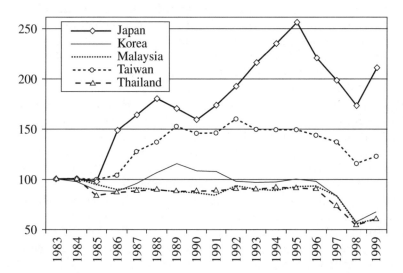

Note: Dollars per currency with July 1983=100. Upward shifts denote a weaker dollar.

Source: Federal Reserve Board.

Figure 3.3   Normalized exchange rates relative to the dollar, five East Asian countries, 1983–99

considerations in these nations' policies. Second, and most important, is the fact of heavy state involvement in the allocation of resources. This has been referred to in the literature as the developmental state (Johnson, 1995) or late industrialization (Amsden, 1989). For example, until the recent crisis period, the Korean government provided temporary import protection for domestic markets introducing new products or technologies, channelled the development of high-tech production capabilities to a small number of diversified companies (called *chaebol*), allocated credit toward priority industries and technologies, and tightly regulated the cross-border movement of money. At the same time, the government selectively opened markets to import competition and imposed export performance criteria in return for government aid to insure that key industries achieved world-class efficiency. Such heavy involvement in investment and savings flows is present even when the apparent level of government involvement is relatively slight, as in Taiwan. Strong government guidance is, of course, antithetical to neoliberalism, but it did lead to high investment levels, as Figure 3.4 illustrates. The US investment share of GDP hovers just under 20 per cent; Malaysia's and Taiwan's shares have trended downward to about 25 per cent; but Japan's share has remained at about 30 per cent. Investment shares in Korea and Thailand have climbed over 35 per cent in the 1990s.

The Asian economies are tightly integrated. This close relationship is demonstrated in Figure 3.5. The US GDP growth rate is relatively independent of the East Asian rates, which instead vary closely with Japan's cyclical growth rate. In 1996, about 52 per cent of Asian exports, and 54 per cent of its imports, were intra-regional (UNCTAD, 1998, p. 27). The apparent pattern of dependence on Japan is not surprising given the sheer scale of the Japanese economy, whose GDP is about 12 times as large as Korea's. That the Korean economy was, until the 1997 crisis, the eleventh largest in the world, makes this mismatch all the more remarkable.

Another theme of East Asian development has been deferred gratification for consumers. Tight constraints have been imposed on the domestic consumer goods market in order to free up resources for investment and exports. Current consumption has been sacrificed for high rates of capital accumulation, and thus for future consumption. The guiding idea has been that household needs would be met by the sheer pace of growth.[8]

Finally, East Asia has been understood to be reasonably free from the overt capital–labour conflict that has often characterized Western labour markets and labour processes. The exchange of the security of lifetime employment for worker loyalty in pursuit of company objectives is often seen as a key component of the Japanese and Korean 'miracles'.

But the deferred-gratification/low-conflict features of the Asian model should not be exaggerated or romanticized. Rapid growth, relatively flat

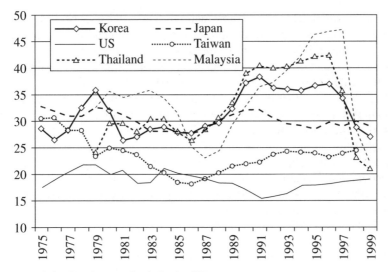

Source: Asian Development Bank, Bank of Korea.

Figure 3.4   Gross investment as a percentage of GDP, selected countries, 1975–99

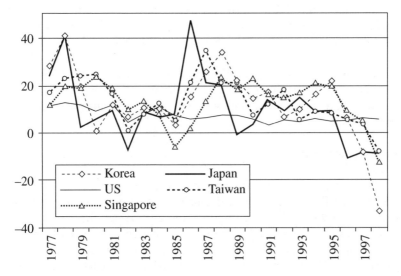

Note: Changes in GDP are measured here in nominal US dollars, and thus reflect changes in both economic activity and exchange rates.

Source: Bank of Korea.

Figure 3.5   Growth in GDP measured in dollars, selected countries, 1977–98

pay scales, and flexible supervisory methods have often kept capital–labour conflict in the background. But political repression including the destruction of independent, democratic and militant unions has played a crucial role as well – and continues to do so in the restructuring processes imposed by the IMF after the crisis began. Further, the avoidance of overt capital–labour conflict is due in part to the heavy industrial use of female labour in the context of longstanding gender-based oppression. But the case of Japan shows that the long-term price of playing the gender card in industrial development is the 'revolt' of women, which can jeopardize the reproduction of social relations in several ways (see Naff, 1996). Further, housing remains inadequate, especially for lower-income people (Ha, 1995; W.J. Kim, 1997). And democratic participation has been restricted – at times outlawed, encouraging the entrenchment of powerful economic and political elites (E.M. Kim, 1997).[9]

3.4   THE EMERGENCE OF THE EAST ASIAN CRISIS: AN OVERVIEW

In this section we make two arguments. First, that the fundamental structural incompatibility between the neoliberal regime and the East Asian model guaranteed that the Asian economic miracle would inevitably be disrupted at some time, in some way. Second, that the financial liberalization imposed on Asia by external and internal elites, in the context of the global financial regime, set the stage for the timing and character – the conjunctural and contingent characteristics – of the Asian crisis of late 1997. We see these two arguments as addressing, respectively, the ultimate and proximate causes of the crisis.

Structural Incompatibility

It is not just a coincidence that Japan, Korea and Taiwan created and consolidated their East Asian models during the golden age. Northern growth was rapid and the demand for imports grew even faster. Since only a few Asian countries were vying for shares of Northern import markets, and were starting from a small base, their success posed no immediate threat to host countries. Cold War politics made the US hesitant to treat these countries too harshly; on the contrary, it provided substantial grants and loans to assist their development. Plus, the US pumped money into Asian countries in the course of prosecuting the wars in Korea and Vietnam. Finally, note that for much of the period, the movement of financial capital across national borders was slow, and controlled by national governments.

But the rise of the neoliberal regime has created multidimensional tensions with developing countries that have adopted the Asian model. For one thing, East Asia's success offered proof that an intelligent and flexible combination of state regulation and market forces could achieve a combination of economic growth, productivity, technological progress and income equality superior to anything neoliberalism could offer. Until 1997, the unparalleled success of the Asian model was seen by many as proof that the idea embodied in the 'Washington consensus' that 'there is no alternative' to neoliberalism was just an ideological slogan, not a fact. For another, it was true even in the golden age that export-led growth in the South could never be a permanently successful strategy for every developing country given limits to the growth of low- to mid-tech global export markets. But the evolution of the neoliberal regime with its chronically inadequate aggregate demand growth and structurally determined excess supply made these limits bind earlier and bite harder than otherwise would have been the case. Asian countries could not continue forever to increase exports at 8 per cent a year in a global economy whose developed economies were growing at 2 per cent a year. These constraints meant that sometime, somewhere, export-led developing countries were likely to experience severe problems.

As a result of conflicts between the structure of the East Asian models and the ideological and material interests of the G7 nations and multilateral institutions, enormous pressure was applied to East Asian countries in the late 1980s and 1990s to deconstruct key components of their economic systems. Northern powers pressed with special vigour for liberalization of both domestic and international financial markets, and elimination of trade management and investment oversight. This pressure arose in part because the profits that firms, banks and rentiers outside East Asia could earn from its economic miracle was severely restricted by Asian governments' controls and regulations. Beyond this, Asia's government-directed economies represented the last significant obstacle to the consolidation of global neoliberalism. Western interests believed that they were in a 'war' with East Asia over what kind of capitalism would dominate the early twenty-first century – US capitalism or East Asian capitalism; and they intended to win. Though they used many weapons in this war, financial liberalization was clearly central to their battle plans.

Financial Liberalization, Short-Term Capital Flows and the Outbreak of Crisis

That the sought-after financial liberalization was in fact achieved is demonstrated by the surge of capital inflows to East Asia in the 1990s. Figures 3.6 and 3.7 provide data on yearly inflows of short-term and long-term capital

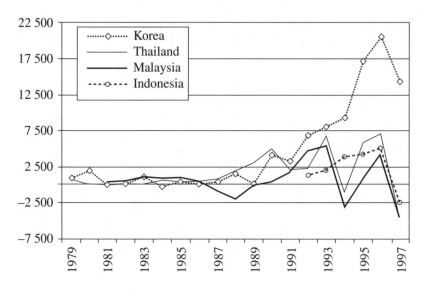

Note: Figures include portfolio and other short-term inflows.

Source: Asian Development Bank.

Figure 3.6   Short-term capital inflows, four East Asian countries, in millions of dollars, 1979–97

in four East Asian economies. These economies all experienced a substantial rise in short-term capital inflows in the 1990s. Long-term capital inflows rose in three of the four countries as well. It is important to emphasize the shift toward short-term lending, depicted in Figure 3.8. The short-term character of much of this capital reflects global lenders' perceived need to maximize their liquidity – the ability to unwind any position quickly and with minimum loss, and created the potential for a lightning-fast bout of capital outflow. These short-term financial inflows created the preconditions for Minsky crises, especially in South East Asian countries such as Malaysia and Indonesia that lack deep financial markets, adequate regulation and lender of last resort institutions.[10] The inflow of so much money in such a short time to so many different East Asian countries created the possibility of region-wide panics, contagions and financial crises.

Moreover, the East Asian model is an integrated and coherent whole. Its impressive successes were the result of all key components working together. Breaking down some parts of the system while leaving others intact courted disaster. Opening Asia to unregulated capital inflows before making all the other changes that financial deregulation required made no sense. In particular, the deregulation of domestic and international

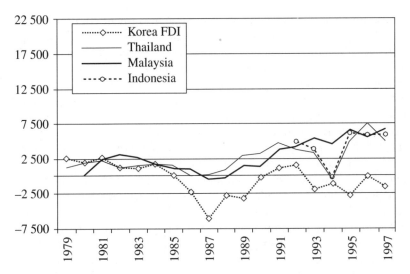

Note: Includes foreign direct investment and other capital with maturity of over one year.

Source: Asian Development Bank.

Figure 3.7   Long-term capital inflows, four East Asian countries, in millions of dollars, 1979–97

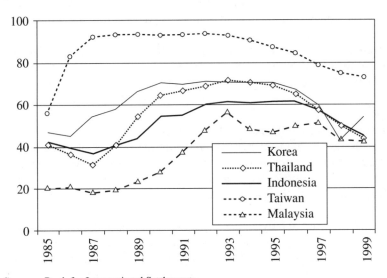

Source: Bank for International Settlements.

Figure 3.8   Short-term debt as a share of all debt for BIS-reporting institutions, selected East Asian countries, 1985–99

financial markets and the elimination of state investment coordination in the context of traditional corporate and bank leverage ratios was a recipe for crisis. Corporate debt–equity ratios of three or four are inherently vulnerable to profit or interest or exchange rate shocks.[11]

The huge and variable capital inflows to Asia set up a Catch-22 dilemma for Asian exchange rate regimes, which raised yet higher the likelihood of crisis. As Figure 3.3 shows, most East Asian countries adopted de facto fixed exchange rate regimes in the 1990s. This insured foreign investors against exchange rate losses. Fixed rates also required that national authorities control inflation and limit budget deficits – policies favoured by foreign rentiers; they thus helped generate glowing evaluations by the IMF and World Bank as to the soundness of these economies, which only accelerated the speed of capital inflows. However, de facto fixed exchange rates made it impossible to eliminate current-account deficits. So when deficits did arise, governments had to use their limited reserves to defend the exchange rate. When investors began to withdraw funds because current account deficits threatened the exchange rate regime in 1997, governments were forced to use their exchange reserves even faster. When the exchange rate pegs were finally abandoned in the heat of the crisis, remaining reserves were too small to cover foreign debt repayment commitments. Default or IMF supervision were then the only remaining options.[12]

Under speculative bursts of capital inflows and outflows, however, flexible exchange rate regimes can lead to devastating exchange rate instability. Inflows raise exchange rates, causing current account deficits and domestic credit explosions; large outflows make it impossible for domestic firms and banks to repay foreign denominated debt. No small, trade-dependent country can tolerate the extreme exchange rate volatility inherent in the neoliberal regime. That is why capital controls are essential for such countries.

Thus, once neoliberal forces had successfully orchestrated the liberalization of domestic financial markets and international capital flows, and weakened the structures of trade management and investment coordination, the Asian countries were placed in deep jeopardy no matter which exchange rate regime they adopted. It was only a matter of time until crisis came.

We will flesh out the dynamics of the Asian crisis and present a more detailed explanation of its causes, with special focus on the case of Korea, in Section 3.6. But first, we look at the strengths and weaknesses of the explanations of the crisis offered by mainstream economists.

3.5.   A CRITICAL EVALUATION OF NEOCLASSICAL THEORIES OF THE ASIAN ECONOMIC CRISIS

Most analyses of the Asian crisis have focused on the cycle of short-term capital flows into and out of the recently liberalized Asian financial markets. Outstanding treatments of theory and facts surrounding this financial cycle can be found in the work of non-mainstream scholars such as Wade (1998), Wade and Veneroso (1998), Akyuz (1998), Chang et al. (1998), Grabel (1998), MacLean et al. (1998) and UNCTAD (1998). Of course, many mainstream economists have also presented theories to explain the Asian financial crisis. Before we present a more detailed view of the crisis via an analysis of the course of events in Korea, it will be useful to briefly review the debate within mainstream economics about the causes of Asian crisis. We preface this review by recalling a typology developed by Radelet and Sachs (1998). These authors argue that financial crises can have any of five causes: deteriorating macroeconomic fundamentals; moral hazard in loan markets; financial panic; asset bubbles; and disorderly work-outs. Most economists' writings on the Asian financial crisis incorporate some combination of these elements; indeed, the debate is shaped along these lines. The IMF, for example, emphasizes the first two factors: they trace foreign-exchange and asset-market pressure to either inappropriate macroeconomic policies or flawed systems of financial intermediation and regulation. This coincidence is not surprising in that the list encompasses the research interests of most economists using the core conceptual categories of mainstream macroeconomics. In order, these five causes correspond to: models of efficient markets; asymmetric information models; models with multiple equilibria, especially the Diamond–Dybvig model of bank runs; models of sunspot equilibria and self-fulfilling prophesies; and 'political economy' models with rent-seeking government officials.

There is something here for almost every neoclassical economist. Indeed, there is something exhilarating, almost titillating, for economists about the Asian crisis; for the opinions of a sizable band of economists revered in academia – Joseph Stiglitz, Jeffrey Sachs, Paul Krugman, Lawrence Summers, Martin Feldstein, Stanley Fischer, and so on – have been analysed in excruciating detail in leading journals of world opinion. Political professionals like to say about careers in their field that 'you find a horse and you ride him'. Things are little different for economists interested in making their mark on Noriel Rubini's instantly famous Asian crisis home-page – you find a theoretical take and you ride it.[13]

The fundamental problem with most of this literature is, not surprisingly, the problem one finds in mainstream macroeconomics debates between New Keynesians and New Classicals (and the shades in-between): this debate is conducted using as a point of reference the perfectly coordinated, mistake-free Walrasian general equilibrium model. There is certainly nothing wrong with comparing outcomes in one's model of choice with the Walrasian case. The problem goes deeper, however, to an ingrained habit of contemporary debate in mainstream theory: the idea that the implications of a given idea can be understood – and thus accepted as important – only with respect to the deviations they introduce from Walrasian equilibrium. Models for which the Walrasian case is simply not applicable thus cannot be understood.

The debate over the Asian model has quickly taken on this sort of flavour: the focus is on the mechanism that drives one away from the efficient equilibrium assumed to be the natural resting place of the system. A good example of this approach is a recent paper by Chang and Velasco (1998). These authors adapt the Diamond–Dybvig model (1983) to show that a shortage of global liquidity combined with a shock that adversely affects borrower countries in the presence of short-term capital inflows can generate recessions driven in part by a debt–deflation multiplier. Clearly, these authors have generated a framework capturing many aspects of recent events in a clever and concise way.

The question is, where does an analysis of this sort go next? One move would be to attempt to add in additional realistic features based on stylized characteristics of Asian economies with respect to the labour process, the government sector, a household sector, and so on. But this is asking the Diamond–Dybvig framework to carry a lot more weight than it was designed to bear, given its origin as a simple demonstration of the possibility of bank runs. Not only would such realistic features conflict with the simplifying assumptions required to generate a closed-form equilibrium; but adding them would lead to confusion on the part of mainstream economists as to which realistic feature is generating what amount of inefficiency in the resulting second-best equilibrium. To pertain more fully to the unfolding crisis in Asia, this (and other) framework(s) must be stretched this way; but to do so takes them quickly beyond the formal limits that generated their explanatory force in the first place The problem derives, at root, from theoretical economists' insistence on assuming that the Walrasian maintained hypothesis is meaningful – that in the absence of whatever mechanism is emphasized, the economy would be at (or near) an efficient economic outcome. It is possible to ask, 'what else is missing?' only within the straitjacket imposed by whatever formalism underlies an author's results. To insist on bringing in factors that require loosening that straitjacket invites the suggestion that one doesn't understand the rules of this game.

Another problem is empirical. One would like to move toward an empirical implementation of an idea like Chang and Velasco's. However, the formal restrictions required to generate equilibrium in their model do not permit the construction of a set of empirical propositions. A reduced form must be used, one that presumably includes the list of variables that could shift the parameters of central interest in this formulation. However, this reduced form will be almost indistinguishable from those generated by models based on very different premises – in this particular case, from the Hardy and Pazarbasioglu (1998) model discussed in note 13, which assumes efficient markets (and does not bother with the information asymmetry at the root of the Chang/Velasco framework). Suppose one found that variables representing structural features of the banking system, as Hardy and Pazarbasioglu do, matter empirically? It is unclear whether one is showing: *à la* Chang and Velasco, that the banking system has malfunctioned because of international liquidity shortages; *à la* Hardy and Pazarbasioglu, that lack of regulatory oversight and other structural problems in domestic banking systems are to blame; or something else altogether. Still, the sheer difficulty of getting significant coefficients with small time-series/cross-section samples poses a barrier, even if one swallows the objections raised in note 1.

We can sum up this discussion by generalizing a remark that Jeffrey Sachs made about IMF economists in his *Financial Times* article of December 13, 1997, 'it defies logic to believe that the small group of 1000 economists on 19th Street in Washington' – or for that matter a self-conscious academic elite not afraid to substitute a simplifying assumption for an institutional investigation – 'should dictate the economic conditions of life to 75 developing countries with around 1.4 billion people' – or that their own debating conventions should dictate the terms on which matters of such importance must be understood.

Following every nuance of the burgeoning economic literature would be exhausting, if not impossible, in the manner of a cat chasing its own tail. The remainder of this section identifies the three central threads along which debate has flowed.

The Asian Model on Trial: The Neoliberal/Neoclassical Perspective

The neoliberal view of the Asian crisis is espoused by economists at the IMF and World Bank, by business economists, and by conservative, largely US-trained academic economists, including many in elite universities in Asia and Latin America. Neoliberal economic theory is the official ideology of the neoliberal regime. This view finds the roots of the Asian crisis in the inherent incompatibility of the external (neoliberal) global environment and most Asian nations' internal economic structures and policies.

This incompatibility is traced in part to self-dealing and rent-seeking, 'crony capitalism', which the March 1998 issue of *Finance and Development* sees, *inter alia*, as the root of the crisis in South East Asia (see Grey and Kaufman, 1998). In countries where corruption is not present, the IMF position is that something must be wrong with either macroeconomic management or institutions. Since Asia's afflicted economies generally had strong macroeconomic fundamentals prior to the crisis, blame focuses on 'weaknesses in financial systems and, to a lesser extent, governance' (IMF, 1998).[14]

This approach asserts that market fundamentals should drive observed outcomes, and government intervention can only worsen outcomes. Since only the neoliberal approach fully embodies this view, 'there is no alternative' to neoliberalism. No East Asian model of centralized control over capital movements and investment can be permanently sustained because its costs – price distortions, misallocated resources and restricted access to Northern goods and financial instruments – will eventually become too large to bear. The crisis is thus not attributable to external forces such as currency speculation, but to the cumulation of internal inefficiencies. Any transition from government-controlled allocation to decentralized market allocation will, it is admitted, impose temporary costs of adjustment, but in the neoliberal view, the permanent costs of not opening capital and product markets clearly exceed the one-time costs of transition.

The Asian Model on Trial: Economic Theory Weighs In

Broadly speaking, contemporary theoretical models can be divided into those with unique and those with multiple equilibria. The unique-equilibrium models invariably describe efficient outcomes along steady-state growth paths; the multiple-equilibrium models permit deviations from efficient outcomes for reasons ranging from missing information, to perverse parameters, to asymmetric information, and so on. Models of the second type, which as already mentioned encompass almost the entire research agenda of applied microeconomists and macroeconomists using mainstream methods, are being widely and variously applied to the Asian crisis. The apparent facts of the case fit well with the notion of a good equilibrium which is replaced by a bad one.

Models of this type have been used to identify problems in Asia. For ease, we consider just one strand within this stream – microfoundational models in which bubbles emerge due to incentive problems under asymmetric information. The fundamental problem is incentive incompatibility between a well-informed loan applicant and a less-informed lender: in finite-horizon games in which loan applicants pay interest and keep residual returns, applicants have an incentive to undertake riskier projects than lenders want to underwrite. The potential for *overlending* and/or a *bubble* then arises if lenders do not exercise adequate vigilance. Banking systems in which risks are guaranteed are especially likely to fall prey to this sort of moral-hazard problem. This general approach has been used to indict deposit insurance as the culprit in the 1980s US savings and loan crisis and the Latin American debt crisis.[15]

Paul Krugman's web-published January 1998 paper proposes a moral-hazard theory of the East and South East Asian financial crisis incorporating these elements. Specifically, he argues that each nation has a class of assets – especially land – that is fixed in quantity but has a variable return. Suppose the return to land can be either high or low with a given probability. Then under risk neutrality a fair price for this land is, (Probability of high return) × (Value of high return) + (Probability of low return) × (Value of low return). Krugman argues that a bubble in land values emerges when one set of bidders on these assets discards the low return, and thus bids their price up to the high-return value. The culprit is the domestic banking system, which supports this bidding-up because it is backed by implicit governmental guarantees against failure. The asset bubble then bursts when low returns occur, generating losses for banks that governments are unable to absorb. This sets off a contagion effect when depositors at banks holding overvalued assets of this sort realize that they stand to lose the next time a low-return outcome is drawn.[16]

Second Thoughts about the Neoliberal Regime: Economic Theory Changes its Mind

But what economic theory gives, it also takes away. The same asymmetric-information framework used by Krugman to demonstrate weak points in the Asian model has been deployed to defend it and cast suspicion back on the neoliberal regime itself as the possible culprit. This counter-offensive draws strength from the fact that neither of the aforementioned attacks on the Asian model fits the facts very comfortably. *Vis-à-vis* the IMF's two-level attack, note that some countries affected in the current crisis have succeeded because of state-directed, interventionist macroeconomic and microeconomic policies, not despite them. Further, the spread of the Asian crisis to Latin America has hit hardest countries such as Brazil and Mexico that have made sustained efforts to rebuild their economies after the debt-crisis years using precisely the orthodox policies championed by the IMF. If the IMF was right, Latin America should have stayed clear of the Asian meltdown of 1997–98. Further, while Krugman's asset-bubble argument may apply to some features of recent South East Asian experience, it doesn't fit the situation of Korea at all, not to mention Latin America. As Dymski (1998) observes, Korea's land and stock market bubble peaked nearly a decade ago; a variety of policy steps had reined in the worst excesses of that bubble before this crisis broke out.

This general line of attack is set out in a 12 March speech in Manila by Joseph Stiglitz, now Chief Economist at the World Bank (Stiglitz, 1998). According to Stiglitz, 'Curiously many of the factors identified as contributors to East Asian economies' current problems are strikingly similar to the explanations previously put forward for their success.' Here Stiglitz is referring to core results from applications of the asymmetric-information framework to the developing-country case, a method he pioneered.[17] Stiglitz argues that because asymmetric information and incentive incompatibility are fundamental features of unregulated credit markets, those markets are prone to market failure. East Asia has defended against market failure in several ways – government coordination of resource flows, limited scope for interest-rate movements, and close instead of arm's-length relationships between borrowers and lenders. The success of these measures contributed to the rapid development of these economies. Indeed, he points out that the East Asian solution to credit-market failure permitted Asian governments to channel a remarkably high proportion of national output as savings into capital accumulation without chronic market instability. Stiglitz admits that there was some misallocation of credit in East Asia. But macroeconomic fundamentals there were strong, and these credit-misallocation problems do not prove that these systems are fundamentally flawed. Instead 'the buildup of short-term, unhedged debt left East Asia's economies vulnerable to a sudden collapse of confidence'. Thus, he concludes, it was financial deregulation followed by excessive short-term capital inflows, not corruption or credit misallocation attributable to government guarantees or regulatory laxity, that plunged East Asia into crisis.

Clearly, then, mainstream theories of the Asian crisis are inherently incapable of explaining either the successes or the failure of the Asian model. They are thus an inadequate foundation on which to build policies for reconstructing prosperity in Asia and the rest of the world.

3.6. THE TRIPLE CRISIS: KOREA, ASIA AND THE NEOLIBERAL REGIME

We focus our analysis of the Asian crisis in this section on events in South Korea. Highly diversified, family-owned conglomerates, called chaebol, dominate Korea's key export markets as well as many of its essential domestic markets. The chaebol were the vehicles used by governments over the past decades to build Korea's technological, productivity and growth 'miracle'. Indeed, one might say that the Korean 'model' consisted of state regulation of the creation and evolution of the chaebol, largely, though not exclusively, through its control of credit flows.

In the 1990s many of the chaebol's key export markets – including semiconductor, autos, shipbuilding, steel, petrochemicals, construction, capital goods and electronic equipment – suffered from the chronic excess supply and secular deflationary pressure discussed above. They thus faced fierce competition in their struggle to maintain and increase market share. At the same time, Korea's long period of tight labour markets, in concert with key political changes after the 'revolution' of 1987, strengthened the labour movement, building steady upward pressure on the growth of real wages. Caught between rising labour costs and downward price pressure in product markets, the chaebol sought relief through high rates of productivity growth in their domestic operations, and the movement of many of their lower tech operations into the cheap labour pools of South East Asia, just as Japan had done earlier. Both objectives required high rates of capital investment in the face of the low profit rates coercive competitors brought to these industries.

Meanwhile, a global pool of liquid financial capital ready to cross borders in pursuit of high short-term profits had risen to gargantuan proportions through the expansion of neoliberalism – by 1997 about $1.5 trillion moved through the foreign exchange markets every day. Partly in response to the dearth of high returns available in Northern markets in the early 1990s, an increasing proportion of hot money began to move in the direction of Asia. Heated competition developed among global bankers and investment fund managers to get the best opportunities that East Asia, South East Asia and China had to offer. Loan 'pushing' became the order of the day, just as it had been in the Latin American debt buildup of the 1970s. By 1996 over $300 billion a year of foreign capital was flowing into developing economies; over $90 billion of these funds went to the five Asian nations that were to be hardest hit by the 1997 crisis.

Of course, Korean markets would not have been open to the inflow of hot money if the traditional tight control of capital flows into and out of the country we associate with the East Asian model had been kept intact. But powerful global agents such as the G7, the OECD, the IMF, the World Bank, and multinational banks and firms had exerted enormous economic and political pressure on Korea and other Asian countries to deregulate domestic financial markets and capital flows, and to reduce barriers to imports and FDI. Those who resisted this pressure were threatened with restricted access to Northern goods and financial markets and hostile treatment from international agencies. Especially in the 1990s, after the Cold War ended, external neoliberal agents bullied the countries of the South without restraint.

Meanwhile, many of the East Asian banks, industrial and commercial firms, and elite families that had prospered and grown powerful as a result of the decades-long 'miracle' came to believe that their future economic interests were tied more closely to developments in global than in domestic markets. They came to believe that their personal prosperity was less dependent on national well being than on unrestricted access to foreign markets. They knew that such access would not be forthcoming unless their own governments gave in to external pressures to liberalize domestic markets. These agents created a rising internal demand for liberalization that reinforced the external pressures faced by area governments.

In Korea, the internal pressure for liberalization came primary from the families that owned the chaebol. As noted, the chaebol felt they had no choice but to increase investment spending to survive the coercive competition they faced in their primary export markets. But their motives for undertaking this investment expansion were not simple or unidimensional. The long history of success they had achieved in gaining a foothold in increasingly important global markets led chaebol leaders to believe that they could become even bigger global players. Sometime in the early 1990s the chaebol developed excessively and unrealistically ambitious plans to become serious competitors to the most powerful Northern multinational corporations, contesting markets with them all over the globe through exports as well as foreign direct investment. The rise in the value of the yen after 1993, which the chaebol believed reflected a long-term trend, may have contributed to their ambitions. Thus, both pressure to survive and ambition to become more powerful – defensive and offensive motivations – combined to induce the chaebol to undertake huge investments in new capacities and in new technology at home and abroad.

Though the chaebols' gross profit rates were modest, contrary to popular belief, they were not much out of line with their foreign competitors (see Chang, 1998, Table 2). However, their high debt/equity ratios generated oppressive interest burdens, which forced net profit rates well below average. As a result, the chaebol needed a great deal of new credit to finance this new investment. Toward this end, they allied themselves with external neoliberal forces to pressure the government to accelerate the pace of domestic financial market deregulation. In response, the government of Kim Young Sam permitted the establishment of 9 new merchant banks in 1994 and 15 more in 1996, most of them started by people who had made their fortunes in the informal curb market and had little or no experience in standard commercial banking. According to sources in the banking industry, the government exercised little regulation or control over these banks. They even failed to monitor them. The government apparatus had no idea what these banks were doing with either their asset commitments or liability structures. This total lack of banking oversight constituted a dramatic break with traditional East Asian practices. The chaebol took significant ownership positions in many of the new merchant banks, and borrowed extensively from them; most of this debt was short term. Thus, the chaebol became even more indebted to domestic institutions than was usual in the high debt-to-equity tradition of the Korean and Japanese models.

The chaebol and the new merchant banks also wanted unlimited access to foreign credit markets, in part because global interest rates were as much as 50 per cent lower than those available in the still semi-regulated Korean market.[18] They therefore pressured the government to prematurely and excessively liberalize short-term inward capital flows – bank loans and portfolio capital. Liberalization of the capital account was also a requirement for membership in the OECD, which the chaebol sought in order to guarantee themselves access without discrimination to Northern goods and investment markets (Amsden and Euh, 1997). But the Korean government, under strong pressure from the chaebol, liberalized capital flows even faster than was required by the agreement with the OECD.

Thus, as a number of heterodox economists cited in Section 3.5 have noted, the preconditions for the outbreak of the crisis were created not by too much government interference in the private sector, or too much 'cronyism', but by the failure of the government to maintain its traditional responsibility to monitor and control economic activity in the national interest. We would argue, however, that one cannot fully understand why this excessive liberalization took place without an evaluation of the internal contradictions and tensions within Korea. External neoliberal forces may be the main villains in this sad story, but they are not the only villains.

Thus, just when global financial markets were flush with money seeking to move into the new 'hot' markets of Asia, some Asian governments were tearing down the barriers that had previously prevented their free entry.[19] Fed by the ongoing euphoria associated with the East Asian boom, global investors exhibited their usual herd behaviour. Short-term foreign funds poured into Korea in 1994 through 1996, mostly in the form of bank loans. Some of the loans were directly to the chaebol, most were made to Korean banks, which relent much of the money to the chaebol. It is believed that the merchant banks used a significant part of their foreign borrowings to speculate in financial assets around Asia.

The result of the liberalization of short-term capital inflows in these circumstances was a doubling of foreign bank debt between 1994 and 1997 from about $60 billion to about $120 billion (not counting the debts of foreign branches of Korean banks). Total foreign debt was still not grossly out of line with the experience of other countries; the key problem was that over 60 per cent of this debt was short-term, due within one year.

The chaebol had thus financed an ambitious and risky long-term capital investment boom primarily with short-term loans, a large part of which were owed to foreign lenders and therefore due in foreign currency. And the government, which had traditionally regulated and restrained the chaebol in the nation's interest, helped them do it.

It was not so much the expansion programme itself that was the main source of danger, though it was risky and probably excessively ambitious. After all, in response to the same competitive pressures confronting the chaebol, major Northern MNCs were engaged in similar programmes of capacity expansion across the globe in industries such as autos, steel and semiconductors, all of which were plagued by excess capacity. This is an era in which huge oligopolies are engaged in a competitive struggle to determine who will dominate global markets. The big question is: which firms will be left standing when the excess capacity created in this struggle is destroyed by deep recession, mass insolvency and bankruptcy. General Motors was expanding more or less in the same way as the Korean chaebol. The key difference in the Korean case was in the short-term and foreign mode of finance of the investment boom.

Despite the fact that both the IMF and the World Bank certified that the Korean economy was in sound condition in mid 1997, the stage was now set for the generation of a domestic and external financial crisis. Any one of a large number of not-unlikely developments would now trigger both kinds of financial crises: a devaluation of the won (which would require more won to pay back a given debt in dollars or yen), an undervaluation of the yen (which could erode export markets), increasing foreign interest rates, a domestic recession, a slowing of growth in key export markets, or any other source of profit problems for the chaebol.

Under such conditions, domestic financial turmoil could quickly induce a foreign exchange crisis, while any problem in external markets would tip the razor's edge balance of the domestic economy. Foreign banks that begin to fear defaults on their short-term loans and portfolio investors that suspect a currency devaluation both know that the first banks and the first investors to withdraw their funds from the country will be the least likely to suffer. If the chaebol had trouble servicing their domestic loans, foreign banks and portfolio investors were likely to pull their money out of Korea. The situation was thus ripe for a panic or contagion, which would accelerate the collapse in the currency, raising the likelihood of the mass defaults that everyone feared. That the Korean government maintained an inadequate volume of foreign reserves, an amount perhaps equal to three months of imports, made the situation even more precarious.

Of course, events in the mid 1990s did build toward a crisis. Devaluation of the Chinese yuan in 1994 and the Japanese yen after 1995, along with falling demand in key export markets such as steel, autos and, especially, semiconductors, led to a rising current account deficit after 1994. In 1995 it rose slightly, to about 2 per cent of GDP, but the deficit hit $24 billion or near 5 per cent of GDP in 1996. The government in the past had usually been quick to devalue the won in the face of deterioration in the current account, but despite evidence that the won was perhaps 10 per cent overvalued in 1995 and 1996, several factors blocked such action. For one thing, the huge inflow of foreign capital in this period maintained upward pressure on the won that could not be easily offset through sterilization. Further, foreign investors had come to expect and to count on relative exchange rate stability in Asia; a sharp devaluation might spook them. Finally, the government feared that a falling exchange rate would make it harder for Korean firms and banks to pay back their rising foreign debt.

Korea's current account problems did not last long; the country moved back toward balance by mid 1997. Unfortunately, they lasted just long enough, given the other developments of the period, to help tip the country into crisis. Declining export growth led to declining profits and increasing excess capacity for the now highly-leveraged chaebol. This resulted in some key loan defaults and an increase in domestic nonperforming bank loans in the first half of 1997. Whether Korea would have been able to weather this disturbance in the absence of further problems will never be known, because in July 1997 the sharp devaluation of the previously fixed-rate Thai baht triggered an outbreak of financial panic across Asia. But we do know this: if Korea's mid 1997 debt problems had been exclusively domestic, the economic collapse that began later that year and accelerated after the imposition of the IMF agreement in December would *not* have occurred. Korea would have suffered slower growth and financial difficulties to be sure, but not a depression and loss of economic sovereignty.

When the Asian crisis erupted there was a general flight of investor capital from Asian markets and Asian currencies. Foreign banks now refused to roll the loans over. Real and financial asset prices plummeted around the region, and exchange rates went into free-fall. After losing reserves in a futile attempt to support exchange rates, countries raised interest rates to try to stop the panic. The initial declines in asset prices in turn induced further 'forced' asset sales by investors unable to meet their interest payments.

The destructive neoliberal financial infrastructure within which Asia was now embedded meant that the onset of financial crisis in any country in the area would pull everyone down, the strong as well as the weak. The won lost about 20 per cent of its value in the period before early December, when the IMF made its deal with Korea. Firms and banks with large dollar or yen debt were pushed toward bankruptcy and their desperate demand for dollars and yen kept downward pressure on the won. Interest rates rose again in response to a sharp upward re-evaluation of risk, while banks pushed near default began to refuse to extend credit to smaller businesses. Economic growth slowed and unemployment, almost unknown in postwar Korea, rose – from 2 per cent in November to almost 3 per cent in December. A self-reinforcing cycle of declining growth, falling profits, rising unemployment, rising interest rates, falling interest coverage ratios and rising bankruptcies was now well under way.

As the world watched in amazement and fear, a number of Asian countries turned from economic miracles to economic disasters in a matter of weeks! The *New York Times* pointed to 'the transformation of South Korea from industrial giant to industrial pauper' (22/11/97). Neoliberal economists, who previously insisted that the success of the East Asian miracles had been generated by free-market policies, not state-led industrial policy, now claimed that the crisis was caused by the same powerful but inefficient state industrial policies whose existence they had previously denied. With many of its banks and corporations unable to meet the mounting interest and principal repayment demands of foreign bankers, and thus on the verge of private sector foreign loan defaults on a mass scale, the Korean government, after initial resistance, accepted in December a virtual takeover of their economy by the US-controlled IMF.

Pouring Fuel on the Fire: The Agreement between Korea and the US–IMF

We have argued that the evolution of the global neoliberal regime made the eruption of a financial crisis in Asia at some time virtually inevitable. But the main agents of the neoliberal regime did *not* intentionally create the Asian crisis. The crisis was the unintended outcome of its laws of motion, not the conscious objective of some international conspiracy. However, an examination of the core elements of the IMF agreement will make clear that the forces of the neoliberal regime *did* consciously use the opportunity presented by the crisis to try to permanently defeat the Asian alternative to Anglo-American capitalism and open Asia to the fullest exploitation by external economic interests. Paradoxically, the consequences of the victory of the neoliberal regime over Asian-style capitalism have fuelled a global firestorm that is likely to scorch the neoliberal regime itself as well as its constituent elites before it dies out.

The IMF agreements in Asia mandated institutional and policy changes which are unprecedented in their breadth and severity. The key elements of the IMF agreement with Korea were as follows:

- austerity macroeconomic policies, including high interest rates and restrictive budget or fiscal policy;
- independence of the Korean Central Bank from the rest of the government;
- stringent banking regulations, requiring Korean banks to take immediate steps to meet the minimum capital/asset ratios specified in the 1986 Basle Accord;
- labour law reforms allowing firms operating in Korea to fire workers at will;
- the removal of restrictions on imports, including Korea's virtual prohibition of the importation of Japanese autos;
- the removal of restrictions of foreign ownership of Korean banks and firms;
- the elimination of all forms of government influence over both domestic and international capital flows – including short-term capital inflows, which had triggered the immediate crisis.

The imposition of sky-high interest rates (including short rates as high as 30 per cent at the beginning in December and January), restrictive fiscal policy and tough new banking standards devastated output, employment and financial resiliency. Korean banks have always operated with lower equity/asset ratios (higher debt/equity ratios) than are permitted by the free-market oriented Basle standards. When the loan defaults of the crisis left them near insolvency, the imposition of the Basle standards forced banks to drastically cut loans, especially to small and medium-size businesses. The resulting credit crunch then forced more firms into loan default, leaving banks even further away from compliance with the Basle standards. Together these policies created an ever-deteriorating cycle of bankruptcies, bank failures, declining production and rising unemployment. The vastly understated official unemployment rate has approached 8 per cent, the highest rate in decades, and may climb above 10 per cent – this in a country without a social safety net.

While devastating to the Korean economy, this wave of destruction created advantages for external forces and, to some extent, the chaebol. The collapse of the Korean economy has led to a large current account surplus – perhaps $35 billion in 1998, gained solely through a massive collapse of imports. This surplus will provide the dollars needed to repay foreign banks and the IMF. And the depressed stock market and undervalued won associated with the crisis make it possible for foreigners to buy Korean firms and banks at rock bottom prices. Labour law 'reform', in turn, has already severely weakened the Korean labour movement, and in so doing, has begun to create the labour market 'flexibility' demanded both by the chaebol and by foreign multinationals wishing to buy Korean firms.[20] The independent Bank of Korea, as expected, has pursued the objectives of domestic and foreign rentiers rather than those of the Korean people. It maintained high interest rates right through mid-summer, even as the credit crunch worsened and the economy collapsed. And, of course, some of the IMF dollars that came with the agreement were recycled to foreign lenders, thus avoiding at least temporarily a severe crisis of the global banking system.

The last three elements of the agreement open the Korean economy to unrestricted foreign exploitation. The US had been trying for decades to penetrate the Korean economy with only moderate success: it looks like the IMF will finally get the job done. Note that at present, about 99 per cent of cars purchased in Korea are made by Korean firms. This will change dramatically when Toyota and Honda have unrestricted access to the market next year.

Taken together, the full implementation of these provisions would dismantle the structures and policy tools used by successive Korean governments to regulate business in the national interest – and hence to create the Korean economic 'miracle'. For example, these conditions eliminate the government's ability to allocate domestic credit flows and regulate cross-border capital flows – the cornerstone of the Korean development model. If these agreements are permanently implemented, Korea will lack the tools needed to reconstruct a non-neoliberal, East Asian style system. Korea will then end up neoliberalized – like Mexico, Argentina and Brazil before it.[21] Elite families and some powerful banks and firms may prosper; but the labour movement will deteriorate and two-thirds of the Korean population will face persistent economic insecurity and falling wages.

Internal and External Elites Come Together in Asia: Why the Korea Government Accepted the IMF Agreement

Most Koreans believe that the government had no choice but to accept whatever demands the US and IMF made, no matter how harmful to Korea's sovereignty and its economic future, because the costs of debt default or even a temporary debt moratorium would have been more catastrophic.

But it is quite likely that Korea could have held out for a less destructive agreement. To succeed at this, the government would have had to make a credible threat to proceed without an agreement if IMF and US demands became excessively destructive. For example, the government could have threatened to let Korean banks and firms default on their foreign bank loans. Alternatively, the government could have imposed a temporary moratorium on principal repayments (such as the one later imposed by Russia). The crucial point is that Korea did not need a 'good' fallback position in order to credibly threaten to reject the devastating agreement offered by the IMF. In a bargaining situation, a threat whose enactment would severely damage its maker can be effective if it is sufficiently dangerous to the other participants as well. Prospective large-scale Korean defaults did pose a severe threat to other parties directly and indirectly involved in the negotiations. The risk was not just to Japanese, European and American banks: the international financial system itself could have been thrown into crisis if investors lost confidence in the IMF's ability to organize and lead an all-powerful global creditors' cartel. In sum, it would have been irrational for the IMF to refuse to aid Korea and risk a global financial crisis just because the government would accept some, but not all of its demands. The costs of a collapse of negotiations to the IMF and its backers would have exceeded the benefits from holding out for the disputed demands.

Why then did the government accept this remarkably onerous agreement? Answering this question again takes us back to the evolution of the neoliberal regime. By the 1990s, internal and external elites had, to a significant degree, adopted similar beliefs concerning economic policies and structures. Powerful internal forces in Korea wanted much of the IMF deal for their own interests.

Discussions we held in March with representatives of the chaebol and with government officials established, to our surprise, that the chaebol were generally positive about the IMF agreement – though they were not at all happy with its imperious mode of its design and implementation. While they objected to some elements of the agreement, especially the dangerously high interest rates and the opening of the Korean economy to unrestricted Japanese imports, they believed the IMF deal would help them accomplish two key domestic economic and political objectives. First, the agreement would permanently undermine the power of the labour movement, paving the way for falling wages, labour market flexibility and permanent job insecurity. Second, the agreement would give the chaebol complete independence from government regulation. If fully implemented, the agreement would create freedom for the chaebol to pursue company profits and owning-family financial interests inside Korea or around the globe, no matter what effect their decisions might have on the majority of the Korean people. So with the most powerful force in Korea now ready to substantially align itself with IMF objectives, a credible government threat of default or debt moratorium failed to emerge.

An analysis of the Korean side of the negotiations leading to the IMF agreement reinforces a key point made earlier. The evolution of the neoliberal regime helped create economic and political elites in Asia that eventually saw their material interests as being aligned more closely with external neoliberal agents than with the workers and citizens of their own countries. They became a domestic fifth column, working to destroy the foundations of the traditional Asian models from within.

The Asian IMF Agreements and the Future of the Neoliberal Regime

The IMF agreements in Asia were clearly understood in the West to signal the final defeat of Asian-style capitalism in the war between the systems. Former US Secretary of State Henry Kissinger commented that 'what we are trying to engineer in some of these countries is clearly a revolution', while Federal Reserve Chairman Alan Greenspan proclaimed that 'one of the most fundamental effects of the Asian crisis was "a worldwide move toward the Western form of free market capitalism" instead of the competing Asian approach that only a few years ago looked like an attractive alternative model for nations around the world' (*New York Times*, 13/2/98). This triumphalism was summed up nicely by a *Wall Street Journal* headline which simply stated, 'We Won'.

But our analysis suggests that this will turn out to be a Pyrrhic victory. The ultimate cause of the Asian crisis lies in the contradictions of the global neoliberal regime itself, most fundamentally in its chronic deficiency of aggregate demand. The policies of the IMF constitute one of the system's many sources of demand restraint. In response to the outbreak of recurrent financial crises built into the structure of the neoliberal regime, the IMF has imposed austerity policies on scores of developing countries. Asia had been the only high-growth area in the world over the past 20 years. In the 1990s about half the growth in global GDP took place in East and South East Asia, even though only about 25 per cent of global production originates there. By 'conquering' Asia and forcing it into deep recession and perhaps depression, the IMF has increased global demand deficiency qualitatively. This cannot help but accelerate the ferocity of predatory and destructive competition sweeping global markets, creating even more severe problems of profitability, excess capacity, financial instability, banking crises and commodity price deflation.

Current estimates of the expected rate of *decline* of real GDP in Asia in 1998 include: 2.5 per cent in Japan, 15 per cent to 20 per cent in Indonesia, 7 per cent in Malaysia, 8 per cent in Thailand, 5 per cent in Hong Kong and 8 per cent in Korea (*New York Times*, 2 October, 1998). The impact of this economic collapse and the massive capital flight accompanying it has already spread to Russia, Latin America and to US financial markets. Forecasts of a mild US recession in 1999 are now commonplace. With 40 per cent of global GDP generated by countries already in recession, the end of growth in Europe and the US would quite likely lead to a global depression and deflation of historic proportions. In the end, even the global elites who created the neoliberal regime and have received disproportionate shares of its booty will be unable to insulate themselves from the destructive dynamics they have unleashed.

3.7.   POLICY IMPLICATIONS

Our analysis of the Korean crisis puts substantial emphasis on the large flows of short-term foreign capital that flooded the recently liberalized Korean economy in the mid 1990s. Such emphasis is consistent with the focus placed on large, volatile short-term capital movements in most mainstream and heterodox writings on the Asian crisis. Clearly the $105 billion change in net capital flows to Korea, Malaysia, Indonesia, Thailand and the Philippines – from a $93 billion net inflow in 1996 to a $12 billion outflow in 1997 – an amount equal to more than 10 per cent of the area's pre-crisis GDP, played a major role in triggering the problems under review. This would be equivalent to a change in net capital flows of about $850 billion in the US economy, which would create an unimaginable degree of instability in US financial markets.

However, we have also attempted to look beneath unstable cross-border financial flows to the structure of the global economic regime within which these financial dynamics were taking place. A complete understanding of the causes and consequences of the Asian crisis, encompassing ultimate as well as proximate causes, requires an investigation of the basic contradictions of the global neoliberal regime. But we stress the importance of a theory of the neoliberal regime not just because it helps us better understand the current crisis, but also because it creates a policy perspective quite different from the one associated with most mainstream and heterodox crisis studies.

Neoclassical economists who acknowledge the existence of flaws in global capital markets have proposed that developing countries that experience foreign exchange problems be permitted to utilize certain kinds of temporary controls on inward, but not outward, short-term capital movements. Many heterodox economists go further. They support the use of permanent capital controls as part of the reconstruction of new versions of the East Asian model, ones better suited to current economic conditions and based on more genuine democratic control of the state than were their predecessors. See, for example, Chang (1998).

But our analysis of the crisis suggests that neither of these policy positions is fully adequate, either to repair the damage caused by the current global economic crisis, or to guide the creation of a global economic environment within which long-term, sustainable, egalitarian, high-employment growth is possible in both the North and the South. If we are correct, no new golden age era will be possible unless and until the fundamental structures and policies of the global neoliberal regime are destroyed and replaced by institutions that support buoyant global aggregate demand, facilitate egalitarian national public and private sector institutions and rules-of-the-game, and tolerate different national paths to economic development. Of course, our argument does not suggest that pursuit of objectives short of a reconstitution of the structures of the global economic system are not of the utmost importance. On the contrary, the reimposition of national capital controls in pursuit of the reconstruction of effective and progressive national industrial policies are quite likely preconditions for success in the larger project. The key point is this: if we do not create global institutions that support such progressive national programmes, it is far less likely that anyone will be able to successfully construct and maintain them.

POSTSCRIPT

Two years have passed since this essay was published in *International Papers in Political Economy*. Our analysis, like many others at that time, emphasized the singular importance of the Asian financial crisis. In our view, market forces unleashed in this crisis had largely broken the power of the global economy's only significant remaining bloc of government-directed economies. And with the passing of the 'Asian economic miracle', the possibility of an alternative to neoliberal policies was severely wounded. Now, much more is being written about the re-emergence of Asian economic growth. While the World Bank subtitled its September 1998 retrospective on East Asia 'The Road to Recovery', its mid 2000 update, 'Recovery and Beyond', reports with some relief, 'East Asia is once again the world's fastest growing region' (p. v). Why has this occurred? And what then is the meaning of the Asian financial crisis?

A postscript cannot hope to definitively answer these questions. Instead, paralleling the logic of our 1998 paper, we first comment on changes in the global context of the Asian crisis. We then dissect the substance of the East Asian recovery by examining Korea post-crisis.

East Asia

The World Bank sets out its views about the questions above in 'Recovery and Beyond'. The Bank argues that 'harsh but quick adjustment' has done its job; now further steps permitting integration with the global economy are needed. And 'the international community can help by developing a framework that makes capital flows more manageable and less volatile and by continuing to reduce trade barriers' (p. 2). The report's ensuing pages point out that growth in the five most affected large countries (Indonesia, Korea, Malaysia, the Philippines and Thailand) shifted from −8 per cent in the fourth quarter of 1998 (on a year-over-year basis) to +8 per cent as of the third quarter of 1999. A closer reading finds a less euphoric picture. Korea's rebound in 1999 is most dramatic, but should not be overstated, as we discuss below. And Thailand's 1999 rate of growth was less than its 1998 decline, while Indonesia had negative growth in both 1998 and 1999.

How has this partial recovery been achieved? Have Japan, the US and Europe's advanced economies been behind these trends? It seems unlikely. US economic growth is robust, but may be unsustainable. For one thing, US growth appears to be built on the unstable ground of a consumption boom linked to consumer debt accumulation and rising asset prices, and to an increasingly debt-heavy corporate sector. Further, this growth has led to an historically unprecedented trade deficit. The combination of a booming stock market, government surplus, trade deficit, and capital-account inflow can be sustained only under increasingly implausible scenarios.

By contrast, other advanced nations' growth has slowed or behaved erratically. In particular, Germany's growth rate fell from 2.3 per cent in 1998 to a lower level in 1999 before recovering slightly in early 2000. China's growth rate has also slowed. The exception to this pattern is Japan. It reversed its 1998 negative growth of −2.8 per cent and climbed to a still anaemic 1 per cent growth rate. Given that Japan's growth rate is the tail that wags the pace of East Asian expansion, as Figure 3.5 suggests, Japan's reversal may explain much of the overall East Asian recovery. This is hardly an encouraging sign, since Japan remains mired in an intractable structural crisis involving political paralysis, a tottering banking structure, and a numbed and dissatisfied population.

It is important to remember that before the crisis, East Asia was the world's growth leader on the basis of its models of state-led growth. With the subsequent damage to and even dismantling of these models, there is no reason to believe that East Asia will resume this global role. East Asia's remarkable growth has resulted in part from dense trade and investment interrelations, but also from exports to other nations, especially advanced countries. Now, this region's growth depends even more on the pace of demand in the rest of the world economy.

And what about global growth? Overall, world economic growth fell from a pace of 4.2 per cent in 1997 to 2.5 per cent in 1998 before rising again in 1999 and early 2000. Much of the renewed pace of global expansion is driven by the historically unprecedented US trade deficit, which has helped East Asia's recovery both directly and indirectly (by absorbing EU exports and facilitating EU import demand). This good news is offset by two factors: first, the revived growth rate remains anaemic relative to the pace of global labour-force growth; second, the US trade deficit is unsustainable in the long run, a fact reflected in the increasing turbulence of US financial markets. In sum, if the picture of global stagnation we described in 1998 has brightened at all, it is only at the expense of deeper global structural imbalances.

Our 1998 paper attributed weak global growth rates to the mutually reinforcing problems of insufficient growth in aggregate global demand and to chronic excess aggregate supply. Weak aggregate demand was in turn traced to five factors: forces holding down wages and mass consumption; high real interest rates; restrictive fiscal policy; the level and character of global investment; and the IMF. Among OECD nations, wages have increased only anaemically since 1997; interest rates have climbed even higher; fiscal policies remain tight; and investment spending still flows systematically to lower-wage locations in both the developed and the developing world. So four of the five factors remain operative. The only exception is that the IMF has at least temporarily lost its grip as an enforcer of neoliberal discipline. This has given developing economies more scope for pursuing policy mixes that have permitted recovery. But these policies' effects are dampened because they are being pursued while the advanced countries are pursuing go-slow economic policies.

For the five crisis countries, recovery from the brink is due to structural adjustments associated with wrenching downturns. These nations have rebuilt their reserve via large trade surpluses. These have been compiled despite flat export performance through the collapse of imports. Facilitating this recovery, as the World Bank noted, has been a shift toward looser fiscal policy. Budgetary surpluses relative to GDP have become more negative; from a 1997 range of zero to -1 per cent, these five nations' ratios by 1999 had slipped to a range of -3 to -7 per cent. Note that this shift occurred during a period in which external pressure and 'partnership' with the World Bank have forced the IMF to back off.

These five countries' structural improvements have not come without cost. All five experienced a severe contraction in investment, as Figure 3.4 documents. Already heavy debt levels have worsened, and banks' non-performing loans have reached unprecedented levels: 40 per cent in Thailand, 35 per cent in Indonesia and 20 per cent in Korea. Poverty has become more widespread, and households generally are contending with far greater economic insecurity.

The IMF, World Bank, and advanced countries' leadership have taken a distanced view of these adjustments and trends; for example, the above-mentioned World Bank report mentions 'Legacies of crisis – and the new vulnerability' (p. 11) without any apology. But by identifying effects without naming causes, this official discourse raises more questions instead of answering them. Consider the World Bank's discussion of looser fiscal policy as a factor in East Asian recovery. Do the larger deficit/GDP ratios signal activist policies that have helped in the resumption of growth, or are these ratios the (passive) result of the collapse of public revenues? Are the IMF and other capital providers now permanently permitting nations to maintain larger negative deficit/GDP figures without punishment? Or is this an emerging point of difference between the World Bank and the IMF?

Korea

We now revisit Korea, addressing three important questions about Korea's experience under IMF-sponsored economic restructuring since late 1997. First, has the Korean economy undergone the miraculous economic recovery that neoliberals have claimed? Second, how have labour and the broad majority of the Korean people fared under neoliberal restructuring? Third, to what degree have the forces of global neoliberalism transformed the Korean economy from its state-guided past to its intended market dominated future?

In the last year and one half, Korea's economy has become a poster child for IMF restructuring. The Asian Development Bank describes Korea's 'economic recovery and financial stabilization' following the crash of 1998 as 'remarkable'. By creating 'flexibility' in Korea's notoriously 'rigid' labour markets, aggressively tearing down the remaining barriers to imports and to real and financial capital inflows, shoring up the collapsing financial sector, and replacing the dead hand of government with private market forces, neoliberals argue, President Kim Dae Jung has brought Korea back from the edge of depression to a long-term, high-growth path in record time.

Evidence in support of this view is not hard to assemble. After falling almost 7 per cent in 1998, Korean real GDP grew over 10 per cent in 1999. While this two-year growth of 3 per cent is dramatically below the 15 per cent that might have been expected in the absence of the Asian crisis, it does seem impressive given the trying circumstances of the period. The rate of unemployment, which peaked at 8.4 per cent in early 1999, is approaching 4 per cent in 2000 as the expansion continues. Korea's balance of trade, which had slipped to −5 per cent of GDP in 1996, was a record $40 billion in 1998 – over 10 per cent of GDP, and $25 billion in 1999. In combination with a huge inflow of foreign capital, these trade surpluses rebuilt Korea's foreign reserves toward comfortable levels. Most important, in the view of G7, IMF and World Bank leaders, has been the dramatic economic restructuring under President Kim's strong leadership: the transformation of a corrupt and inefficient pre-crisis 'crony capitalism' to an open, market-driven economy, though still incomplete, assures that the initial post-crisis rebound will be self-sustaining.

A closer look at the data, however, suggests that the recent Korean 'miracle' may not be all that miraculous. The modest GDP growth between 1997 and 1999 was created solely by a huge swing in the trade balance. GDP minus net exports was actually 9 per cent lower in 1999 than in 1997. And the large cumulative trade surplus was achieved not by a significant rise in export earnings, but through a collapse in imports brought on by the deep recession and a dramatic fall in Korea's exchange rate. Per capita real gross national income – an index of economic performance that takes account of the impact of deteriorating terms of trade on national living standards – fell almost 20 per cent over these two years. Figure 3.5, which depicts several nations' GDP in dollar terms, gives some indication of the scale of this decline. Moreover, future export performance will obviously deteriorate unless the US continues to run record trade deficits, European growth does not decline, and exchange rates in China and Japan do not turn against Korea. Even under present favourable external conditions, the trade balance is approaching zero. Turning to non-trade categories, real consumption only attained pre-crisis levels in 2000, with much of its 1999 rebound driven by the increased spending of upper-income families enriched by increasing inequality. Fixed capital formation in 1999 was 18 per cent below 1997's value, and is only now rebounding towards pre-crisis levels. Finally, note that after the initial period, in which the US and IMF brought the Korean economy to its knees by insisting on balanced government budgets and sky-high interest rates, both monetary and fiscal policy became quite expansionary. But neoliberal authorities are now demanding a shift to fiscal and monetary conservatism to guard against inflation. In sum, the bounce-back after 1998 was based on temporary, not sustainable developments, and longer-term growth prospects are nowhere near as rosy as neoliberals claim.

Beneath the macro level, the effects of the crisis on the labour movement and the bottom 80 per cent of the income distribution suggest that the situation is even worse. The IMF's most important demand in its negotiated deal with Korea, reflecting the priorities of both domestic and foreign capital, was for deep, immediate 'reform' of Korea's flexibility-constraining labour laws. And in February 1998, mass firings as a managerial prerogative were legalized, even in Korea's giant conglomerates. Taking advantage of their new legal powers and the collapse in demand, chaebol firms fired about 30 per cent of their workers on average. As demand picked up in 1999 and 2000, firms hired mainly part-time or temporary labour. As a result, the percentage of Korean employees with permanent or regular jobs, already among the lowest in the industrialized world before the crisis, fell dramatically, from 58 per cent in 1995 to 47 per cent in mid-2000, causing a sharp rise in worker insecurity. So while the unemployment rate has fallen – almost to 4 per cent, at this writing, still double the pre-crisis rate – the percentage of permanent employees shows no sign of rising. Indeed, interviews with top-level chaebol representatives by one of the authors in June 2000 confirmed that Korean capital is determined to drive this percentage even lower. No OECD country is close to Korea in this index of job and income insecurity; on average, 87 per cent of employees in OECD nations have permanent or regular job status.

The leaders of the militant, democratic Korean Confederation of Trade Unions made valiant efforts to slow the juggernaut of neoliberal restructuring. Days lost to strikes were triple the 1997 level in both 1998 and 1999, and militant labour actions continue. The KCTU even tried to organize general strikes in 1998 and 1999 to break the restructuring momentum. To date, these efforts have not been successful for several reasons. Kim Dae Jung has met labour activism with fierce repression, including the arrest of virtually all union leaders involved in strike activity. The labour movement is still divided: the more conservative, pro-government Federation of Korean Trade Unions has refused to join forces with the KCTU. Moreover, the ever-increasing split in the workforce between permanent and temporary workers makes it increasingly difficult for the KCTU to maintain labour unity. The media is universally anti-labour, and labour has no major allies, because the middle class fears that labour activism will destabilize the recovery, and the once powerful progressive student movement is virtually non-existent now.

While it would be imprudent to rule out a new outbreak of effective labour militance, realistically, prospects for labour do not look good. Continued government repression and chaebol aggression can be expected. Real wages have only now regained pre-crisis levels and job insecurity grows ever greater.

Meanwhile, inequality of income and wealth is rising rapidly. The Gini coefficient, which equalled 0.28 in 1997, now stands at 0.32; and the ratio of the income of the highest quintile of households to that of the lowest quintile has risen by 22 per cent in just two years. Indeed, the real income of the top 20 per cent rose substantially both in the collapse of 1998 and in the recovery of 1999. Meanwhile, the income of the 80 per cent of households constituting the bottom four quintiles fell in both years; the income of the lowest 20 per cent fell by a total of almost 20 per cent. Not surprisingly, poverty has also worsened since the crisis. The urban poverty rate, which stood at 8.5 per cent in 1996, rose to 19 per cent in 1998 before falling slightly to 15 per cent. Korea, a country proud of its tradition of social solidarity, is discovering that there are no exceptions to the rule that neoliberalism generates rising inequality everywhere.

A full discussion of economic restructuring cannot be undertaken here. However, some important trends can be mentioned beyond the structural deterioration of labour rights addressed above. The most pressing problem facing the incoming Kim government was the collapse of a banking system overburdened with bad loans. To deal with this threat, the government injected a huge amount of public funds into the financial system; Standard and Poor estimated the ultimate cost at $125 billion, or about 29 per cent of 1999 GDP. In effect, the banking system was temporarily nationalized. President Kim then used control of the banks to dictate structural change to the heavily indebted chaebol. Under the traditional Korean state-led growth model, high debt–equity ratios for chaebol companies were the norm, but liberalization followed by the outbreak of crisis in 1997 – with its 30 per cent interest rates, bank credit crunch, and collapsing sales – left the highly indebted chaebol in extreme financial risk. Intent on rapidly installing a neoliberal regime, and on taking advantage of the public's hatred of the families that controlled the chaebol, Kim Dae Jung demanded that the chaebol specialize on a smaller set of business areas and cut their debt–equity ratios from approximately 5 to under 2 in two years. He threatened to destroy them if they failed to do so, by cutting off credit from their main banks, which the government now controlled. Of course, in near-depression conditions, these firms could meet this demand only by selling off many of their assets to pay off their debts; since domestic firms were illiquid, such a process was guaranteed to dramatically increase foreign control of Korea's economy. On paper at least, the chaebol have now met this requirement, though their absolute level of debt has dropped only about 10 per cent. Most of the improvement has come in the denominator of the ratio, as firms raised the accounting value of their assets and issued new stock.

Just as President Kim intended, the forced sale of stock and real assets opened the door to an unprecedented rise in foreign ownership and control of the Korean economy. Foreign direct investment poured into Korea. After running between one and two billion dollars for most of the 1990s, inward FDI from early 1998 through early 2000 totalled almost $30 billion. It is projected to reach $20 billion in 2000 alone. Almost all of these inroads were achieved via mergers and acquisition; Korea thus gained few new real assets in return for this massive transfer of corporate control to outsiders. The full opening of the Korean stock market to foreigners, along with the outpouring of new stock offerings by chaebol firms pressed to lower debt–equity ratios, vastly increased the function of the stock market as a market for corporate control, and increased its volatility – the KOSPI stock price index was 350 in late 1997, rose to near 1000 in mid 1999, and dropped to about 600 in September 2000. About $10 billion of net foreign money has flowed into the Korean stock market in the past two years. Foreigners owned only 12 per cent of the Korean stock market in late 1997, but 30 per cent by early 2000.

Mainstream economists applaud the contribution these inflows of foreign capital to Korea's foreign exchange holdings. But these inflows have a longer-run downside: Korea is clearly losing control of its economic destiny to those who do not have its interests at heart. Much of the recent economic expansion was concentrated in a few key industries – such as semiconductors, telecommunications and autos, all of which are falling under strong foreign influence. *The Korea Times* (17 July 2000) reported that foreigners owned 44 per cent of semiconductor shares, and 21 per cent of telecommunication shares. The situation in autos is well known. Renault bought Samsung auto (at about 10 per cent of the value of its assets), Daimler-Chrysler is increasing its influence over Hyundai-Kia, and Kim Dae Jung has announced that Daewoo, Korea's largest auto maker, *must* be sold to foreign interests, even though its sale will bring little money, perhaps $3 billion, less than 3 per cent of the cost of the government's bailout of the financial system. *The Financial Times* (27 June 2000) sees 'the possibility that the entire [Korean auto] sector, the second largest in Asia, could soon be dominated by foreigners'. *Forbes* (18/9/126), in an article titled 'If You Can't Beat Em, Buy Em', predicts that the cash-rich Big Three in autos will soon take control of Daewoo and Hyundai for the express purpose of preventing the Korean firms from becoming serious competitors in the most profitable parts of the market – SUVs, sedans and mini-vans. That is, they wish to keep these companies from developing – hardly a wonderful prospect for the Korean economy.

In our view, then, the widely advertised neoliberal Korean 'miracle' is largely fraud. The sources of growth to date are unsustainable, intermediate-term impediments to growth are numerous, and the restoration of long-term growth at historic rates is unlikely. The labour movement and the vast major-ity of the Korean people are clearly worse off because of neoliberal restruc-turing. Even the chaebol – who are delighted by the decline in labour's power

– might sometimes wish they could put the genie back in the bottle, as their independence from foreign control rapidly vanishes. The trends in FDI and stock ownership, including the recent rise in foreign ownership of financial institutions, clearly reinforce a key concern raised in the body of our article in late 1998: Korea has moved substantially if not irrevocably towards a situation in which future Korean governments will be structurally incapable of guiding or regulating the Korean economy in the interests of the people of Korea.

NOTES

*   The authors are, respectively, Professor of Economics at the University of Massachusetts, Amherst, and Associate Professor of Economics at the University of California, Riverside. The authors' research for this paper was supported by the Pacific Rim Research Program of the University of California, and by faculty research funds at their respective institutions. They thank their friends and colleagues in Korea, and owe a special debt to Soo Haeng Kim and Hyeon-Hyo Ahn for their help during the authors' visit to Korea during March 1998. Antonio Callari helped in translating the quote from Gramsci, and the editors provided useful suggestions for improving the ideas developed here.

1. This concept is introduced and explored in Glyn et al. (1990).
2. One reason why wage effects of foreign direct investment are dismissed is that the tests designed to measure its impact are badly flawed. See Crotty et al. (1997), on which this section draws heavily.
3. Another factor depressing global wages was the entry of workers from China, the former Soviet Union and India into the global labour pool in this period.
4. See Crotty (1993) on the importance of this shift in competitive regimes.
5. See Dymski and Isenberg (1998) and Dymski (1999).
6. Galbraith (1998) analyses recent global exchange-rate trends. Blecker (1998) documents the global contractionary bias of government policy.
7. For example, Korea's industrial strategy was made over substantially in the 1970s, and again in the early 1980s, both to correct policy mistakes and to respond to an evolving international environment; see E.M. Kim (1997).
8. This aspect of East Asian economies has gradually changed. Government expenditures on social welfare and housing have risen rapidly in most countries, albeit from a low base.
9. Of course, the US and its European OECD partners hardly have clean hands when it comes to the eradication of social inequality, gender oppression, and the coddling of entrenched elites.
10. Dymski (1998) and Kregel (1998) discuss the relationship between Minsky's framework and the Asian financial crisis.
11. See Wade and Veneroso (1998). The high debt ratios of the Asian model follow logically from the fact that profits are low, while household savings and capital investment are high. High corporate debt levels are the inevitable result of using a banking system to transfer large volumes of household savings to the corporate sector to finance investment.
12. The *Wall Street Journal* of October 16, 1998 makes the same argument about the untenability (hence Catch-22 aspect) of both fixed and flexible exchange rates, noting that 'misalignments and currency crashes are equally likely under pegged and flexible exchange rate regimes. In the 116 instances between 1976 and 1996 when currencies plunged 25 per cent or more, half were operating with flexible exchange rate systems' (while obviously the other half were fixed or pegged).

13. The most extreme example of this is perhaps the empirical sub-literature on whether banking and financial collapses (like those in Asia) have generally been foreshadowed by deteriorating macroeconomic or structural fundamentals. The one-time character of any given occurrence of financial crisis leaves too few degrees of freedom for a reliable test. Some enterprising economists have tried to overcome this constraint by building up a panel of different occurrences of banking and financial crisis in contemporary economic experience; by stretching the definition of crisis and the allowable range of countries, they are able to generate 50 or more events. This in turn makes it possible to use a multi-nomial probit model to test whether a number of macroeconomic and financial variables collected for these various events are useful indicators of banking crises. For example, Hardy and Pazarbasioglu (1998) build a model of this sort, then apply the parameters they obtain to the case of East Asia. They find that variables capturing the vulnerability of the banking and corporate sector predict the subsequent crises, but macroeconomic variables do not. One problem with this exercise is that it requires the assumption that, say, the US savings and loan crisis of the 1980s, the Japanese banking crisis of the early 1990s, and numerous bank runs in smaller countries around the globe in the past 20 years can be put into a uniform data set and manipulated using models that require a high degree of statistical regularity.

14. This argument trips over itself. The governments in crisis are blamed both for permitting weaknesses to emerge in financial systems (through the aforementioned over-regulation of flows) and for their inadequate financial supervision. The contradiction herein is resolved if one considers that it refers to financial systems already in transition from government directed to market-based methods of allocation. Interestingly, a paper produced independently by economists at the IMF (Demirguc-Kunt and Detragiache, 1998) summarizes some empirical tests which conclude that financial liberalization increases the probability of banking crisis.

15. The standard asymmetric-information models of the LDC debt crisis are Sachs (1984) and Eaton et al. (1986). These models advance the proposition that the debt crisis arose because the penalty for non-payment was too low and contractual terms could not be enforced. The recurrence of two currently prominent names from this earlier discussion gives pause. As Yogi Berra put it, 'It's deja vu all over again.'

16. A macroeconomic approach building on the same factors as Krugman's microfounda-tional model is McKinnon's 'overborrowing syndrome' model, which focuses on the inadequate regulation of domestic banks with access to overseas financial borrowing. This approach was operationalized empirically by Kaminsky and Reinhart (1996), a con-tribution which has now provided a launching point for many applied papers on the Asian crisis.

17. For example, Stiglitz and Uy argue that, 'Several characteristics of financial sector inter-ventions in East Asia stand out: they incorporated design features that improved the chances of success and reduced opportunities for abuse; interventions that did not work out were dropped unhesitatingly; and policies were adapted to reflect changing economic conditions' (Stiglitz and Uy, 1996, p. 249). They go on to argue, in opposition to Krugman's emphasis on moral hazard and government intervention in financial crises, that: 'financial crises occur with remarkable frequency in the absence of government intervention. Private monitoring apparently does not suffice to prevent a financial crisis. Moreover, no single financial institution will exercise sufficient care on its own to avoid financial distress.'

18. The difference between US and, especially, Japanese interest rates led to a wave of so-called 'carry trades' in which multinational banks would borrow in Japan or the US at low rates, then relend the money to Korean firms or banks at rates that were high enough to create attractive margins, yet were still well below domestic rates in Korea.

19. Of course, those governments that chose not to liberalize rapidly, such as Taiwan and China, stayed relatively insulated from the immediate effects of the subsequent financial crisis.

20. The struggle in Korea in the aftermath of the IMF agreements is described in Crotty and

Dymski (1998a, 1998b, and 1998c). These articles pay particular attention to the attempt by the Korean Confederation of Trade Unions, the more independent, democratic and militant of the two major Korean union federations, to prevent the implementation of radical neoliberal restructuring in Korea.

21. Interestingly, in June 1998, when it had become clear that the economic collapse *per se* was not leading to a spontaneous economic restructuring of the sort the neoliberals had in mind, the government stepped in and took direct administrative control of the restructuring process. We thus see once again that the neoliberal commitment to free markets and disapproval of government interference in economic activity apparently evaporates when the interests of its constituent agents are not being well served by market processes alone.

REFERENCES

Akyuz, Yilmaz (1998), *The East Asian Financial Crisis: Back to the Future?*, Geneva: United Nations Commission on Trade and Development.

Amsden, Alice (1989), *Asia 's Next Giant*, New York: Oxford University Press.

Amsden, Alice and Euh Yoon-Dae (1997), 'Behind Korea's Plunge,' *New York Times*, 27 November.

Blecker, Robert (1998), 'International capital mobility, macroeconomic balances, and the risk of global contraction', Technical paper, Economic Policy Institute, June.

Chang, Ha-Joon (1998), 'Korea: the misunderstood crisis', mimeo, Cambridge University.

Chang, Ha-Joon, Park, Hong-Jae and Yoo Chul Gyue (1998), 'Interpreting the Korean Crisis: Financial Liberalisation, Industrial Policy, and Corporate Governance', *Cambridge Journal of Economics*, **22** (6), August.

Chang, Roberto and Velasco, Andrés (1998), 'Financial crises in emerging markets: a canonical model' Working Paper 98-10, Federal Reserve Bank of Atlanta, July.

Crotty, James (1993), 'Rethinking Marxian investment theory: Keynes–Minsley instability, competitive regime shifts and coerced investment', *Review of Radical Political Economics*, **25** (1) (March), 1–26.

Crotty, James and Dymski, Gary (1998a), 'The Korean struggle: can the East Asian model survive?', *Z*, July–August.

Crotty, James, and Dymski, Gary (1998b), "The Korean struggle intensifies', *Z*, September.

Crotty, James and Dymski, Gary (1998c), "The Korean struggle and the Asian crisis', *Dollars and Sense*, November.

Crotty, James, Epstein, Gerald and Kelly, Patricia, (1997) 'Multinational corporations, capital mobility and the global neoliberal regime: effects on Northern workers and on growth prospects in the developing world', *Seoul Journal of Economics,* **10** (4), Winter, 297–340.

Davidson, Paul (1998), "Quack's cure for depression won't quiet our fears', *The Guardian*, 14 September.

Demirguc-Kunt. Asli and Detragiache, Enrica (1998), 'Financial liberalization and financial fragility', IMF Working Paper 98/83, Research Department, International Monetary Fund, Washington, DC, June.

Diamond, Douglas and Dybvig, Philip (1983), 'Bank runs, deposit insurance, and liquidity', *Journal of Political Economy,* **91**, 401–419.

Dooley, Michael P. (1997), 'A model of crises in emerging markets', NBER Working Paper No. 6300, December.

Dymski, Gary A. (1998), 'A spatialized Minsky approach to asset bubbles and financial crisis', Mimeo, University of California, Riverside, September.

Dymski, Gary A. (1999), *The Bank Merger Wave: The Economic Causes and Social Consequences of Financial Consolidation*, Armonk, NY: M.E. Sharpe, Inc.

Dymski, Gary A. and Isenberg, Dorene (1998), 'Housing Finance in the Age of Globalization: From Social Housing to Life-Cycle Risk', in *Globalization and Progressive Economic Policy*, Dean Baker, Gerald Epstein and Robert Pollin (eds), Cambridge: Cambridge University Press.

Eaton, Jonathan, Gersovitz, Mark and Stiglitz, Joseph (1986), 'The pure theory of country risk,' *European Economic Review,* 30, 481–513.

Galbraith, James K. (1998), 'The butterfly effect', mimeo, University of Texas, Austin.

Glyn, Andrew, Hughes, Alan, Lipietz, Alain, and Singh, Ajit (1990), 'The Rise and Fall of the Golden Age', in Stephen Marglin and Juliet B. Schor (eds), *The Golden Age of Capitalism*, Oxford: Oxford University Press.

Grabel, Ilene (1998), 'Rejecting exceptionalism: reinterpreting the Asian financial crisis', *Cambridge Journal of Economics,* **22** (6), August.

Gramsci, Antonio (1996), *Prison Notebooks*, Volume 2, Edited and translated by Joseph Buttigieg, New York: Columbia University Press.

Grey, Cheryl W. and Kaufman, Daniel (1998), 'Corruption and development', *Finance and Development*, **35** (1) (March), 7–10.

Guitián, Manuel (1998), 'The challenge of managing capital flows', *Finance and Development*, June.

Ha, Seong-Kyu (1995), 'Housing and Poverty', Chapter 5 in *Combating Poverty: The Korean Experience*, Seoul, Korea: UNDP.

Hardy, Daniel C. and Pazarbasioglu, Ceyla, (1998), 'Leading indicators of banking crises: was Asia different?', IMF Working Paper 98/91, Monetary and Exchange Affairs Department, International Monetary Fund, Washington, DC, June.

International Monetary Fund (1998), 'The IMF's response to the Asian crisis', International Monetary Fund, Washington, DC, June 15.

Jeong, Seongjin, (1997), 'The social structure of accumulation in South Korea', *Review of Radical Political Economics*, **29** (4), December, 92–112.

Johnson, Chalmers (1995), *Japan. Who Governs?* New York: W.W. Norton.

Kaminsky, Graciela and Reinhart, Carmen, (1996), 'The twin crises: the causes of banking and balance of payment crises', International Finance Discussion Paper No. 544. Washington, DC: Board of Governors of the Federal Reserve, March.

Kim, Eun Mee (1997), *Big Business, Strong State: Collusion and Conflict in South Korean Development, 1960–1990*, Albany, NY: State University of New York Press.

Kim, Woo-Jin (1997), *Economic Growth, Low Income, and Housing in South Korea*, London: Macmillan Press.

Kregel, Jan (1998), 'Yes, "It" did happen again – a Minsky crisis happened in Asia', Jerome Levy Economics Institute Working Paper No. 234, April.

Krugman, Paul (1994), "The myth of Asia's miracle', *Foreign Affairs,* **73** (6), November/December, 62–78.

Krugman, Paul (1995), 'Dutch tulips and emerging markets', *Foreign Affairs,* **74** (4), July/August, 28–44.

Krugman, Paul (1998), 'What Happened to Asia?', MIT Department of Economics, January.

MacLean, Brian, Bowles, Paul and Croci, Osvaldo (1998), 'Understanding the Asian Crisis and its Implications for Regional Economic Integration', in G. Boyd and A. Rugman (eds), *Deepening Integration in the Pacific*, Aldershot: Edward Elgar.

McKinnon, Ronald I (1993), *The Order of Economic Liberalisation. Financial Control in the Transition to a Market Economy*, 2nd edn, Baltimore: Johns Hopkins University Press.

Naff, Clayton (1996), *About Face*, Tokyo: Kodansha International.

Radelet, Steven, and Sachs, Jeffrey (1998), 'The onset of the East Asian financial crisis', mimeo, Harvard Institute for International Development, Harvard University, March.

Sachs, Jeffrey (1984), 'Theoretical issues in international borrowing', *Princeton Studies in International Finance*, 54, July.

Sachs, Jeffrey (1998), 'Global capitalism: making it work,' *The Economist*, September 12.

Singh, Ajit (1996), 'Savings, Investment and the Corporation in the East Asian Miracle', *East Asian Development. Lessons for a New Global Environment*, Study No. 9, Geneva: United Nations Conference on Trade and Development, March.

Stiglitz, Joseph E (1996), 'Some lessons from the East Asian miracle', *World Bank Research Observer,* **11** (2), August, 151–177.

Stiglitz, Joseph E (1998), *Sound Finance and Sustainable Development in Asia*, Washington, DC: The World Bank, March 12.

Stiglitz, Joseph E and Uy, Marilou (1996), 'Financial Markets, Public Policy, and the East Asian Miracle', *World Bank Research Observer,* **11** (2), August, 249–276.

United Nations Conference on Trade and Development (UNCTAD) (1998), *Trade and Development Report, 1998*, Geneva: United Nations.

Wade, Robert (1990), *Governing the Market: Economic Theory and the Role of Government in East Asian Industrialization*, Princeton: Princeton University Press.

Wade, Robert (1998), 'Gestalt shift: from "miracle" to "cronyism" in the Asian crisis', *Cambridge Journal of Economics,* **22** (6), August.

Wade, Robert and Veneroso, Frank (1998), 'The Asian crisis: the high debt model vs. the Wall Street–Treasury–IMF complex,' *New Left Review,* 228, March–April.

World Bank (1998), *East Asia: The Road to Recovery*, Washington, DC: World Bank.

World Bank (2000), *East Asia: Recovery and Beyond*, Washington, DC: World Bank.

4. Financial derivatives, liquidity preference, competition and financial inflation

Jan Toporowski

> He [John Law] told Pitt that he would bring down our East India stock, and entered into articles with him to sell at 12 months hence, a hundred thousand pounds of stock at eleven per cent under the present current price. (Hardwicke, 1778, vol. ii, p. 589)

Towards the end of August 1719 Thomas Pitt, Lord Londonderry, dined in Paris with John Law who was shortly to be appointed Contrôlleur-Général des Finances, effectively Prime Minister, to the French King Louis XV. Law was then in the process of organising the repayment of the French national debt by his Mississippi Company, and was consumed with a sense of his own financial genius. He seems to have believed that France, under his financial direction, was destined to push Britain into the margins of finance and trade, causing investors to abandon British securities for shares in his Mississippi Company, the market for which was being inflated using credit created by Law's own Banque Royale.[1] A contract with Lord Londonderry was drawn up and signed on the 29 September 1719. Under this contract, His Lordship was to pay Law £180 000 in exchange for £100 000 of shares in the East India Company, a year thence. At the end of September 1719, East India shares cost £192 per £100 of shares. By June 1720 their price had risen to £420. Law made various margin payments on the contract but, in the months that followed, the Mississippi Company collapsed, and in December 1720, Law fled France. It is unlikely that he ever fully settled his contract with Lord Londonderry (Murphy, 1997, pp. 241–2).

Law's contract was what would today be called a forward contract, that is, a future financial commitment whose terms are agreed when it is entered into, rather than the standardized futures contract traded in futures markets. That agreement was the prototype of today's financial derivatives.

4.1. LIQUIDITY PREFERENCE AND THE CONVENTIONAL APPROACH TO FINANCIAL FUTURES

Financial futures may be regarded as a particularly neoclassical answer to what Keynes regarded as his quintessential contribution to political economy, his theory of liquidity preference. According to his theory, uncertainty causes economic agents in general, and rentiers in particular, to prefer to hold liquid assets rather than engage in long-term investment. This is supposed to prevent the capital market from functioning properly because rentiers demand higher interest rates on their long-term financial assets, to compensate them for the possibly lower liquidity of those assets. These higher long-term interest rates then discourage entrepreneurs from investing, leading to under-investment (Keynes, 1936, chs. 15 and 23; 1937). From the neoclassical point of view of their purveyors, uncertainty, the cause of Keynesian pessimism about free market capitalism, may be banished by projecting a web of certain prices into an uncertain future, through financial futures and the apparently spontaneous and ardently competitive set of markets in those instruments.

However, the limitations of existing financial futures markets in this regard seem fairly obvious. These include the short-term nature of their contracts and the narrow range of predominantly financial parameters which may be secured through them. In terms of effecting an intertemporal general equilibrium, financial futures markets are deficient because they deal in nominal values, rather than relative prices. Less obvious are the nature of the competition in those markets, the actual operations of the agents in those markets, the resulting market mechanisms, the effects of these on liquidity in the economy, and the role in all this of capital market inflation. These are the subjects of this chapter.

Insofar as neoclassical theorists consider financial futures as part of a more general economic analysis, they tend to view these instruments as part of a perfectly intermediated world, thereby approaching more closely that intertemporal general equilibrium in which social welfare is maximized (see Rybczynski, 1988). One interpretation of Keynesian uncertainty is that, in a non-ergodic or continually changing world, financial parameters are the link between a certain present and an unknown future. Financial parameters are therefore held to affect in particular entrepreneurial investment in fixed capital and the spot (that is, for immediate delivery) markets for bonds and money.[2] However, Steindl suggested that, in financial markets, uncertainty is associated with the unpredictability of the consensus on the value of financial parameters that market traders will arrive at on a particular day in the future (Steindl, 1990). Participants in financial futures markets enter into contracts in order to profit from the consensus that eventually arrives. The liquidation of the resulting structure of short-term financial claims and liabilities results in financial flows that may be more destabilizing than the volatility of the underlying financial variables.

The neoclassical view of financial futures markets is that they are a facility which projects certain values into an uncertain future, or at least replaces uncertain values with a 'certainty-equivalent value' that reflects future 'risks'. If this were the case then, other things being equal, one would expect a reduction in the liquidity preference due to uncertainty as the use of financial futures has proliferated since the 1970s. Since other things have not been equal since the 1970s, one cannot observe this because of the difficulty of distinguishing between increased usage of financial futures and the increasing volatility of financial parameters which causes companies and investors to resort to these instruments.

However, the uncertainty associated with financial futures depends on the use to which a financial future is put: If the purpose of using financial futures is to fix financial parameters, then this would indeed reduce uncertainty and may reduce liquidity preference (other things being equal!). But, if the purpose of using financial futures is to obtain a profit, then these instruments may actually increase uncertainty. In the first case an uncertain parameter is fixed enabling a profit from some underlying activity to be calculated with less uncertainty. But in the second case the profit depends on the difference between the fixed financial parameter and its uncertain value in the future. Such differences are likely to be even more volatile than the parameter itself. In other words, where financial futures are used for investment, the profit is not made more certain, but may be less so. The Basle Accord's regulations imposing capital requirements on banks' financial futures liabilities (a form of compulsory liquidity preference) is an implicit recognition that financial futures do not create greater certainty.

The conventional textbook analysis of financial futures, based on time-series analysis of price data, holds that the values of financial futures instruments are determined by the fundamental values of the underlying assets, so that the rationale for financial futures exists because there are market imperfections. For example, exchange rates deviate from 'equilibrium' rates, stock prices deviate from 'fundamental' values, price differences have not been arbitraged away, or private information has not yet become public information (that is, the markets are not strongly efficient). Neoclassical (market efficiency) theorists view financial markets as consensus-creating systems of information exchange. In the neoclassical system, the consensus emerges around fundamental capital asset values. By contrast, Keynes, in his beauty contest analogy of capital markets, in which participants rate

stocks according to how they think *average opinion* will rate them, regarded
that consensus as purely conventional (Keynes, 1936, pp. 152–61).

Theories about financial markets in general, and financial futures in particular, describe how markets operate and determine prices. A good price
theory should explain how markets operate in order to bring about the
prices described by the theory. But even the most abstractedly mathematical price models make implicit assumptions about the market mechanisms
which bring about the prices postulated in those models. Such models are
commonly empirically validated by price equations of the form:

$$P_t = P_t^* + \varepsilon_t \tag{4.1}$$

Typically, the conventional neoclassical theories measure the deviations,
ε_t, of actual prices, P_t, from fundamental values, P_t^*, and filter out those
components of ε_t which coincide with 'significant' events such as
announcements of company results, trade and inflation statistics.

At its most systematic the neoclassical theory presupposes that a competitive equilibrium will determine fundamental values (P_t^*). Futures decisions are then dependent on a presumption that the state of perfect market
equilibrium (proxied by average prices in the capital asset pricing models
used to determine P_t^*) will be approached in historical time. Given a fixed
volatility in the price of the underlying asset,[3] no income on that asset, constant short-term interest rates, perfectly elastic supply of credit at given
rates of interest, a tax regime that is neutral in respect of trades, and zero
transaction costs, relatively simple mathematical formulas can be derived
to show the value of an options or, more generally, a futures contract (see
Black, 1989). Broadly, it is then worthwhile entering into a financial futures
agreement providing that its price or premium, f_t, is below the deviation of
the actual price from the perceived fundamental value, that is,

$$\text{buy if } f_t < (P_t - P_t^*) \text{ or } f_t < \varepsilon_t \tag{4.2}$$
$$\text{or sell if } f_t > (P_t - P_t^*) \text{ or } f_t > \varepsilon_t \tag{4.2'}$$

where ε_t represents the current deviation from fundamental value.[4]

Future deviations from fundamental values are allowed for in
Black–Scholes and Cox–Ross methods of futures pricing by averaging
recent deviations. The residual from average prices, and the variance of that
residual, is treated as a probabilistic measure of the risk that the average
price (presumed to be the fundamental value) will not be realized by the
maturity date of the futures contract. There is an implicit assumption that,
at the maturity date of the contract, the most probable price of the underlying security will be some *average* of past prices. In line with modern port-

folio theory this is treated as a proxy for the fundamental value of that security (Markowitz, 1990). Other possible values of that price are distributed around that mean in a normal distribution completely described by that mean and the standard deviation from it. Accordingly, the frequency of 95 per cent of possible maturity values is supposed to be encompassed within 2.46 standard deviations of that mean.

But the future is never like the present, or the past. Because economies and markets change over time, each day in those markets has its unprecedented developments, so that the past is not a *complete* guide to the future. Indeed, speculation would be impossible if the past could provide such directions about the future, while financial innovation may be regarded as an optimistic attempt to distinguish the future from the past. There is a degree of uncertainty (lack of knowledge) about the future which cannot be proxied by deviations from historical averages. In the equations above, ε_{t+n} (the deviation on the maturity of a futures contract) may not be in any stable relationship with the array of past ε. The absence of any such stable relationship is all the more likely when capital markets are irregularly inflated by financial inflows.

To the degree that there is some trend at work, evolution can be approximated by weighting the recent past more than the distant past. But there remains a fundamental limitation of probability calculations based on statistical inference for serious academic research and financial market practice. Here it is necessary to distinguish between, say, a lottery, a routinely repeated action which gives rise to different outcomes of a particular frequency distribution, and events in markets which are not routinely repeated. Market events occur not because they are probable, but because their antecedents and circumstances cause them to happen. An event that occurs with a perceived probability of less than 1 per cent is much more real than all the possible outcomes with higher probabilities that did not happen. It can only be seriously explained or anticipated by examining how it happened and why. Probability cannot explain in this logical sense (Keynes, 1921). In a market, price determination is a series of events that are decided by the financial inflow into that market, rather than a lottery (see Toporowski, 2000, Part I), even if subsequently price statistics may be drawn up as frequency distributions. As financial markets become more volatile, probability becomes a less and less adequate guide to analysis. A fundamental methodological contradiction arises between the growing volatility of financial markets, which is the rationale for the existence of financial futures, and the widely used models for analysing and pricing financial futures, based on the relative stability of financial markets. This volatility brings financial research into the domain of business-cycle theory, rather than probability analysis.

The neoclassical pricing theories have a certain practical significance in that the higher is the proportion of traders following these pricing methods the more likely they are to give the correct valuation, in the sense of anticipating a consensus view. In a comment on the practical significance of the Black–Scholes method of valuing options, the Chairman of the Chicago Board Options Exchange, William Floresh, described that significance as 'staggering' because 'without a mathematical model that could predict comfortably where options prices could fall, we would not have had the participation of big investors that we have seen'.[5] In other words, the value of Black–Scholes is not that it gives 'correct' answers, but that it gives answers which enable investors to use options markets on a larger scale.

Students learning about strategies of investment in financial futures markets are commonly taught valuation formulae as the vehicles for understanding values in those markets. Even recently fashionable models which deviate from the assumptions of perfectly competitive equilibrium, such as theories of bubbles, 'information cascades' and 'chaos' postulate equilibrium values which are the reference point for somewhat longer and more extreme deviations (Allen and Gorton, 1993; Bikhchandani et al., 1992; Hsieh, 1991). However, such values cannot be independent of the way in which those markets operate. There are other trading strategies that are just as practical as using mathematical models for valuing futures instruments and which may be even more rational in the sense of being based on some understanding of what is happening in the markets. Traders may, for example, disaggregate recent deviations into those systematically associated with particular events and developments, and then anticipate how these will evolve in the future, and what the resulting deviations will be. This is not necessarily what is commonly called a 'fundamentalist' strategy, because that usually means an assumption that deviations from fundamental values will eliminate themselves (that is, that ε tends to zero). A more realistic view simply supposes that deviations will continue to occur, but that they will be deviations from past values, rather than some underlying equilibrium. This already happens in, for example, the foreign exchange market, where traders continually anticipate, often in a relatively ill-informed way, the consequences for their market of a continuous stream of official and unofficial statistical announcements ('statsbabble, the process by which economic and financial statistics are propelled around the market by traders using them to arouse speculative intents and desires among investors'[6]).

A more subjective, but still rational, strategy that is highly appropriate to open-outcry financial futures markets, is Keynes' 'beauty contest' approach, anticipating the future valuations of other traders and how these may differ from current valuations of P_t and f_t. In this approach, fundamental values, and therefore deviations from them, are not even considered. Trading strategy is here determined by psychological analysis of other traders' sentiments, wishes and desires. A third strategy may be to analyse the liquidity position and liabilities of traders and their claims against each other to determine where the most profitable 'forced' sales of assets, or their future purchases, will occur.

These 'alternative' strategies are all more realistic, in that they are based on induction from observed events and behaviour, than the mathematical models based on deductions from unrealistic assumptions of perfectly competitive equilibrium. But for practical purposes, their greater realism has to be set against the disadvantage of the lengthy, serious analysis that they require before the value of a trading decision becomes apparent. This limits their usefulness to long-term, more considered investment than the rapid-fire deals in the open-outcry trading that prevails in the main financial futures markets. In those markets, the neoclassical Black–Scholes and Cox–Ross methods are superior: With computers to make the calculations, they provide virtually instantly programmable trading decisions. An individual trader may make many more trades during a trading day, making up in volume for the smaller profit margins that he may expect to obtain on the most commonly traded contracts. The computer-programmable neoclassical valuation models are therefore an important factor in facilitating fuller utilisation of trading capacity, through the proliferation of inter-broker dealing (see Section 4.4 below).

There is also an institutional inconsistency in the neoclassical pricing analysis, which becomes very important when conclusions are drawn from it for the regulation of financial futures trading. The analysis supposes that financial futures instruments are bought for profit, so that any losses are the result of an inadequate analysis of risk (that is, an incorrect specification of ε) or an incorrect trading strategy, and large profits (and by implication large losses) are supposed to be eliminated by arbitrage in near perfectly competitive markets. In this way, that element of the analysis with the weakest ontological foundation, namely fundamental values, proxied in empirical analysis and practical pricing application by some average of past prices, is absolved of any blame when the market equilibrium fails to arrive. This happens, for example, when pricing strategies go wrong, when traders such as Barings' Nick Leeson try to corner a market, or when serious losses accrue. Such events suggest that trading in markets occurs out of equilibrium, that there is no perfectly competitive, or any other, equilibrium 'out there' in the markets, other than the accounting balance between purchase and sale, and that the equilibria or fundamental values used in finance theory are a useful and calculated, but no less arbitrary, fiction.

4.2.   DERIVATIVES USE BY INDUSTRIAL AND COMMERCIAL FIRMS

In the orthodox, neoclassical theory, the agents in futures markets are all investors, that is, individuals and firms possessing wealth and seeking a return on that wealth, either in capital gain or in income through buying and selling assets in financial markets. Financial futures are treated as merely a form of financial asset on which a profit may be made. Industrial and commercial users of financial futures instruments are assumed to be either acting as investors, or merely servicing in an undefined way their commercial activities without affecting what is happening in the financial markets. But a clear and widely accepted rationale for financial futures is not to profit from these contracts, but to avoid losses from activities in the real economy, in industry and commerce.

For industrial and commercial firms (entrepreneurs for short), financial futures are a form of insurance against adverse movements in financial parameters (such as interest rates and exchange rates) which affect their business. If financial futures can project certainty into an uncertain future, then the scope for their application is truly enormous, and covers virtually all economic activity in virtually all economies. If markets for financial futures are as close to perfect competition as we are often assured, then the use of these instruments should indeed be widespread. However, among non-financial firms they are used by only a handful of large companies, and market literature, while paying lip-service to the future 'risks' which may be avoided by using financial derivatives, emphasizes the profitable applications of financial futures, and the large losses which they may cause. Financial investment for such hazardous profits requires a long pocket to be able to sustain losses, and the large capital that needs to be tied up in supporting operations in these markets is clearly a deterrent to the wide-spread use of financial futures.

The reason why only a small number of large companies use financial futures to avoid risks is because such instruments are inferior to the much more commonly used liquidity preference as means of avoiding financial risks. They are inferior because liquidity preference, in the sense of holding or accumulating a hoard of liquid assets from which occasional cash flow deficits may be met (what Keynes called the 'precautionary motive' for liquidity), brings a positive and certain return in the form of interest on bank deposits, or some equivalent profit on liquid savings, such as holdings of short-term company paper. Financial futures are also inferior because liquidity preference is more versatile: liquid assets may be used to meet cash deficits arising from a very wide range of circumstances, whereas financial derivatives, like insurance policies, specify very particular losses which may be covered. Indeed, with financial innovation, financial futures become more complex and new contracts become available for fixing the values of less commonly used financial parameters. By narrowing the scope of the possible losses covered, such financial innovation makes the resulting contracts even more inferior to liquidity, which has the capacity to insure all losses.

This dual function of financial futures, as a source of profit and as an insurance, has been pointed out elsewhere.[7] It gives rise to a contradiction over the socially optimal pricing of these instruments. If, on the one hand, they are sources of profit, then it is in the regulatory interest for the price to be high enough to discourage reckless trading. This is implicitly recognised in the Basle Accord, which originally required banks to set aside capital against the total value of their futures contracts, effectively raising the price of those contracts by the cost of the additional capital which has to be set against them. If, on the other hand, financial futures are an insurance against losses due to changes in financial parameters, then it is in the social interest that financial futures prices should be as low as possible, with minimal margin requirements, in order to spread their benefits among the largest number of users. Neoclassical market theorists would argue that there is no contradiction here since the prices at all times should cover the risk entailed. However, equilibrium pricing according to current market supply and demand may not give the same result as actuarial calculations of possible future loss, because of uncertainty about future returns, and because imperfect liquidity handicaps market arbitrage. Hence the regulatory issue of how to set margins and capital adequacy requirements remains open to dispute.

In this chapter distinct classes of agents in financial markets are examined. Each of them has its own distinctive interest and, together with the financial market authorities, these classes form a complete description of the agents in those markets. These agents are entrepreneurs (industrial and commercial companies), who use financial futures to avoid losses, rentiers (nowadays financial investment institutions), who use financial futures to obtain profits, and banks or brokers, who act as intermediaries and issue financial futures contracts. The existence of these three distinct classes of agents has been in practice concealed by two aspects of the way in which financial markets in developed capitalist economies have evolved. The first is the entry of large industrial and commercial companies to join specialist financial investment managers trading in financial markets. This is due to companies' own liquidity preference, which has enabled them to accumulate large stocks of liquid financial assets. That liquidity preference has been enhanced by the companies' overcapitalization, which requires them to hold large amounts of liquid reserves against their larger obligations to the capital markets (Toporowski, 2000, ch. 1; 1993, ch. 3). Industrial and commercial companies' treasury divisions now effectively operate as separate cost and profit centres within these large companies. At the peak of the boom in Tokyo's financial markets at the end of the 1980s, many large Japanese companies were reported to be making more profit from their treasury activities than from their traditional commercial, manufacturing and exporting business.

The second aspect of financial markets which has tended to conceal the distinctive operations of industrial and commercial companies is the relatively recent emergence of modern financial futures in the era of financial instability, following the breakdown of the Bretton Woods system of fixed exchange rates, and the widespread abandonment of Keynesian monetary policy aimed at holding interest rates low. This instability has affected financial parameters as well as financial flows. Financial futures markets are supposed to offer ways of avoiding such instability, commonly not by fixing the parameters, but by guaranteeing to pay the difference between the contract or strike price and the actual price. Such instability is held to affect virtually all companies, but in actual fact most of its consequences are purely notional, or valuational (Toporowski, 2000, ch. 2). Except where a change in an exchange rate or interest rate has a significant effect on actual cash flows, changes in such financial parameters should not affect an industrial or commercial company's income and expenditure. To the chagrin of the purveyors of financial futures contracts, most industrial and commercial companies do not make any use of financial futures. As noted above, they use more practical and less costly ways of managing their cash flow (for example, increasing their liquidity preference by holding large precautionary deposits, engaging in leads and lags for foreign exchange conversion, and borrowing or issuing securities at fixed interest rates). The main users of financial futures instruments remain banks and brokers.

Notwithstanding the recent dabbling of large corporations in financial speculation, the characteristic activity of entrepreneurs is making profits from production and trade, rather than operations in financial markets. Insofar as they use financial markets, it is to transfer payments, to borrow and to raise capital to finance and refinance their trade and production activities. These financial operations are subsidiary to and in principle should be designed to accommodate the main purpose of entrepreneurs' activity, which is to secure a return on their capital in the form of profits on the production, exchange and transport and distribution of goods and nonfinancial services. When acting as entrepreneurs rather than rentiers, industrial and commercial companies may use financial futures instruments to avoid anticipated losses on these non-financial activities. Hence, entrepreneurs tend to use exchange rate futures, interest rate agreements and currency swaps, rather than more strictly financial derivatives instruments like stock index futures, in order to protect their cash flow arising from adverse changes in exchange rates, interest rates, and commodity prices.

Let us call the financial parameter whose adverse movement is being anticipated P_e. The entrepreneur will consider a financial futures contract in P_e at time t if he fears that the parameter's future value, $P_{e,\,t+n}$, will be greater than his preferred future value, $P^*_{e,t}$, in the case of a cost or cash outflow, or $P_{e,t+n}$ will be less than $P^*_{e,t}$, in the case of a revenue or cash inflow, at time $t+n$ when the inflow or outflow is due. This price difference, multiplied by some scalar of the company's operations that are affected by the financial parameter, q, shows the loss which the company is anticipating. For a cost, or cash outflow, this anticipated loss, $L^*_{c,t}$ is therefore given by the expression:

$$(P^*_{e,t} - P_{e,t+n})\, q_{c,t+n} = L^*_{c,t} \tag{4.3}$$

For a revenue or cash inflow, this anticipated loss is:

$$(P_{e,t+n} - P^*_{e,t})q_{r,t+n} = L^*_{r,t} \tag{4.3'}$$

In the case of a parameter affecting costs and revenues, this expected loss is the sum of the above expressions (see Davidson, 1997):

$$(P_{e,t+n} - P^*_{e,t})q_{r,t+n} + (P^*_{e,t} - P_{e,t+n}) = L^*_t \tag{4.3''}$$

In a world in which expectations are frequently and irregularly confounded, it is also possible that the financial parameter in question may actually move in a favourable way for the company, that is, $P_{e,t+n}$ may be greater than $P^*_{e,t}$, in the case of a revenue or cash inflow, or it may be less in the case of a cost or cash outflow. If this is expected, then clearly the company will not consider using financial futures contracts, because it will profit from the movement of the financial parameter. If this favourable movement is not expected, then the company will have committed itself to a financial agreement which is less favourable than the benefit from not having entered into the agreement at all. However, this is a notional loss, rather than an actual one: it is very reasonable to suppose that the financial parameter being fixed by the futures contract is set at a level that gives an expected profit to the company from the commercial transaction represented by the scalar q. As a result of fixing that parameter, the expected profit is realised or, at least, any shortfall is not due to the contract entered into but is due to the company's uncovered operations. These may have been uncovered because the markets do not have contracts for such contingencies (for example, competitive pressures, business cycle fluctuations) or because the company preferred to make its own internal arrangements for coping with the contingency, or because the price at which the contract is offered is above what the company is willing to pay for it, so that the company is induced by the futures price offered in the market to make its own internal arrangements for accommodating the loss.

This leads on to the question of how much the company will be prepared to pay for a financial futures contract guaranteeing it a price of $P^*_{e,t}$ at time $t+n$. In principle, L^*_t should be the upper bound on the fee that the company will be prepared to pay in order to eliminate the loss that it expects to make as a result of the expected shift in financial parameter P to $P_{e,t+n}$. It would be irrational for the company to pay in excess of L^*_t for the contract, since it would then be paying more to eliminate the anticipated loss than it expects the loss to be. Its willingness to pay any price below L^*_t depends on the size of the projected loss, relative to its total profit – a small enough loss may be deemed negligible and not worth the transaction costs of the contract. Furthermore, there are alternative ways of eliminating or reducing the expected loss: in the case of the foreign exchange example which are given below, these would be leads and lags, foreign currency deposits and matching transactions. Using a foreign currency cash inflow to pay bills in the same foreign currency is, in form at least, Minsky's least risky form of financing, hedge finance. Obviously the lower is the price of the financial futures contract, the more likely the company is to consider it preferable to these alternative methods. In brief the entrepreneur's willingness to use financial futures is in proportion to the relative size of his exposure to fluctuating financial parameters, and in negative proportion to the price of a financial futures contract that would protect them against a loss due to such fluctuations, relative to the size of that loss.

Three other remarks may be made about the financial futures contracts to eliminate entrepreneurs' expected losses from variations in financial parameters. First of all, only realized expected losses appear in the accounts of a company. The actual profits or losses entered into the income and expenditure accounts of the entrepreneurial company arise out of the commercial and industrial activity of the company, whereas the expected losses considered here are the revenues lost (or the additions to costs) due to anticipated changes in the financial parameters to which the company's activities are exposed, including expected changes that never occurred. Expected losses are notional, or contingent, losses which depend on the entrepreneur's subjective evaluation of future changes in financial parameters. Because of uncertainty about those changes, and their industry-specific nature, the realism of these evaluations cannot be programmed by computer, or decided by outside financial advisers, although they may be informed by them. They depend principally on the situation of the company in its markets, and on the experience of its managers.

Secondly, commercial and industrial companies, as such, do not enter into matching financial futures contracts, in the sense of exactly equal and opposite contracts. In other words they do not hedge their futures contracts in the financial futures market. The interest of these companies is in stabilizing the cash flow generated by their non-financial business, rather than in generating additional cash flow. Moreover, if contracts are exactly matched, then the gain on one would equal the loss on the other, and the company would have to pay in addition the two fees or commissions that would be the price of the contracts.

Thirdly, there is in practice not just one preferred financial parameter P, or its expected level in the future. There will be a whole range of possible values of P, which the company can array in its order of preference. There will also be a range of future values of P, which the market will order according to the fee for a standard contract (see Section 4.4 below). In general when industrial and commercial companies use financial futures contracts to secure more preferred values of P, they enter into contracts to pay fees that are less than their expected loss. If companies had known the stable preference functions for particular values of P, and financial futures brokers had fixed and stable pricing policies, a market equilibrium could be determined, providing that there is some overlap between the prices that companies are prepared to pay for fixing preferred parameters, and the prices that brokers require for those parameters. However, company preferences are determined by their commercial business and, like that, they evolve over time. By contrast, pricing policies in financial futures markets depend on the current conjuncture in financial markets, volatile expectations about it, the individual brokers' need to hedge or match uncovered positions, as well as changes in the most commonly used futures pricing models.

The financial futures activity of industrial and commercial firms can be illustrated in the following example. Let us suppose that a company manufactures a particular product for export to Germany, where its sales are invoiced in Deutschmarks. All production costs are in the UK, but the company is clearly exposed to the risk that the Deutschmark will depreciate against the pound sterling. It may convert DM300m of sales proceeds in a year's time. Let us further suppose that the current rate of exchange of DM3 per UK£ would give the company sales proceeds of £100m, and the company finds this rate of exchange acceptable because it offers an adequate return on its capital. But the company expects the Deutschmark to depreciate to DM3.50 per UK£ in a year's time, which would give it sterling sales proceeds of £85.7m, and a notional loss of £14.3m, due to that depreciation. This notional loss £14.3m therefore represents the limit on what the company is prepared to pay to avoid this loss by entering into a futures contract to convert DM300m into sterling in one year's time at a rate of DM3 per UK£.

Clearly the company will not pay more than this, since the contract would then cost more than the loss that it anticipates. Whether the company would be willing to pay £14m, or £1.4m, or any money at all, to fix the rate for the DM300m at DM3 per £ depends on the alternative methods available to the company for dealing with the projected loss: in this case it may be able to use leads and lags to avoid the depreciation by converting on a different date, simply holding the foreign currency for a longer period of time, that is, increase its liquidity preference. The company's willingness to pay a particular price for fixing the exchange rate also depends on its attitude towards the projected loss of £14.3m. This depends not just on those deeply subjective factors that are the staple of risk and expectations analysis, that is, its so-called 'risk-aversion'. It is also influenced by what is happening to other competitors (who may be even worse affected by the depreciation) and therefore reporting smaller losses than those competitors may actually be to the advantage of the company; by its fiscal position; and by the degree of (capital market) pressure for the company to maximize the return on its capital.

The projected loss of £14.3m will not appear in the company's statement of income and expenditure. Even if the company ends up converting its export sales proceeds at the depreciated rate, what will actually appear will be sales revenue of £85.7m, rather than the £14.3m lost because of the less favourable exchange rate. In this sense the losses due to changes in financial parameters are notional, because they are always relative to some more or less arbitrary (and hence, less or more realistic) preferred level in those parameters from which the loss is measured.

Finally, the company will not enter into matched contracts to sell and buy DM300m in the future, because the company's actual exposure to exchange rate fluctuations arises out of its commercial business, which leaves it with that amount of foreign currency to convert. If its commercial business was exactly matched, so that it had exactly DM300m of costs to set against revenue of this amount at the time of its receipt, the equation (4.3″) would show no projected loss, and the company would have no commercial or industrial need to enter into sterling–Deutschmark futures contracts.

4.3. DERIVATIVES USE BY RENTIER INSTITUTIONS

There is a second class of agents operating in the financial futures markets with unmatched positions. These are investors, or rentiers as they may be called, to distinguish them from industrial and commercial investors in fixed capital or material and manufactured stocks. Rentiers in the past were individuals who held their own portfolios of financial investments. Today they are principally insurance companies and pension funds, and various investment managers managing financial assets on behalf of insurance and pension funds. The characteristic feature of rentiers is that they seek a return on their capital by trading in financial markets, and hence have, or control, assets in a range of financial markets. Thus the essential difference between entrepreneurial and rentier capital is the kind of operations from which they seek their return. The simplifying assumption that firms operate either as entrepreneurs, or rentiers, or the bankers/brokers described in the next chapter is maintained. In Section 4.5 some of the consequences of removing this assumption are considered.

The rentiers' mode of using financial futures instruments differs from that of entrepreneurs in another very fundamental way. Entrepreneurs use financial futures contracts to avoid the consequences of deviations from preferred values of financial parameters because entrepreneurs have little influence over those parameters and deviations. In contrast, rentiers by and large themselves determine those financial parameters but determine them as a class. For rentiers, financial parameters are endogenous data. They fix them by the daily creation and re-creation of a consensus among the leading traders in the markets on the values of those parameters, through arbitrage, reputation, tacit understandings, covert rumour, overt trading and the exchange of information in the financial press.[8] Financial futures trading therefore takes place in a semi-informed ignorance of what the eventual consensus will be, as a way of profiting from it as well as influencing it.

In financial futures trading, the rentier, or in practice his fund manager, estimates the future value of a financial parameter by any rational (or irrational) means. This is his $P^*_{ri,t+n}$. He next compares this with the future values indicated by other traders in screen trading quotations, or on the boards in board trading, or the calls in open outcry trading, or the financial press and information system. Let us suppose that these indicate different expected values among them, say, a value $P^*_{rj,t+n}$ ($P^*_{ri,t+n} \neq P^*_{rj,t+n}$). If in the process of finding out this market view on the future of this financial parameter he remains convinced of his own initial estimate, then a clear profit opportunity arises. The size of the expected profit depends on the difference between this view from the market and his own estimate, and the amount of money that the rentier is prepared to invest in the contract (and the value of the contract that the counterpart holding the view $P^*_{rj,t+n}$ is prepared to accept). This amount of invested money is a scalar, $q_{p,r}$, applied to the price difference. It may be the full value of the contract, if a deposit against the full amount of it is necessary when the contract is agreed, or it may be a much larger amount, if only a margin payment is required and the rentier intends to sell the contract before it matures. The total expected profit, $\Phi_{i,p,t}$, on the contract is therefore given by the expression:

$$|P^*_{ri,t+n} - P^*_{rj,t+n}| \cdot q_{p,r} / m = \Phi_{i,p,t} \tag{4.4}$$

where m is the margin that is being traded.

$\Phi_{i,p,t}$ also sets the upper limit on the fee that the rentier will be prepared to pay for the contract. Deducting this fee, $F_{p*,t}$ from the expected profit gives the net profit on the contract, $\Phi_{i,p,t} - F_{p*,t}$. Therefore,

$$\frac{(\Phi_{i,p,t} - F_{p*,t})}{(P^*_{ri,t+n}) \cdot q_{p,r}/m}$$

represents the expected rate of return. Standardizing it for the amount of time in which his capital ($P^*_{ri,t} + {}_n[q_{pr}/m]$) will be tied up, the rentier may compare a standardized expected rate of return with that on other financial instruments available for investment by the rentier. In general then, the lower the fee (or the margin requirement), or the greater the difference between his estimate of the future value of the financial asset and that of the market, the more profitable the contract will appear to be, and hence the greater will be the demand for it. But the more that the rentier's views on the future coincide with those of the emerging market consensus, the smaller is the expected profit likely to be because brokers offering the contract are more likely to demand a fee equivalent to that anticipated profit and their corresponding anticipated loss (unless they can profitably hedge their contract – see section 4.4 below).

It should be noted that this expected profit is not an amount that is ever likely to find its way into the rentier's accounts, unless his expectations are fully realized. The value of the contract when it matures, or when it is sold, will reveal an actual profit or loss on the transaction that depends on conjunctural flows of funds between markets, and the market consensus on that conjuncture, which jointly determine the values of financial parameters in the spot and futures markets at any one time. Such is the caprice of financial market sentiment that this conjuncture and the market view on it may be, and frequently is, totally uncorrelated with the consensus at the time when the contract was entered into.

Unlike entrepreneurs who only need futures contracts to fix parameters or prices for financial inflows and outflows generated by their normal commercial business, rentiers who do not engage in industrial or commercial enterprise need to be able to secure an inflow of the underlying financial asset which a futures contract obliges them to deliver, or secure purchasers for deliveries made to them. Financial futures markets use one of three kinds of operations to settle such obligations on the maturity date of the contract. These may be met by transactions in the cash market, equivalent bank credit transfer, or hedging in the futures market. Hedging in the cash market consists of buying or selling the financial instrument specified in the futures contract in the market for immediate delivery of the instrument, that is, the foreign exchange market, or the stock market. However, in the case of stock market index futures and interest rate futures, settlement usually consists of a bank credit transfer of the difference between the value of the financial instrument specified in the futures contract, and the instrument's value in the cash market ($\Phi_{i,p,t}$ in equation (4.4)). The third type of hedging is simply buying a matching futures contract which supplies the underlying asset to settle the obligation entered into under the original contract.

While all these operations enable rentiers to settle a financial futures contract, they do not ensure that it will be profitable. In the case of the first two settlement operations, profitability depends on the difference between the price specified in the contract and the price in the cash market. This is the gain or loss that the futures contract fee would have to cover, if there were no possibility of hedging in the futures market. Hence, in general, when fees are related to the expected gain or loss on a contract, the profit from speculating in such a contract is limited, or negligible.

However, if the fee is driven by competition below the expected gain or loss (see Section 4.4) then a substantial profit may be obtained, depending on movements in the cash market, in the case of cash settlement, or on changes in the consensus in the futures market that enables a hedging contract to be bought, fixing a profit on the initial contract. Therefore, once a 'position is taken' in the futures market, and a futures contract is entered into, it is in the speculator's interest to influence the market consensus in the cash and the futures markets by publishing information and disinformation, and even conspicuous trading. This kind of 'dirty' speculating makes a mockery of neoclassical notions that active financial markets disseminate information more efficiently (see Toporowski, 2000, Introduction and ch. 1).

Financial futures markets are not only sensitive to developments in the spot market and financial flows in the economy as a whole. Fees in futures markets are also affected by the supply of and demand for particular contracts. Moreover, in today's markets investors need not hold any contract to maturity, but may sell and rebuy as often as they wish. Because of the relatively short maturity periods of financial futures instruments (three months is usual, and over six months is exceptional) rentiers' portfolios of futures contracts are much more changeable than portfolios of other financial instruments. Therefore at any one time there will be, in addition to new contract demands from rentiers and entrepreneurs, a stock of outstanding contracts about to mature or available for resale. This makes supply and demand for particular contracts, and the resulting prices charged for them, very fluid and volatile.

As with entrepreneurs, a simple example illustrates the way in which rentiers operate in financial futures markets. Let us suppose that the rentier expects the Deutschmark to appreciate against the pound sterling in a year's time to DM2.50. However, for a certain fee, the rentier can get from the market a contract to buy Deutschmarks in a year's time at DM3 per UK pound. Providing that the fee is less than 16.66 per cent of the contract value (that is, the amount by which the rentier expects the Deutschmark to appreciate), it is profitable for the rentier to enter into contracts to buy Deutschmarks in a year's time at DM3 per UK£. To illustrate the point about the fluidity of futures portfolios, it may be noted that should the Deutschmark start to appreciate, and the market offer a contract to sell Deutschmarks at DM2.50 per UK£ for a sufficiently low fee, then it is possible for rentier to secure his profit in advance, entering into that contract to sell at DM2.50 and thereby hedging his original contract.

Two aspects of this transaction should be noted. First of all, in order to profit from this transaction it has to be unmatched: the rentier will not enter into two contracts to buy *and* sell a given quantity of Deutschmarks (or any other financial asset) at the same rate, because the pre-fee profit on one transaction would exactly equal the loss on the other transaction. But by entering into an unmatched contract, the rentier creates an exposure to adverse changes in financial markets. If, instead of appreciating, the Deutschmark depreciated, the rentier would make a loss, and would certainly be unlikely to secure his profit by entering into the second 'hedging' contract to sell Deutschmarks for a sufficiently low fee. Even if the currency appreciated, a loss could still be made on the contract if the appreciation failed to cover the fee paid for the transaction. Hence, a lower fee reduces the potential loss. At zero fee, the only possible loss is if the currency depreciates. Notwithstanding the fee paid, the exposure due to unhedged futures commitments is the important element in the rentier's risk in investing in financial futures. Normally traders secure themselves against this risk by hedging their original exposure in the futures market, that is, entering into an opposite contract at a different rate. However, their ability to guarantee their profit in this way depends upon a contract becoming available at a favourable rate, and at a sufficiently low fee.

Furthermore, where the contract is covered by a transaction in the 'spot' market (in this case, if Deutschmarks bought when the futures contract matures are sold in the cash market) then this may cause difficulty in the cash market. So, for example, derivatives trading inspired the large-scale selling of stock that caused the 1987 stock market crash (Toporowski, 1993, pp. 120–27).

The other noteworthy aspect of the transaction is the view of the counter-party, since the profit of the rentier (excluding the fee) is the loss of the counter-party issuing the contract. If he has the same information and expectations as the rentier then, to cover himself against that loss, the counter-party should charge a fee or premium that is at least as large as the profit that the rentier is (commonly) expected to make. But if the counter-party does this, then the rentier will not enter into that contract because it would earn no profit after the fee was paid.

There are only two possible reasons why a counter-party should expose himself to the loss that the rentier expects to earn as a profit on the transaction. The first possible reason is that of divergent expectations: the counter-party in this case expects the currency to depreciate, or at least not appreciate by as much as the rentier does. This may be a factor in the willingness of traders to enter into futures contracts, but it is likely to be a marginal one. The theory of efficient markets argues that once private information is made public, prices will come to equal those warranted by the fundamentals determining asset values (see Toporowski, 2000, ch. 5; Fama, 1991). In this view, financial derivatives markets are transitory markets before expectations converge on correct evaluations. Once they do, then rentiers will no longer find counter-parties for their transactions in financial futures because, in our example, all of them will wish to buy Deutschmark futures at DM3 per UK£, and the excess demand for these contracts will raise the fee for them to the level that exactly equals the rentiers' profit (and the counter-party's loss).

Insofar as there is any truth in this theory it is that financial market expectations converge. This is not so much because traders cognitively realize fundamental values but, more plausibly, because after an exchange of views, of which financial futures trading may be a part, a market consensus emerges (Toporowski, 1993, pp. 113–17). Hence in practice the prices of financial futures instruments are volatile because, as soon as a consensus has formed, the price of any futures contract designed to profit from that consensus view would rise to cover the loss that a counter-party would expect to make. In this situation, financial futures trading would indeed be truly marginal, dependent on quixotic, eccentric or particular sentiments among counter-parties, were it not for entrepreneurs, whose expectations are formed in industrial and commercial activity, rather than in the financial markets, and a third class of traders, namely financial futures brokers or banks. Their mode of operation in the financial futures reveals a second and somewhat more durable reason why a counter-party should expose himself to the loss that a rentier expects to earn as a profit on a financial futures contract.

4.4.   THE BROKING OF FINANCIAL FUTURES

Financial futures brokers, or banks, act as intermediaries for entrepreneurs and rentiers, issuing contracts for them and acting as their counter-party. Because of this intermediary function these agents are here called banks. In general, virtually all modern banks in the advanced capitalist economies trade in some or a variety of financial futures instruments. Like entrepreneurial companies and rentiers, this class of agent is distinguished by the source of its revenue, and its mode of operating in the futures markets. In the previous section it was assumed that entrepreneurial companies earn their profits from industrial and commercial activity and use financial futures markets to avoid foreseeable losses, while rentiers earn their profits from investing in financial markets, using financial futures instruments to gain profits. Banks may use financial futures instruments to secure themselves against losses (for example, using forward interest rate agreements to indemnify themselves against losses on fixed interest loans). But their principal income from the financial futures markets is from the fees charged for entering into agreements as counter-parties with other banks, entrepreneurs and rentiers.

However, as noted above, with unmatched contracts, the rentiers' expected profit, or the expected loss passed on by an entrepreneur, represents an equivalent expected loss to their counter-parties the banks. The only way in which they can avoid this loss is by entering into matched or hedged agreements. In the example used above, if a bank agrees to buy Deutschmarks from the entrepreneur in a year's time at DM3.00, the bank's expected loss is eliminated by agreeing to sell those Deutschmarks in a year's time, at that same rate to the rentier. A profit may be foregone, but any loss is eliminated, and a fee is obtained from both parties. Alternatively, the bank may 'hedge' by finding another bank, rentier or entrepreneur to agree to buy those Deutschmarks at a different rate, perhaps below DM2.50 to make a profit for the bank.

This possibility of eliminating losses by matching or hedging contracts[9] enables the banks to charge a fee that is less than the expected loss on a contract, due to the appreciation or depreciation of the underlying financial asset. Such income from fees, replacing the loan business lost due to the inflation of capital markets (see Toporowski, 2000, ch. 2) is undoubtedly a factor in the enthusiasm of banks since the 1990s for financial futures business. Moreover, whereas the charging of fees equal to the expected loss or profit on a contract would quickly eliminate investors' enthusiasm for the market, the charging of fees less than expected losses or profits has enabled financial futures markets to flourish in recent years.

So far this discussion has dealt with a rather simple concept of the price of a futures contract, taking as a representative contract a standard currency future, in order to distinguish between the operations of different classes of agent in the market, and to show how the price of a futures contract may be reduced below the expected gain or loss from it. This analysis can be extended in order to distinguish different types of futures contracts, according to the degree of competition in their respective markets, and to clarify the process of innovation and the role of diverse expectations in derivatives markets.

Let us suppose that there exists only one financial futures contract in a competitive market. Competition will tend to drive the price of the contract down to the point where the fee or commission for it will barely cover the brokers' transaction costs: the risk premium is reduced to the fee for the matching contract through which brokers eliminate their risk. If new brokers are entering the market, then the price may be reduced even below transaction costs, as new brokers try to establish market share by loss-leading, and established brokers accept losses in order to maintain their market share.

Given the common technology of different kinds of futures, in the sense that no new equipment is required to produce a new type of financial future contract, it is profitable for brokers to engage in monopolistic competition by introducing new types of contracts (Toporowski, 1993, pp. 51–2). This may be for a new underlying financial asset, for an established contract at a new maturity date, or for a new value of an underlying asset already traded in financial futures markets. A new contract is brought into the market by a broker who is now in a monopoly position as supplier of that contract and the counterparty to any client who wishes to trade in that contract. This contract is in effect an over-the-counter forward agreement. In essentially faddish markets, the demand for this contract among fund managers and traders may be boosted by its novelty, but it may also be limited if investors expect its market to be less liquid because one broker only issues it. Furthermore, because it is less frequently traded among fewer institutions, its future value will be the subject of similarly limited exchanges of market opinion. Expectations concerning the gain or loss from it (for example, on resale or against a hedging transaction in the spot market for the underlying asset) are less likely to converge on a market consensus. The broker's minimum price will therefore be his expected loss or the gain foregone.

However, as the contract, or similar contracts, comes to be traded among other brokers, two possibilities arise. The first is that a more liquid contract comes to be more easily hedged in the futures market itself. For brokers this means that they can eliminate the risk of being a counter-party to a contract by more immediately buying a hedging contract. This allows brokers to offer the contract at prices below the expected loss or gain foregone. Secondly, as the contract comes to be more commonly traded, traders arrive more rapidly at a consensus value for the contract.

The relationship between market structure, innovation, the expected values of the underlying assets, and prices of futures contracts may be illustrated by means of a simple non-linear equation showing the price of a contract as a function of the difference between a broker's offered contract value of an underlying asset in the future at time $t+n$ ($P^*_{b,t+n}$) and the market's consensus of the value of that underlying asset at time $t+n$ ($P^*_{b,t+n}$), that is,

$$F_{p*,t+n} = C + (P^*_{b,t+n} - P^*_{b,t+n})^\sigma \quad \sigma \geq 0 \tag{4.5}$$

where $F_{p*,t+n}$ is the fee for the contract offered, and C is the transaction cost of the contract. σ is a parameter reflecting the degree of competition between brokers in the market for the contract for the underlying asset priced by broker b for maturity at $t+n$ in the future at $P^*_{b,+n}$. If there is perfect competition across the whole range of possible values of $P^*_{b,+n}$, then σ will equal zero. This would imply that a futures contract could be purchased for the transaction costs of issuing that contract for any future value of the underlying assets.

In the example which is used above, perfect competition would mean that the same (minimal) fee would be charged for converting Deutschmarks in the future at DM3 per UK£ as at DM0.5 per UK£, or at DM100 per UK£. Such an extreme state of affairs could only be brought about because, under the assumptions of perfect competition, namely free entry and exit and numerous firms competing by price in all markets, any broker offering a contract at DM0.5 per UK£ would as easily find a counter-party for a matching or hedging contract as at DM100 per UK£, and would therefore suffer no risk of having to match the contract with a purchase or sale in a cash market where only one exchange rate holds at any one time.

In practice, however, competitive conditions only obtain around the market consensus for the expected value of the underlying asset ($P^*_{b,t+n}$)

Hence σ is in practice greater than zero. A broker making markets across a range of values of P^* expected in time $t+n$ would publish his fees list as a U-shaped function against $P^*_{b,t+n}$ (see Figure 4.1 below).

The greater the difference between the market consensus view of the future value of the underlying asset and an offered future contract value (or strike price) of that underlying asset, the higher is the fee for the contract, because there is less probability that the broker will be able to hedge with an exactly matching contract. The more competitive are futures markets in the underlying asset, the flatter will be the curve of function $F^*_{b,t+n}$. Competition here does not just depend on the ways in which brokers operate in the market for a particular futures contract. It is also affected by competition in other futures markets. In the first instance competition in the market for the hedging contract affects the brokers' ability immediately to lay off all risk by hedging a contract entered into for a client. In other futures markets, the ability to hedge effectively all his other contracts also affects brokers' willingness to price a particular contract competitively. In this sense, competition is a condition of the market-place in which trade in various contracts takes place, as well as a feature of the particular market for a contract.

An analysis of imperfect competition in financial derivatives trading is a

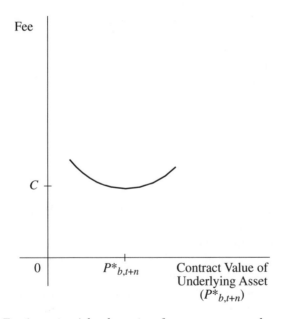

Figure 4.1 Fee (premium) levels against futures contract values (strike price) of an underlying asset

critical part of understanding such markets. Contrary to the widespread view that these markets are characterized by a state of competition approaching what economists regard as perfect competition, there is evidence suggesting that markets for financial futures instruments are highly concentrated. For example, an OECD study found that among banks operating in the world's largest futures markets, those of the United States of America, in 1992 seven derivatives dealers accounted for 90 per cent of all bank derivatives activities (OECD, 1995). In London, a central banker noted that in 1992 the ten most active principals in financial derivatives had a combined overall share of the market that was 'materially higher' than 43 per cent (Quinn, 1993).

This degree of concentration cannot just be considered as a factor distorting the operations of a price system which would otherwise correspond to that obtaining under perfect competition. It also reflects a peculiarity of financial markets that has a direct bearing on the efficiency of the financial intermediation mechanism. In general, firms 'producing' goods and services need to sell those commodities to customers who are not the firms producing the commodities. Car companies, for example, will sell cars to households, governments and companies, but rarely if ever sell their cars to each other. However, the profit that may be obtained from purchasing investment services has a much more universal appeal. Financial instruments are therefore commonly purchased for profit by other firms in the same business, except where market regulation explicitly forbids intermediaries or brokers to act as principals in their market (as for example in the case of stockbroking in the London market before the 1986 reforms). In the case of financial futures, most contracts are intra-market trades between brokers hedging their positions or trading for profit. Precisely what proportion of trades is intra-market is not commonly revealed, but candid traders will informally admit that most of their trade is with other traders as principals. Indeed this accounts for the high degree of concentration in the futures markets that was noted above.

This has a number of consequences for our understanding of how financial futures markets work. First of all, the figures on the numbers of contracts traded in the various financial futures markets, widely published in comparisons between those markets, are not a reliable indicator of the usefulness of financial futures for the economy in general, and retail customers outside the financial futures markets in particular, as is sometimes implied by markets publishing such data. Because of the high share of intra-market trading in total turnover, the published figures on market concentration reveal little about particular firms' share of retail financial markets, and intra-market hedging of retail market exposures.

Secondly, excess capacity, which is the normal microeconomic mainspring of competition and business fluctuations in markets outside the financial system (see Steindl, 1976, part I), is smaller in those financial markets where intra-market trading is common. Financial firms with insufficient retail customers can expand their business activity simply by trading with each other. Cyclical activity in their markets is therefore not generated by excess capacity but by inflows and outflows of funds (see below and Toporowski, 1993, ch. 5).

Thirdly, where excess capacity is kept down in this way, and competition between firms in the financial futures market to find retail customers is correspondingly weak, financial firms tend to orientate their trading strategies towards their more immediate customers in the same business. The result is emulatory competition that is 'conservative in practice and faddish in innovation' (Toporowski, 1993, p. 52) and trading for reputation, because reputation gives dealers and their firms market power to influence prices and the pace and direction of innovation. What are commonly called competitive pressures in financial markets are in fact pressures to emulate market leaders, defined by their reputation in the markets. While this may speed the emergence of consensus in particular markets, it may be as much through the exchange of disinformation and rumour as by the exchange of those prices and trading intentions that are the basis of neoclassical theories of financial markets from Walras onwards. Because the business of financial firms is so dependent on reputation among other financial firms, pressures for conformity may seriously inhibit competitive behaviour, of the kind envisaged by neoclassical theorists, and destabilize markets (Steindl, 1990, pp. 374–5). In particular, the arbitrage which most finance theorists believe keeps prices equal and low in such markets may be confounded by 'reputation premiums' which may allow prestigious firms or markets to maintain higher fees for their services. Competition for reputation among fellow-traders or between markets may also direct innovation towards contracts favoured by other traders in the same business rather than such contracts as are of general social use. Arguably then, the above-cited fragmentary figures on market concentration in financial futures markets understate the degree of imperfect competition in those markets.

4.5. FINANCIAL DERIVATIVES AND FINANCIAL FRAGILITY

If microeconomic crisis is caused by the draining of liquidity from an individual company (or household) macroeconomic crisis or instability, in the sense of a reduction in the level of activity in the economy as a whole, is usually associated with an involuntary outflow of funds from companies (or households) as a whole. Macroeconomic instability is defined as a 'real' economic phenomenon, rather than as a monetary phenomenon, the sense in which it is used, for example, by the International Monetary Fund to mean price inflation in the non-financial economy. Neoclassical economics has a methodological predilection for attributing all changes in economic activity to price changes, specifically the price changes that undoubtedly accompany economic fluctuations. But there is sufficient evidence to indicate that falls in economic activity follow outflows of liquidity from the industrial and commercial company sector (Kindleberger, 1993, ch. 15; Minsky, 1986, 1975, ch. 6; Hyndman, 1932; Toporowski, 1993, ch. 5). Such outflows then lead to the deflation of economic activity that is the signal feature of economic recession and depression. This section examines how financial futures markets may contribute to this kind of macroeconomic instability.

Such a discussion must start with a consideration of how vulnerable financial futures market themselves are to illiquidity, since this would indicate whether the firms operating in the market are ever likely to need to realize claims elsewhere in order to meet their liabilities to the market. Forced liquidations of this kind were a factor in transforming, for example, the 1929 stock market crash into the 1930s depression (Galbraith, 1980, pp. 179–80).

Paradoxically, the very high level of intra-broker trading is a safety mechanism for the market, since it raises the velocity of circulation of whatever liquidity there is in the market: traders with liabilities outside the market are much more likely to have claims against other traders to set against those claims. This may be illustrated by considering the most extreme case of a futures market dominated by intra-broker trading, namely a market in which there are only two dealers who buy and sell financial futures contracts only between each other as rentiers, in other words for a profit which may include their premium or commission. On the expiry date of the contracts, conventionally set at three-monthly intervals in actual financial futures markets, some of these contracts will be profitable, some will be loss-making. (Margin trading, however, requires all the profitable contracts to be fully paid up in order for their profit to be realized.) The trader whose contracts are on balance profitable therefore cannot realize his profits until he has paid up his contracts with the other broker. The other broker will return the money in paying up his contracts, leaving only his losses to be raised by an inflow of money. Thus the only net inflow of money that is required is the amount of profit (or loss) made by the traders. However, an accommodating gross inflow is needed in the first instance in order to make the initial margin payments and settle contracts so that the net profit or loss may be realized.

The existence of more traders, and the system for avoiding counter-party risk commonly found in futures market, whereby contracts are made with a central clearing house, introduce sequencing complications which may cause problems. Having a central clearing house avoids the possibility that one trader's default will cause other traders to default on their obligations. But it also denies traders the facility of giving each other credit, and reduces the velocity of circulation of whatever liquidity is in the market. Having to pay all obligations in full to the central clearing house increases the money (or gross inflow) that broking firms and investors have to put into the market as margin payments or on settlement days. This increases the risk that a firm with large net liabilities in the financial futures market will be obliged to realize assets in other markets to meet those liabilities. In this way, the integrity of the market is protected by increasing the effective obligations of all traders, at the expense of potentially unsettling claims on other financial markets.

This risk is enhanced by the operations of rentiers, or banks and entrepreneurs operating as rentiers, hedging their futures contracts in other financial markets. The hedging of index futures in the stock market gave rise to such coordinated selling in 1987 that stock markets ceased operations because of insufficient buying interest. However, while such incidents generate considerable excitement around the markets at the time of their occurrence, there is little evidence that they have caused involuntary outflows from the corporate sector on such a scale as to produce recession in the real economy (Toporowski, 1993, ch. 8). This is because financial futures are still used by few industrial and commercial companies, and their demand for financial derivatives instruments is limited by the relative expense of these instruments and their own exposure to changes in financial parameters (which may more easily be accommodated by holding appropriate stocks of liquid assets, that is, liquidity preference (see Section 4.2 above)). Therefore the future of financial futures depends largely on the interest in them of the contemporary rentiers in pension, insurance, and various other forms of investment funds. Their interest, in turn, depends on how those funds approach their 'maturity'.

Despite the prevalence of widows, pensioners, and Belgian dentists in the folklore of the financial markets, the typical contemporary rentier is not an individual, but a large pension or insurance fund, or fund managers trading on their behalf. The premium or contributions inflow to these institutions has had an income elasticity significantly greater than unity in recent decades. This is reinforced by a strong contractual element in these inflows, with the result that these funds, since the 1970s, have been 'immature', that is, premium and contribution inflows have largely exceeded outflows on pensions and insurance claims. To keep down unpredictable liabilities, investments in financial futures, like other highly speculative investments in, say, venture capital or emerging markets, have been limited to small fractions of investment fund portfolios. With rare exceptions, such as the Orange County Pension Fund collapse in 1994, these institutions have, through their prudence and their fortunate cash flow situation, been able to avoid or absorb cash flow losses in the financial futures markets.

However, the decline of pension fund surpluses poses important problems for the main securities markets of the world where insurance and pension funds are now the dominant investors, as well as for more peripheral markets like emerging markets, venture capital and financial futures. A contraction in the net cash inflow of investment funds will be reflected in a reduction in the funds that they are investing, and a greater need to realise assets when a change in investment strategy is undertaken. In the main securities markets of the world, a reduction in the 'new money' that pension and insurance funds are putting into those securities markets will slow down the rate of growth of the prices in those markets. Moreover, a reduction in the net cash inflow of an investing institution makes its portfolio of assets less malleable. When the cash inflow is large, it is possible to change the proportions of particular assets, and classes of assets by concentrating buying on those assets whose greater representation in the portfolio is desired. When the cash inflow is negligible, proportions cannot be changed without selling less favoured assets. The stability of asset markets then depends on the size of the net inflow into the rentier sector and the balance between 'bullish' and 'bearish' expectations in those markets (Keynes, 1930, pp. 25–2; Steindl, 1990, pp. 374–5). Since expectations tend to converge, fund managers tend to seek similar portfolio adjustments. With less cash inflow to devote to preferred investments, more money to finance such investments must be raised from the sale of less preferred assets. The convergence of views on what are less desirable assets, and which ones are worth buying, will tend to polarize markets between booming speculative markets, and precipitately falling markets. The fall in the institutions' net cash inflow impinges most severely on the more marginal markets, such as emerging markets, venture capital and financial futures, depending on how institutional portfolios are managed in the period of declining net contributions inflows.

In general, investment managers in their own firms, or as employees of merchant or investment banks, compete to manage institutions' funds. Such competition is likely to increase as investment funds approach 'maturity', that is, as their cash outflows to investors, pensioners or insurance policyholders rise faster than their cash inflow from contributions and premiums, so that there are less additional funds to be managed. In principle, this should not affect financial futures markets, in the first instance, since, as argued above, the short-term nature of their instruments and the large proportion in their business of intra-market trade makes them much less dependent on institutional cash inflows. However, this does not mean that they would be unaffected by changes in the portfolio preferences of investment funds in response to lower returns from the main securities markets. Such lower returns make financial investments like financial futures, venture capital and emerging markets, which are more marginal because they are so hazardous, more attractive to normally conservative fund managers. Investment funds typically put out sections of portfolios to specialist fund managers who are awarded contracts to manage a section according to the soundness of their reputation and the returns that they have made hitherto in portfolios under their management. A specialist fund manager reporting high, but not abnormal, profits in a fund devoted to financial futures, is likely to attract correspondingly more funds to manage when returns are lower in the main markets securities, even if other investors in financial futures experienced large losses. In this way, the maturing of investment funds could cause an increased inflow of rentier funds into financial futures markets.

An inflow of funds into a financial market entails an increase in liabilities to the rentiers outside the market supplying those funds. Even if profits made in the market as a whole also increase, so too will losses. As was noted above, while brokers commonly seek to hedge their positions within the futures market rentiers have much greater possibilities of hedging their contracts in another market, where they have assets. An inflow into futures markets means that on any settlement day there will therefore be larger net outstanding claims against individual banks or investment funds in respect of their financial derivatives contracts. With margin trading, much larger gross financial inflows into financial futures markets will be required to settle maturing contracts. Some proportion of this will require the sale of securities in other markets. But if liquidity in integrated cash markets for securities is reduced by declining net inflows into pension funds, a failure to meet settlement obligations in futures markets is the alternative to forced liquidation of other assets. In this way futures markets will become more fragile.

Moreover, because of the hazardous nature of financial futures, high returns for an individual firm are difficult to sustain. Disappointment is more likely to be followed by the transfer of funds to management in some other marginal market that shows a temporary high profit. While this should not affect capacity utilization in the futures market, because of intra-market trade, it is likely to cause much more volatile trading, and an increase in the pace at which new instruments are introduced (to attract investors) and fall into disuse. Pension funds whose returns fall below those

required to meet future liabilities because of such instability would normally be required to obtain additional contributions from employers and
employees. The resulting drain on the liquidity of the companies affected
would cause a reduction in their fixed capital investment. This would be a
plausible mechanism for transmitting fragility in the financial system into
full-scale decline in the real economy. But because of the low commitment
of pension funds to financial futures trading, with signal exceptions such
as the Orange County Pension Fund, its effect is likely to be small.

Instability in financial markets presents the ultimate challenge to
financial derivatives. If the neoclassical story is correct, then growing
financial instability will be matched by increasing use of financial derivatives to hedge against such instability. Economies will move closer to the
Arrow–Debreu ideal in which everyone can buy everything that they will
want to buy and sell everything that they will want to sell at prices which
can be determined now, placing the world in an intertemporal general equilibrium with no uncertainty. While an Arrow–Debreu world offers an imag-
inative solution to the technical and sequencing problems of intertemporal
general equilibrium, more worldly consideration suggests an alternative
view, that growing instability in financial markets is more likely to induce a
higher liquidity preference among rentier institutions and companies and
a declining interest in financial futures.

There are three principal reasons for this pessimism about the prospects
for financial futures. First of all, as was argued in Section 4.1, financial
futures give a specific indemnity against loss in the sense that the circumstances, the time and usually the amount of the indemnity are specified in
the futures contract. Maintaining a stock of liquid assets gives a much
more general insurance against losses which do not have to be specified in
advance, and which can be indemnified at the discretion of the economic
unit holding such liquidity.

The second reason arises out of the uncertain value of financial derivatives as investment assets. As was argued above, financial derivatives may
reduce the uncertain future value of financial flows generated by industrial
and commercial activities, or by financial investment in other markets. But
as financial investments themselves the return on them is hazardous. Hence
the problems that some industrial and commercial companies have brought
upon themselves in investing in these instruments as assets (rather than to
hedge their normal business activities). Even investment institutions only
allocate a tiny proportion of their portfolios to such instruments, and
prudent institutions hold liquid assets against the possibility of losses due
to these contracts. As maturity reduces the liquidity of these institutions,
even less of their investment inflow will be allocated to such assets.

The third reason is that there is no evidence that financial futures can protect companies and rentier institutions from the major financial disasters that worry them. The Mexican, East Asian and Russian crises were notable for the effective disappearance of credit guarantees and exchange rate futures contracts that could have protected investors in those markets: where such contracts remained on offer, it was at monopoly premiums that compensated the broker for his risk in issuing the contract, rather than the investor for the loss from which he sought protection (see Section 4.4). But even if one were to suppose that these lacunae could be overcome by even more financial innovation and the further development of the futures markets, it is difficult to see how this could be done without imposing higher costs on someone. Greater financial instability would then be matched by larger payouts from the financial futures markets and larger liabilities by counterparties. In turn, these will require larger amounts of liquidity set against greater potential liabilities. Rentier institutions with serious financial liabilities, such as insurance companies and pension funds, are unlikely to wish to devote larger amounts of their decreasing liquidity to support more hazardous operations in financial futures markets.

If the analysis in this is correct, then in time we will come to see financial futures less as a class of financial innovations that can secure us all against financial instability, and more as peripheral, speculative markets that flourished in the era of finance at the end of the twentieth century and fired the imaginations and commercial acumen of fund managers and their advisers when money was more freely available to invest in such innovations.

NOTES

1. Apart from his financial schemes, Law is nowadays best known for advocating the use of bank credit as money instead of specie (gold or silver). Since the United States dollar was taken off the gold standard in 1971, bank credit has become the virtually universal form of money. See Law (1750).
2. Davidson (1988). See also Davidson (1997); and Imperato (1997, chapter 2).
3. The Cox–Ross formula for valuing options allows volatility to vary in proportion to the price of the asset.
4. A similar formula is given in Davidson (1997).
5. Fischer Black obituary in *The Financial Times* 2 September 1995. His obituary in *The Economist* revealed that within a year of publishing his 1973 paper on the valuation of options, Texas Instruments was advertising in the *Wall Street Journal* that 'You can find the Black–Scholes value using our calculator' (*The Economist*, 9 September 1995). On the possibility of using such probabilistic methods of estimating future values, Keynes remarked that the 'conventional method of calculation will be compatible with a considerable measure of stability in our affairs, *so long as we can rely on the maintenance of our convention* . . . Thus investment becomes reasonably "safe" for the individual investor over short periods, and hence over a succession of short periods however many, if he can fairly rely on there being no breakdown in the convention and on his having an opportunity to revise his judgement and change his investment, before there has been time for much to happen' (Keynes, 1936, pp. 152–3).

6. Toporowski (2000, p. 41). A recent study showed that the company analysts who are employed by brokers do not understand much of the data which they circulate, but that their priority is 'to get earnings news to fund managers at speed because, in the long run, this (service) can help generate commission income' (J. Kelly, 'Power of magic numbers', *Financial Times,* 2 July 1998).
7. Toporowski (1993, pp. 63–8). When the organic structures of cause and effect that give rise to changes in financial markets are obscured by probabilistic conjectures, investment in financial futures appears indistinguishable from gambling. Accordingly, in April 1998, a court in Moscow ruled that 'some forward contracts were best viewed as gambling contracts under chapter 58 of the Russian civil code, and were therefore not enforceable under local law' (*Financial Times,* 6 July, 1998).
8. This is reflected in Keynes's 'beauty contest' theory of investment or speculation. See Toporowski (1993) pp. 115–17; and the Introduction to Toporowski (2000).
9. This kind of risk management is described in Steil (1992).

REFERENCES

Allen, F. and Gorton, G. (1993), 'Churning bubbles', *Review of Economic Studies,* **60** (4).

Bikhchandani, S., Hirshliefer, D. and Welch, I. (1992), 'A theory of fads, fashion, custom and cultural change as informational cascades', *Journal of Political Economy,* **100** (5).

Black, F. (1989), 'How to use the holes in Black-Scholes', *The Continental Bank Journal of Applied Corporate Finance,* 1, Winter.

Black, F., Jensen, M.C. and Scholes, M. (1972), 'The Capital Asset Pricing Model: Some Empirical Tests', in M.C. Jensen (ed.), *Studies on the Theory of Capital Markets,* New York: Praeger.

Davidson, P. (1988), 'A Post-Keynesian View of Theories and Causes for High Real Interest Rates', in P. Arestis (ed.), *Post-Keynesian Monetary Economics: New Approaches to Financial Modelling*, Aldershot: Edward Elgar.

Davidson, P. (1997), 'Are grains of sand in the wheels of international finance sufficient to do the job when boulders are often required?', *Economic Journal* **107** (442), May.

Fama, E.F. (1991), 'Efficient capital markets: II', *Journal of Finance*, 46.

Galbraith, J.K. (1980), *The Great Crash 1929,* London: André Deutsch.

Hardwicke, Philip Yorke, Earl of (ed.) (1778), *Miscellaneous State Papers from 1501 to 1726*, London: W. Strahan and T. Cadell.

Hsieh, D. (1991), 'Chaos and non-linear dynamics: application to financial markets', *Journal of Finance,* **46** (5).

Hyndman, H.M. (1932), *Commercial Crises of the Nineteenth Century*, with a new preface by John A. Hobson, Reprints of Economics Classics, New York: Augustus M. Kelly Publishers, 1967.

Imperato, A. (1997), *Informazione Aspettative ed Incertezza, Napoli: Edizione Scientifiche Italiane.

Keynes, J.M. (1921), *A Treatise on Probability,* London: Macmillan.

Keynes,J.M.(1930), *A Treatise on Money in Two Volumes. 1 The Pure Theory of Money,* London: Macmillan.

Keynes, J.M. (1936), *The General Theory of Employment, Interest and Money,* London: Macmillan.

Keynes, J.M. (1937), 'The general theory of employment', *Quarterly Journal of Economics,* **51**.

Kindleberger, C.P. (1993), *A Financial History of Western Europe*, Oxford: Oxford University Press.

Law, J. (1750), *Money and Trade Considered, With a Proposal for Supplying the Nation with Money*, Glasgow: R. & A. Foulis.

Markowitz, H.M. (1990), *Mean-Variance Analysis in Portfolio Choice and Capital Markets*, Cambridge, Mass.: Basil Blackwell.

Minsky, H.P. (1975), *John Maynard Keynes*, New York: Columbia University Press.

Minsky, H.P. (1986), *Stabilizing an Unstable Economy*, New Haven: Yale University Press.

Murphy, A.E. (1997), *John Law, Economic Theorist and Policy-Maker*, Oxford: The Clarendon Press.

Organization for Economic Co-operation and Development (OECD) (1995), *The New Financial Landscape*, Paris.

Quinn, B. (1993), 'Derivatives – where next for supervisors?', *Bank of England Quarterly Bulletin*, **33** (4), November.

Rybczynski, T.M. (1988), 'Financial Systems and Industrial Restructuring', *National Westminster Bank Quarterly Review*, November.

Steil, B. (1992), 'Regulatory foundations for global capital markets', *Finance and the International Economy. The Amex Bank Review Prize Essays*, No. 6.

Steindl, J. (1976), *Maturity and Stagnation in American Capitalism*, New York: Monthly Review Press.

Steindl, J. (1990), 'The Dispersion of Expectations in a Speculative Market', in J. Steindl, *Economic Papers 1941–88*, London. Macmillan.

Toporowski, J. (1993), *The Economics of Financial Markets and the 1987 Crash*, Aldershot: Edward Elgar.

Toporowski, J. (2000), *The End of Finance. The Theory of Capital Market Inflation, Financial Derivatives and Pension Fund Capitalism*, London: Routledge.

5.   The endogeneity of money

Peter Howells

5.1.   INTRODUCTION[1]

The core of the endogeneity thesis consists of two propositions. The first is that the money supply is determined by the demand for bank lending ('loans create deposits' in the jargon). The second is that the demand for bank lending is causally dependent upon other variables in the economic system. The short version of this is that the demand for loans is driven by the 'state of trade', essentially the level of nominal output. Since this is normally rising, as the result of some combination of price and volume changes, the normal case is for the *stock* of bank loans to expand, that is to say that there is normally a demand for new lending in excess of repayments, so that the *flow* of new lending, and new money, is positive. Expansion is the norm. The role of the central bank is then to set the level of official short-term interest rates. Banks will charge this rate plus some mark-up on loans. Changing official rates thus changes the cost of borrowing, influencing in turn the demand for and the flow of new lending. Since the central bank has no alternative but to supply reserves to validate the lending, varying the level of interest rates is the sole instrument of monetary control available to the central bank. In these circumstances, it is reasonable to conclude that the supply of money is perfectly elastic at the going rate of interest and this, in turn, has encouraged the use of a 'horizontal money supply curve' as the symbol of endogenous money. All of this would be instantly recognizable to post-Keynesian economists, for whose monetary theory endogeneity of money supply is a cornerstone.[2]

The wider significance of the endogeneity thesis is that it offers a direct refutation of the Quantity Theory, by reversing the direction of causation. If the money supply is endogenous, then changes in one, or both, of PY 'cause' money and not the other way round.

> If the money supply is exogenous, as Monetarists believe, then to the extent that changes in the quantity of money are associated with changes in the price level it can only play (by definition) a causal role. If the money supply is often endog-

enous or an effect . . . then anti-inflation policies aimed at restricting the growth of the money supply will be effective only if they restrict aggregate demand. (Davidson, 1988, p. 156)

While the endogeneity of money is now widely accepted, certainly by central bankers throughout the developed world, and by mainstream economists, certainly in Europe, there are still several details in the picture which are either lacking or are contentious. This chapter summarizes what we know about these problem areas and makes a few, too few, suggestions about possible ways forward.

It begins in Section 5.2 by offering a brief but formal contrast between endogeneity and exogeneity. In Section 5.3 we look at the argument that endogeneity of money supply (or exogeneity for that matter) is a characteristic of particular types of monetary system at a particular stage of their development. From there, we follow the sequence of deposit creation. In Section 5.4 we look at whether the demand for loans really does originate solely or even mainly with the 'state of trade'. We then move, in Section 5.5, to the question of why banks seem generally to be unconstrained by reserves in responding to this demand. In Section 5.6 we consider how banks arrive at the appropriate mark-up to impose on borrowers, over and above the cost of reserves. In Section 5.7, we take a critical look at the common practice of symbolizing an endogenous money regime by reference to a horizontal money supply curve. This raises the contentious question of what, if anything, guarantees that the deposits newly-created by the demand for *loans*, will be consistent with the demand for *money*. We discuss this in Section 5.8, while Section 5.9 is simply a brief conclusion.

Since there is widespread agreement in many quarters that the quantity of money is determined endogenously, there is room for the view that raking over some of the difficulties of detail is rather like trying to raise a 'tempest in a teapot' in Basil Moore's memorable phrase (Moore, 1991a, p. 405). But there is, potentially, a big issue at stake. As we said at the outset, the endogeneity thesis is a direct attack upon the Quantity Theory. The nightmare for post-Keynesians is that the resolution of one or more of what look like minor controversies in a particular way may open a chink whereby neoclassical propositions, about the independent causal role of money in particular, may resurface.[3]

5.2. THE ENDOGENEITY THESIS

Expositions of the endogeneity thesis proceed almost always by contrasting its features with those of the allegedly dominant paradigm of exogenous money, where the money supply is determined at the discretion of the monetary authorities, usually through open market operations to manipulate the monetary base. The desire to draw the starkest contrasts between the two is seen in the title of Basil Moore's major (1988a) contribution to the endogeneity literature, *Horizontalists and Verticalists*, and in the enthusiasm for symbolizing endogeneity by reference to a horizontal supply curve (or at least a curve with an intercept on the vertical axis) in contrast to the 'vertical' money supply curve of exogenous money.[4] There are undoubtedly some useful insights to be gained from such an approach, though for UK students it is a practice that sometimes has the appearance of attacking a straw man. Charles Goodhart, whose work has for years combined the analytical insights of economics with a keen appreciation of the *practice* of central banking, has done as much as anyone to encourage a realistic approach to money supply analysis and has largely succeeded, in the UK at least, by frequently denouncing the 'misinstruction' inherent in the base-multiplier model (Goodhart, 1984, p. 188). 'Almost all those who have worked in a [central bank] believe that this view is totally mistaken; in particular, it ignores the implications of several of the crucial institutional features of a modern commercial banking system . . . (Goodhart, 1994, p. 1424).

Consequently, in the UK it is much more common to find textbooks analysing the money supply process through the 'flow of funds' model. Although it does not necessarily entail a commitment to endogeneity, the flow of funds model is a convenient framework within which to analyse endogenous regimes since it focuses not only on flows, but on the 'credit counterparts' (the loans which create the deposits) of the money supply. These two features are apparent in the 'flow of funds identity':

$$\Delta M \equiv PSBR - \Delta Gp - \Delta ext + \Delta BL_p \qquad (5.1)$$

where ΔM is the change in money stock, PSBR is the public sector's total borrowing requirement, ΔG_p and Δext represent the financing of this borrowing from bond sales and external transactions respectively and ΔBL_p is bank lending to the M4 private sector.[5] Note that the focus is upon *changes* in the money supply and the change depends upon the flow of new bank lending to the public and private sectors. And if Goodhart's outspoken comments plus the common use of the flow of funds model is not sufficient evidence of a sympathy towards endogeneity in the UK, we have the recent statement from the Bank's Deputy Governor with responsibility for monetary policy. 'In the United Kingdom, money is endogenous – the Bank supplies base money on demand at its prevailing interest rate, and broad money is created by the banking system' (King, 1994, p. 264).

Unlike Moore and some other US scholars, therefore, our interest in the exogeneity case does not lie in rejecting a plausible rival. That has already been done. We need a reminder of the essentials of exogeneity in order to show later, principally in Sections 5.6 and 5.7, that some controversies within the endogeneity tradition have their origin in a misunderstanding of the paradigm which endogeneity wishes to replace. Ironically, it may well be that expositions of endogeneity have become contaminated by being cast in the base-multiplier framework that they wish to reject.

In an exogenous money regime, the stock of money is a stable function of the monetary base, B, which changes only at the discretion of the monetary authorities. Specifically, the money stock is a multiple of the base:

$$M_s = B \cdot \left(\frac{\alpha + 1}{\alpha + \beta} \right) \tag{5.2}$$

where the value of the multiplier depends upon α and β, the public's cash ratio (C_p/D_p) and the banks' reserve ratio (R/D_p) respectively. If α and β are fixed, then the money supply can change only in response to discretionary changes in B, and the money supply (stock) curve can be drawn vertically in interest-money space, intersecting the horizontal axis at a value, for the money stock, equal to B times m, the multiplier.

The values of α and β are not usually assumed to be fixed, however. In the case of α, the public's cash ratio, the demand for cash is a function of the rate of interest on bank deposits, r_m, and technical considerations relating to the ease and convenience of replenishing cash holdings from cash dispensers and the efficiency of the money (i.e. deposit) transmission mechanism operated by banks, T.[6] Thus we may write:

$$a \equiv C_p/D_p = f(r_m, T) \atop - \quad ? \tag{5.3}$$

(where the sign below the variable denotes the sign of its partial derivative).

Banks' decisions to hold reserves will depend firstly upon the cost of holding reserves, that is to say on the rate of interest earned on reserve assets, r_r, relative to the rate paid on all other assets, r_b. In many systems, the UK included, r_r is zero. The quantity of reserves held will depend also on the cost of being short, that is upon the rediscount rate charged for lender of last resort facilities, r_d. Reserve holdings will also depend upon any mandatory reserve requirement, RR, and, lastly, upon the variability of inward and outward flows to which banks are subject, σ. Hence:

$$\beta \equiv R/D_p = f(r_r, r_b, r_d, RR, \sigma) \atop + \quad - \quad + \quad + \quad + \tag{5.4}$$

Since the money supply depends upon both the base and the multiplier we can write:

$$M_s = f(B, \alpha, \beta) \qquad (5.5)$$
$$ +\ -\ -$$

and knowing (from equations (5.3) and (5.4)) the determinants of α and β we can substitute into (5.5), to yield a money supply determined as follows:

$$M_s = f(B, r_m, T, r_p, r_b, r_d, RR, \sigma) \qquad (5.6)$$
$$ +\ +\ ?\ -\ +\ -\ -\ -$$

A change in B is a change in the multiplicand: changes in all other variables cause a change in the size of the multiplier itself.

Consider now how this appears in interest-money space, in Figure 5.1. Note firstly that the rate of interest on the vertical axis is conventionally the bond rate, r_b. The reason for this is worth bearing in mind, since it becomes an issue in section seven. The purpose of drawing the M_s curve in interest-money space is ultimately to discuss money market equilibria. The rate on the vertical axis *must* therefore be the opportunity cost of holding money. Strictly, in a modern monetary system, this rate ought to be a spread term,

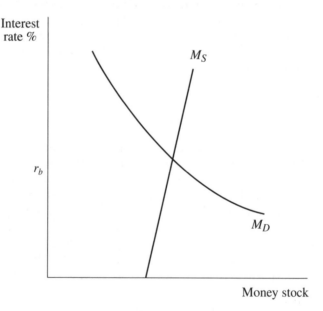

Figure 5.1   Demand and supply of money

representing the difference between the bond rate (appearing as a proxy for the return on 'non-money financial assets') and money's own rate (effectively the weighted average rate on deposits). The bond rate will do, provided we assume that money is non-interest bearing (which of course it generally was when Keynes wrote the *General Theory*, which is where all this originates). The horizontal axis depicts the quantity of money as a *stock*. In this space, equation (5.6) gives a money supply curve intersecting the horizontal (money) axis at a point where $M_s = m \cdot B$ (where m is the multiplier). A change in B changes the point of intersection (the curve shifts). The same results from a change in any of RR, r_d r_r, r_m, σ, T since these cause a change in the value of the multiplier.

Crucial, though, for our later discussions in Sections 5.6 and 5.7, is the effect of a change in r_b, the bond rate. An increase in r_b causes banks to economize on their holdings of (non-interest bearing) reserves, β falls, the value of m increases and, for a given base, the money supply expands. If, as seems reasonable, banks behaviour towards reserves is dependent upon non-reserve interest rates, the 'vertical' money supply curve has some positive slope and the money supply has acquired some degree of endogeneity. Following Davidson (1988, p. 156) one might call this 'interest-endogeneity'. This form of endogeneity is, however, extremely limited. In this framework, a continuous expansion of the money supply (a generally accepted feature of an endogenous money regime) is possible, *ceteris paribus*, only if the level of interest rates r_b rises without limit. But the more normal case of course is that the authorities have some range within which they wish to see r_b remain. In these circumstances, continuous expansion requires the authorities to change one of the other variables in equation (5.6) and we are no longer talking about interest-endogeneity. Notice two features of this analysis. Firstly, nothing happens (to the money stock) unless the authorities will it and intervene directly. It is this picture of stasis by default that makes the MB model congenial to the analysis of exogenous systems. Secondly, whatever variable in equation (5.6) is chosen by the authorities, continuous expansion of the money stock is possible *only with a continuous rightward shift of the curve*. In the MB model as it is normally presented, the variable responsible for shifts of the curve is, of course, the quantity of monetary base, B. We are looking now at 'base-endogeneity' and we come back to this in Section 5.7.

5.3.   THE 'STAGES OF BANKING'

It was Sir John Hicks who said that 'Monetary theory . . . cannot avoid a relation to reality . . . It belongs to monetary history in a way that economic theory does not always belong to economic history' (Hicks. 1967, p. 153). This was a warning that a monetary system in which means of payment was limited to commodity money (gold, for example) was unlikely to function in the same way as a system in which payment involved the liabilities of highly-skilled, profit-making, private sector institutions.

This theme, that 'good' monetary theory needs to be historically and institutionally specific, is widely held amongst post-Keynesian economists (indeed, many would extend it to all branches of theory). The connection between endogeneity, or degrees of endogeneity, and the institutional framework features explicitly in the work of Chick, Niggle, Moore and Wray.

Chick (1986) initially suggested that the evolution of the banking system could be divided into five stages. For the supply of money to be endogenous, two minimal conditions must be fulfilled. First, it must be the case that bank deposits themselves function as means of payment as well as a form of savings, otherwise banks would run the risk that new loans might be quickly turned into notes and coin and reserves would be lost. If deposits are generally acceptable, reserves stay within the system. The second condition is that there is no reserve constraint. Either reserves simply do not matter or they must be available on demand.

In stage one bank deposits are held as savings rather than as means of payment because banks are numerous, small and regionally segregated. In the circumstances, a loan by a bank is unlikely to return to that same bank as a deposit. Worse still, since cash is the dominant means of payment, a loan is likely to be taken in the form of notes and coin and the banking system as a whole loses reserves. In this stage, deposits are exogenous to banks and change only as a result of the creation of high powered money or changes in the public's cash/deposit preferences. Money is unambiguously exogenous.

In stage two banks have amalgamated into fewer larger groups. This, together with customers' increasing confidence in the system, leads to deposits becoming means of payment. In these circumstances, a loan is likely to be held as a deposit, if not with the originating bank, at least somewhere in the system. Reserves are not lost. Banks can now lend a multiple of reserves. Nonetheless, the quantity of reserves remains exogenous to the system changing as before, only as a result of changes in the monetary base or in the public's cash preferences.

In stage three, little happens except that interbank markets develop, enabling individual banks to operate more closely to the minimum reserve ratio of the system as a whole.

The big change comes in stage four when the central bank accepts its lender of last resort obligation. Banks become bolder in their lending since they know that any shortfall in reserves will be made good for the stability of the system. Reserves will be provided at a price and so the rising marginal cost of lending may prove some limit to expansion, but under a policy of stable interest rates even this constraint disappears. As evidence that UK (and possibly the US and most western European) banking had reached this stage by the 1970s, Chick cites the switch in the theoretical literature on bank behaviour from the traditional deposit multiplier approach towards a more microeconomic approach based upon marginal cost (including the price of reserves) and marginal revenue. In stage 4, the money supply is endogenous. The demand for loans is generally met. The loans create deposits and banks have then to find reserves, generally from a compliant central bank. (Notice, in anticipation of Section 5.8, that it is the demand for loans which initiates the causal chain). In stage five, banks become more aggressive, using the various 'liability management' practices to obtain reserves or to economise on the need for reserves when the central bank is reluctant to supply them at the going rate. (We return to this behaviour in the next section).

In 1993 Victoria Chick added a sixth stage. Given the characteristics of stage five (liability management plus the central bank acting as lender of first resort) the only constraints upon the size of banks balance sheets are (a) the amount of creditworthy loan demand that is forthcoming at the current level of interest rates, and (b) the solvency of the banking system as reflected in its capital base relative to outstanding loans, a ratio which might in theory be prudential but which in practice is imposed by regulation, using the Basle Committee recommendations on capital adequacy. In stage 6 banks seek to loosen the constraints in (b) by resorting to securitization and other off-balance-sheet activities. Advances are typically amongst a bank's riskiest assets (as well as its most profitable). Inevitably, therefore, they attract the highest capital requirements. But securitization allows these advances to be exchanged effectively for cash, by 'selling' them to a separately capitalized subsidiary which buys them with funds raised by bond sales to the general public. In this way, banks can concentrate on what they do best – originating loans – leaving the finance of them to the sale of securities.

Niggle puts forward a very similar five-stage schema in two papers (1990, 1991). The first stage consists of a commodity money regime where the money supply is unambiguously exogenous, determined *inter alia* by gold discoveries and mining activity. By stage three, the bank deposit multiplier is again the appropriate model and the money supply is determined exogenously by the availability of reserves. Stages four and five differ from Chick only in detail. The central bank's acceptance of a lender of last resort role is deferred to stage five while liability management and other innovations, including the interbank market shifted back from Chick's stage three, are combined in stage four. It matters little to the argument, of course, which is that endogeneity is the appropriate theory for modern monetary systems, though earlier ones may well have shown signs of exogeneity.

Moore's (1986) contribution to this theme divides the Chick/Niggle schema into two phases at the point of liability management. The argument contains two strands that together amount to saying that the money supply is completely endogenous in conditions of liability management and thus, implicitly, that it was more exogenous before such developments. Moore's illustrations are drawn from the US experience, but while the forces described as driving the movement towards liability management may be peculiar to the US the consequences, of liability management, are common to the US and other systems.

The first of the two strands concerns the nature of bank *assets*. The argument here is that since the 1950s banks' holdings of government and other easily marketable securities have fallen as a proportion of total assets to the minimum level required for secondary reserve purposes. The other part of the picture is a steady rise in bank loans as a proportion of total assets (Moore, 1989, p. 448). Such loans are non-marketable and this in turn increases an asymmetry in the relationship between reserves and other assets. The asymmetry is increased because, while banks can always try to *expand* lending in response to an increase in reserve assets, when non-marketable loans predominate it is virtually impossible for banks to *decrease* lending in response to reserve reductions. Indeed, since loans are made '*at the initiative of the borrower*, not the lender' and 'Loan volume is a *non-discretionary* variable from the point of view of an individual bank' (Moore, 1986. p. 447, emphasis in the original) the determination of the size of banks' balance sheets lies increasingly with borrowers.

The second strand of the argument is that this growth in loans tended to outstrip the growth of deposits during the 1950s because of the effects of interest rate regulation, particularly 'Regulation Q'.[7] Corporate balances were especially hard to attract since their treasury departments were highly skilled at managing demand deposits at the minimum level and holding what might have been precautionary time deposits in the form of treasury bills, for which an active market existed, instead of with banks. The solution was the innovation in 1961 of *negotiable* CDs, enabling banks to pay interest at market-determined rates on what were legally deposits with a term sufficiently long to avoid Regulation Q, but which provided their owners with the liquidity that came from being able to exchange the certificate for cash on demand in a liquid market. The development of negotiable CDs, followed by the development of a market in Federal Funds and of repurchase agreements, has given banks a means by which they can attract the deposits necessary to meet the 'non-discretionary' variable of loan demand.

Although they differ from each other in minor detail, these three accounts stand in stark contrast to Wray's assertion that 'money has always been endogenously created . . . the endogeneity of money does *not* rely on modern institutional relations' (Wray, 1990, p. 24, emphasis in the original). The two chapters in which this argument are advanced are rich both in historical evidence and in attacks upon the 'orthodox' conception of money. One aspect of the latter which suffers badly is the view that early societies moved from barter to market systems of exchange and then had to develop a system of monetary relations to allow these exchanges to take place efficiently. Barter is dismissed as an activity of any economic significance. Its function was usually ceremonial (and 'petty'). Nonetheless, even when market exchange was unusual, most people producing for the majority of their own needs, money had developed but as a unit of account which facilitated borrowing and lending. Keynes in the *Treatise* is quoted favourably as saying that for most important economic and social purposes it is money's role as a unit of account which matters (Wray, 1990, p. 6).

The argument that 'money' has always been endogenous comes in two parts. First, it is argued at the availability of money has never been a constraint on trade. Chapter two yields numerous examples ranging from early Islamic banking practice to the development of commercial banking in the UK after the seventeenth century of the development of various types of credit arrangement which facilitated trade expansion. As a catalogue of financial ingenuity, it is unsurpassed in the literature and should be compulsory reading for any minister of finance or central banker tempted to think that spending can be constrained by regulation. Thus far, there is little that is controversial. Most post-Keynesians, and many of an orthodox persuasion too, would go along with the idea that regulation inspires innovation and that strict monetary control, supposing such a thing were possible, would be quickly offset by velocity-raising practices.

It is the second step in the argument, that these innovations are innovations in the *supply of money* rather than in the supply of credit that controversy strikes. As Wray is perfectly aware, his argument entails some rewriting of conventional definitions.

> money is simply a debt (transferring purchasing power through time from the future to the present), which may or may not serve as a medium of exchange. Thus commercial paper may suffice as money, but might not serve as a medium of exchange. . . . Orthodoxy tends to confuse the medium of exchange with money and emphasizes the medium of exchange *function* of money. (Wray, 1990, pp. 13, 14)

Money, as Wray wishes to define it, is something much wider than a medium of exchange. The purpose of this rewriting of definitions is not clear, but the consequences are far-reaching. On orthodox definitions, monetary restraint whether by high interest rates or direct controls on bank lending, leads to an increase in alternative (non-bank) methods of finance. Spending takes place pretty much as agents intended. The result is a rise in velocity (nominal spending on current output divided by a subset of financial assets called money) and a reduction in the information content of money supply figures. Both consequences are illustrated in one of the most colourful incidents in recent UK monetary history, the 'bill-leak' of 1978–79, where banks switched from further lending (and the profit entailed in the spread between deposit and lending rates) to guaranteeing bills issued by their clients (and the profit from fees charged for such 'acceptances'). Of course, one could divide nominal spending by the newly expanded definition of money, that is by the stock of all those forms of debt which enable purchasing power to be transferred through time, but the resulting figure would be constant since money (new definition) is naturally created to match desired spending.

None of this would matter if no useful purpose were to be served by the conventional practice of limiting the term 'money' to a narrow subset of assets within the larger category of 'debt'. But this case is not made. The case *is* made for the importance of debt instruments which enable consumption to be transferred through time, though it should be said that this case is accepted in more conventional circles by recognising their impact on velocity. There seems to be a difference though between some credit instruments, say IOUs and bills of exchange, and others, say bank loans. Both types enable the debtor legitimately to obtain goods. Furthermore, both entail entering into debt though the bank loan involves a third party. Potentially more serious, however, is the fact that the seller is restricted in the further use of assets such as IOUs and bills of exchange, which are not themselves automatically acceptable as means of payment to third parties, and a transferred bank deposit, which is. The question remains, 'does this matter?' It may do, for the following reasons.

Imagine a situation where there is a surge in the demand for credit and deficit units choose (or are constrained) to issue bills, IOUs or similar instruments. If we assume that this increased demand for credit results from some rise in the price level, or costs of production, or increases in real activity then we have no difficulty with the idea that the demand for (and supply of) credit is endogenously determined, that is, is the *outcome* of events already in the system. The use of these forms of credit enable deficit units to acquire the goods which sellers have exchanged for debt. The critical question is what can the sellers do with this debt? It is not a net addition to their wealth since they have accepted it in exchange for goods and services. One might argue that they are more liquid to the extent that the debt itself can be used for transactions or can be used as security for a loan of money (conventional definition). In both of these roles, debt instruments issued by private households and firms are distinctly limited. In practice, we know that the holders accept such instruments (reasonably) confident that there will, in a short period, be a further adjustment to their wealth when the debts are redeemed for money (conventional definition again). Notice two points. First, although the debt instruments are acceptable as a *means of exchange*, the ability of recipients subsequently to rearrange their wealth is severely constrained and will most likely occur only after the debt has been redeemed. Secondly, on our assumption that deficit units have financed their latest deficit by non-bank borrowing, the redemption of the debt must eventually occur with existing money (when the deficit units have themselves been paid, by their debtors issuing IOUs and so on). In the aggregate, an increased level of nominal activity is being financed with a given stock of (conventional) money by the increasing use of non-bank debt instruments and perhaps by stretching the length of repayment periods. In conventional language, velocity has risen.

Contrast this with a situation at the opposite extreme where new deficits are financed by new bank loans. Sellers now receive payment as cheques drawn on bank deposits. Undeniably, such transfers are acceptable as a medium of exchange (sellers do not even know whether the cheques are drawn on a positive balance or an overdraft). More significantly, any subsequent desire to rearrange wealth, holding fewer bank deposits for example, can be put immediately into effect. How such rearrangements are put into effect is a controversial issue which we return to, mainly in Section 5.8. Plausibly, it will involve some purchase of financial assets (with implications for prices and yields) and of real goods and services (with implications for prices and output).

What are the crucial differences from the earlier case? After all, one might argue that the rearrangement of wealth and its implications would still have followed, albeit only after the debts had been redeemed. Furthermore, one might say that there still remains a debt to be redeemed. In effect, banks have accepted borrowers' IOUs. The crucial difference lies in the nature of the debt instrument that has been created. Bank deposits are acceptable as a medium of exchange ('means of payment' might be a better term) and can be passed directly to third parties, where IOUs and so forth generally can not. Why does *this* matter? It matters because of the scale of additional spending power that is created by new bank loans. Because bank deposits are acceptable, they circulate. Because they circulate, a deposit created by a loan to finance additional first round spending of an amount equal to the new deposit, will continue to circulate. Velocity is greater than one. This is not true for other debt instruments which have to be created on a one-to-one basis.

It seems to us, therefore, that the argument that 'money' is *any* form of debt which enables spending to be shifted through time is unhelpful, at the very least because it is bundling together a variety of instruments which, if one is determined to insist upon their similarity, are distinguished by different velocities. In our view, that is important, and not just because, in lumping all such instruments together, it involves a loss of information. We suggested above that there is a bigger issue and it is the one we touched on at the end of the introduction. If the money supply is endogenously determined, then money is the outcome of prior values taken by other variables in the system. It is an outcome; it cannot 'cause' anything. As such, the endogeneity thesis reverses the causality of the Quantity Theory. If, however, it were possible for the demand for bank loans to generate new deposits on such a scale that they were not willingly held, then awkward questions have to be confronted about what the consequences of that might be. Since new deposits come into existence in order to finance some prior expenditure plan, any possibility of 'excess' must hinge upon the general acceptability of bank deposits and thus their velocity being greater than one. Non-bank credit cannot cause mischief. It is created to finance one round of spending. Defining 'money' to include all debt instruments has a logic, but, intentionally or otherwise, it obscures this issue.

5.4.   THE ROLE OF THE 'STATE OF TRADE'

In what one might call the conventional post-Keynesian view, money is endogenous because the demand for the loans which create deposits is driven by other variables in the economic system, either the price level or the level of output or some combination of both. Production takes time and so, faced with rising costs, producers require an increase in working capital which is supplied by bank loans. This is the scenario for which Moore and Threadgold (1985) found some empirical support in their study of the demand for bank lending in the UK prior to 1985.

If this is the whole story, then one's first thought might be that income velocity would be at least stable, if not constant, over time. Institutional developments might be allowed to shape the trend: cash economizing practices leading to rising velocity, for example, or the increasing payment of interest on deposits leading to a decline. However, in the UK (and to a lesser extent in the US) the income velocity of broad money has declined sharply in the last 25 years, from approximately three in 1970 to approximately one

Table 5.1   UK bank and building society lending by sector (per cent)

	ICC	OFI	Households
1970(4)	42	3	55
1997(1)	0	20	60

Notes: ICC = industrial and commercial corporations; OFI = other (that is, non-bank) financial institutions.

Source: Bank of England, *Statistical Abstract*, 1997(l) table 10.

in 1998. Clearly, therefore, something fairly dramatic has happened to the demand for *money*, but if money is endogenous, then something similarly dramatic must have happened on the credit counterpart side. It is not immediately obvious why, if loans are the outcome of production decisions, the quantity of credit-created deposits should have diverged so dramatically from GDP.

Two pieces of evidence are suggestive. The first is that there has been a substantial shift in the composition of bank lending in recent years. As Table 5.1 shows, while firms may have been responsible for nearly half the demand for bank loans in 1970, by 1997 this demand is swamped by the demand coming from households and 'OFIs' (non-bank financial intermediaries).

The other piece of evidence lies in the data obtainable from the Association for Payments Clearing Systems (APACS) which shows a dramatic increase in the ratio of total transactions to GDP or current output. Figure 5.2 shows this ratio increasing from about 20 in 1970 to 50 in the late 1980s before settling at about 40 now. If we make the reasonable assumption that deficit units borrow in order to finance all types of expenditure not just expenditure relating to production, then it is hardly surprising that total bank lending should increase relative to GDP when there is *both* an increase in the share of bank lending going to agents whose spending is unrelated to production *and* an upsurge in such spending relative to output.

The possibility that the demand for *money* has been driven in recent years by something other than GDP or nominal output is not a complete novelty. For example, Anderson (1993) showed that the boom in mortgage refinancing in the USA had led to an increase in the volume and volatility of financial transactions relative to GDP transactions and that this had measurable effects upon the demand for M1 deposits. More recently, Palley (1995) and Pollin and Schaberg (1998) have demonstrated that money demand estimates in the USA can be improved by recognizing a role for total transactions where the behaviour of the latter is proxied by measures which refer to some part of the property market and to financial activity,

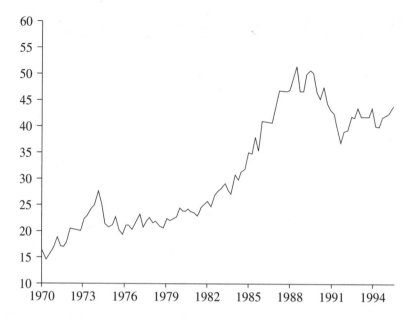

Figure 5.2   The ratio of real total transactions to real GDP

two major categories of spending included in *total* transactions but excluded from conventional measures of GDP. Howells and Hussein (1997) showed that the APACS series itself gave better results than either GDP or wealth in an otherwise standard money demand equation.

The possibility that the same is true for the demand for *credit* has not received the same degree of attention, though it seems an obvious next step for empirical testing. Howells and Hussein (1999) compared the ability of total transactions and GDP transactions to explain the behaviour of bank lending. The results suggest that total transactions is the better series for this purpose.

Once again, the question is 'does it matter if deposits are created by loans granted for purposes other than production?' In one fundamental sense it does not. Provided that the demand for loans continues to originate within the system, the quantity of money remains endogenous. It does not matter, for endogeneity itself, whether loans are granted to finance an upsurge in speculative house purchase (frequently the case in the UK) or to finance incremental production. It does, though, raise one interesting issue.

This is that the quantity of money is now to some extent independent of the needs of production. When Kaldor (1970, 1982) and Davidson and Weintraub (1973) first drew attention to the endogenous nature of the money creation process it was partly a response to a quantity theory analysis of inflation which was popular at the time. A necessary condition for monetary growth to be the 'cause' of inflation was that changes in the quantity of money simply had to be possible, independent of the needs of trade. If the quantity changed only to supply the needs of an increase in output *which was already in the pipeline*, then it could do no harm. If, on the other hand, it changed in response to changes in the cost of production which originated elsewhere, then it was at worst permissive where a rise in the price level was concerned. If, as we have now seen, it is possible for the quantity of money to change independently of the needs of production, then the waters are muddied once more. It is, for example, possible for speculative activities to generate a surge in liquidity which may exceed the growth rate of nominal production. While we measure the rate of inflation largely by changes in the price of current output (rather than asset prices, for example) then it is hard to see why we should rule out in principle the possibility that events in the housing market or in stock, foreign exchange or derivatives markets, might give rise to inflationary pressure through monetary shocks. On the other hand, the increase in money stock resulting from loans demanded to finance an explosion of asset prices may be no more than is required to finance an increase in the asset demand for money, to maintain portfolio equilibrium. Which of these occurs in practice is, of course, an empirical question whose answer depends upon the behaviour of the demand for money in such circumstances. Given the dramatic increase in liquidity that has occurred in the UK over the last ten years and the generally downward trend in inflation, the latter more benign possibility has an edge for now.

5.5.   THE ABSENCE OF RESERVE CONSTRAINTS

If banks are to be able to respond to a demand for loans generated by the state of trade, it follows either that additional reserves must be available to validate the new lending and deposits or that some means must be found for economizing on existing reserves. The former view, that the Central Bank always supplies the necessary reserves at the going rate of interest, is the position adopted by the 'accommodationists'. The alternative view, that banks can modify their behaviour so as to circumvent the main effects of a reserve restriction, is the 'structuralist' position, presumably from the idea that the structure of modern banking systems permits the development of reserve-economizing practices regardless of Central Bank action. This terminology is a little unfortunate since the accommodationist position itself contains two strands, one of which is that Central Banks could restrict reserves if they so chose, but conflicts with other objectives lead them always to supply the required reserves. This may be called 'discretionary accommodation'. The second strand argues that Central Banks have no realistic choice but to supply reserves and the reasons for this, we shall see, lie in the structure of the banking system. It is tempting to call this 'structural accommodation' but it might be safer in the circumstances to call it 'compulsory accommodation'.

The idea that the Central Bank sets the level of short-term rates and then supplies reserves on demand as a deliberate act of policy, is the oldest of the explanations for banks being unconstrained by reserve availability. The argument appears explicitly in Weintraub (1978) and is linked ultimately to his wage theorem. The growth of nominal income (due to a rise in unit labour costs, or in the mark-up on those costs) results in a rise in the demand for active balances. If the level of *real* output is to be maintained, the supply of money must increase. If it does not, or does not do so sufficiently, interest rates will rise and through the normal Keynesian mechanisms this will reduce the level of output and employment. In Weintraub's view, political considerations make this intolerable. Ultimately, the political authorities will instruct the Central Bank to accommodate the extra demand for money.[8] Similar views, that the Central Bank *could* if it chose restrict reserves but chooses not to do so for reasons of policy conflicts, appears in Myrdal (1939) and Lavoie (1985). Thus, under 'discretionary accommodation' endogeneity is made into a political phenomenon.[9]

The weakness of this argument, of course, is that it cannot explain Central Bank accommodation under regimes, like those of Thatcher and Reagan, where the responsibility for the behaviour of output and employment is explicitly renounced and inflation becomes the sole focus of policy. In these circumstances, explanations have to find stronger pressures forcing Central Banks to accommodate. According to Moore (1988a, chs. 5–8) and Kaldor (1982, 1985) such pressures can be found in the structure of modern banking systems. The starting point is that Central Banks, in addition to their role as managers of monetary policy, bear a heavy responsibility for ensuring the stability of their domestic financial systems. This role is commonly referred to as their 'lender of last resort' (LOLR) function. Since financial intermediation always involves an element of maturity transformation, intermediaries are always subject to the risk that they may have calls on their liabilities which they cannot meet from their relatively illiquid assets. In the case of an individual institution in difficulties, borrowing within the system is a realistic solution but in the event of a system-wide shortage of liquidity the general sale of assets will be self-defeating, though it will cause a collapse of asset prices, the threat of insolvency and a general debt deflation. The only safeguard against disaster is the Central Bank's willingness *always* to provide liquidity (Moore, 1988a, pp. 57–65; Kaldor, 1985, pp. 20–25). It needs to be emphasized: this is not a discretionary function. If confidence in the financial system is to be maintained, the public needs to be convinced that this assistance will always be forthcoming. Such reassurance requires an unquestioning response, not a response which is hedged around with conditions (Goodhart, 1984, p. 212).

A second structural feature of modern systems explains why such assistance might often be required. Most textbook discussion of the lender of last resort tends to focus upon the shortage of liquidity caused by net withdrawals of cash ('runs on the bank'). However, the same shortage of liquidity, a fall in the R/D ratio, will occur when banks increase their lending and in many banking systems banks are contractually committed to make additional loans on demand. This arises from the 'overdraft' facility where banks agree to meet all demand for loans up to a ceiling. Customers then use that proportion of the facility that they require on a day-to-day basis. Typically, the proportion of the facility that is in use at any one time is about 60 per cent of total commitments. Thus it follows that if the state of trade requires an increase in working capital to bridge the time gap between firms' additional outlays and the receipts from increased sales, requests for loans will always be met, 'if bank loans are largely demand-determined, so that the quantity of bank credit demanded is a non-discretionary variable from the viewpoint of individual banks, this then implies that the money supply is credit driven' (Moore, 1988b, p. 373). If the state of trade[10] means customers demand more advances, banks have no choice (unless they are to break contractual agreements) but to expand their lending. Advances (and deposits) will rise relative to reserves, interest rates will rise and security prices fall, reducing the value of bank assets. Faced with a general shortage of liquidity, the Central Bank *must*, as we said above, provide assistance. Essentially the same argument is put by Wray (1990, pp. 85–90).

There are two further structural features which make it impossible for Central Banks to resist the demand for reserves. The first is the structure of banks' assets which are overwhelmingly non-marketable loans (rather than marketable securities). Moore highlights the problem by posing a reduction in the monetary base brought about by open market operations of the textbook type. Bank reserves are reduced but banks cannot reduce their balance sheets because calling in loans will bankrupt their customers. This illustration would be more compelling if redesigned to fit into a world of endogeneity where (remember) *expansion* is the norm. In such a setting, we must imagine banks making new loans, in response to demand, expecting the additional reserves to be forthcoming, only to find that they are not because of a change in Central Bank stance. From this point, Moore's argument follows as before. Banks cannot unwind this position without causing chaos.[11]

Lastly, it is worth noting that most monetary regimes which pay any attention to the base/deposits relationship require banks to report on their holding of base at time t, and their holdings of deposits at some earlier period, $t-1$, the system of lagged reserve accounting. The current level of required reserves is thus *predetermined* by the past level of deposits (Moore, 1988b; Goodhart, 1984, p. 212). In these circumstances, there is plainly nothing that banks can do to accommodate deposits to reserves. Any desired ratio can only be met by the Bank supplying the reserves.

For all of these reasons, some a matter of choice, others decidedly non-discretionary, Central Banks accommodate the demand for reserves. Notice, since we return to it as an issue at the end of this section, that in these circumstances the supply of reserves is assumed to be perfectly elastic. We repeat, the Central Bank sets short-term interest rates and supplies reserves on demand.

In the 'structuralist' view of endogeneity, the idea that the Central Bank supplies reserves on demand, and thus that supply of reserves is perfectly elastic, is implausible. It is recognized that Central Banks operate under constraints which vary between regimes and probably over time as well. Thus, while they may well be concerned about the disruption caused by quantity-constrained reserves, the pressure, sometimes from misguided or misinformed financial markets, to tighten reserves may be even stronger. However, this matters little since the structure of modern financial systems enables banks to engage in a number of activities which enable them to avoid the consequences of reserve shortages. In this view it is sometimes said that banks can 'manufacture' reserves though this is a little misleading since most of the practices are aimed at reducing the quantity of reserves that are required. If reserves are defined appropriately as the liabilities solely of the Central Bank then banks can do nothing to avoid a system-wide shortage. What, perhaps, they can do is to economize on reserves so as to avoid the effects of the shortage.

Central to this argument is banks' management of their liabilities. For example, in a period where the Central Bank is consciously seeking to restrain the growth of reserves, and presumably also the money supply, banks will attract funds out of sight deposits which have a high reserve requirement, into time deposits, CDs and other instruments which have lower requirements. The result is that a given volume of reserves will support a higher volume of lending (and a higher volume of total deposits). It also follows that periods of reserve shortage and consequent liability management will be periods of rising interest rates (for a detailed explanation of increasing mark-ups in periods of reserve shortage, see Seccareccia (1988)). Such periods will also be conducive to financial innovation as banks try to find cheaper ways of adjusting to the shortage. An obvious example of this is the development of certificates of deposit where the superior (liquidity) characteristics of the product enables banks to raise funds for a fixed term more cheaply than they could through traditional time deposits.[12]

To date, the only attempt to distinguish empirically between the two positions (for the USA) is by Pollin. The criteria used were threefold. First, Pollin argued, if 'accommodation' were the rule, then we would expect stationarity in the ratio of loans (*L*) to reserves (*R*); secondly, if the Federal Reserve were to provide reserves 'willingly' then borrowed (from the Fed) and non-borrowed reserves would be very close substitutes and there would be no need to develop circumventory products and practices; thirdly, market interest rates would not move independently of official rates (official rates would 'cause' market rates). Formal tests of stationarity in the *L/R* ratio, of elasticities in the demand for borrowed and non-borrowed reserves and of causality between official and market rates, were all claimed to lend support to the structural view (Pollin, 1991).

The controversy remains, however, since some of the results are open to alternative interpretation (Palley, 1991). For example, the discovery that the *L/R* ratio is subject to an upward secular trend is advanced by Pollin as evidence that reserves are constrained. On the other hand, as Palley points out, the need to hold reserves against deposits has been recognized for years in the standard banking literature as acting as a tax upon banking intermediation – limiting the amount of each deposit that can be lent out. The fact that the *L/R* ratio rises over time could merely be evidence that banks are profit seekers wishing to reduce the burden of reserve requirements even when reserves are readily available. Rather similarly, the discovery that there appears to be two-way Sims (1972) causality between Federal and market interest rates (where the accommodationist logic would require unidirectional causality from Fed to market rates) could be accounted for by market rates embodying expectations about future Fed rates.

It has become common practice to cast this argument about the availability of reserves in terms of the shape of the money supply curve. For example, it is often said that a fully accommodative regime gives rise to a horizontal curve. The key to this is the absence of any reason for interest rates to rise with an increase in the volume of money/lending. If the authorities are pegging the official rediscount rate they supply reserves on demand and, with a given mark-up by banks, the supply of money/loans is perfectly elastic at the going rate of interest. In Palley's words:

> The accommodationist view may be summarized as follows. The short-term cost of funds is pegged by the central bank. Banks then act as mark-up pricers making loans that carry a fixed markup over the cost of funds. The loan [*sic*] supply schedule is therefore horizontal, and the level of bank lending is determined by the level of loan demand. (Palley, 1991, p. 398)

The loan supply schedule will not be horizontal, however, if, either, the central bank restricts the availability of reserves and banks have to engage in liability management which raises their costs of funds until some innovation steps them down again, or banks themselves vary the size of their mark-up over costs, perhaps to compensate for increasing levels of risk as loan volume expands.

> When the full implications of this structural endogeneity perspective are drawn out, the differences with the accommodative view become even sharper. For structuralists . . . a crucial point is that the growth of liability management must exert upward pressure on interest rates within a given institutional structure . . . If banks are at least to maintain their interest spread, these higher costs will have to be passed on to their borrowers. (Pollin, 1991, p. 375)

We shall return to this practice in Section 5.7 when we question the value of symbolizing endogenous money by means of *any* curve (horizontal, upward-sloping or even kinked) intersecting the vertical (interest rate) axis. But for now, having raised the possibility that bank mark-ups may not be constant, we need next to consider the circumstances in which they might vary.

5.6. THE PRICING OF BANK LOANS

Within the endogeneity tradition, there are three views about the pricing of loans. First, there is the view that the Central Bank accommodates fully the demand for reserves and the mark-up on the rediscount rate is unchanged, at least in the short run (Moore, 1979, 1985a, 1985b, 1988a, 1988b, 1988c, 1991a, 1991b; Kaldor, 1982, 1985 and Lavoie, 1984, 1985, 1994); secondly, there is the view that the Central Bank may accommodate fully but for reasons of risk and liquidity, mark-ups will anyway eventually rise (Minsky, 1975; Wray, 1990; Dow, 1993, 1996); thirdly, there is the (structuralist) view that Central Banks do not always accommodate and it is the lack of accommodation, forcing up bank costs, which causes interest rates to rise (Earley and Evans, 1982; Minsky, 1985; Pollin, 1991).

Unfortunately, much of this debate has taken place against a background of the implied shape of the resulting money supply curve. The argument is, roughly, that with full accommodation and a constant mark-up the money supply curve is horizontal while, in both other cases, it is sooner or later upward-sloping. The result is that the debate is bedeviled by elementary errors and confusions, of exposition at least, and sometimes of substance, as protagonists have tried to jump prematurely from making sensible points in the pricing debate to indefensible conclusions about the money supply curve. Two things in particular are disquieting.

First, the endogeneity thesis is that banks respond to loan demands and these new loans give rise to new deposits. *If* the banks' response to loan demands involves a rising price for loans, it is reasonable to assume that the return on deposits will also rise (indeed, we have just seen in the last section that a rising marginal cost of deposits may be a *cause* of rising loan costs) *but it does not follow*. The interest rate charged on loans is not the same thing as the rate paid on deposits. It is not even separated from the deposit rate by a constant mark-up. And the rate charged on loans is even further removed from the opportunity cost of holding money, which is the relevant interest rate concept when we come to discussing the shape of the *money* supply curve. Unfortunately, in what follows, we shall see a tendency to describe the behaviour of *lending* rates as evidence of the shape of the money supply curve.

Secondly, even where it is clear that the discussion is confined to bank lending behaviour and its appropriate depiction, it is not always clear whether we are discussing stocks or flows. Endogeneity, as we know, originates in the demand for loans. This results from the 'state of trade'. Consequently, nominal magnitudes are generally increasing. There is a *flow* of net new loans (and deposits). It is one of the strong points of the endogeneity thesis that it recognizes *change* as the norm. Nonetheless, we shall see that much of the discussion appears to be about stocks and to argue that a particular form of bank (or client or Central Bank) behaviour is triggered when a certain level of stocks has been reached is irrelevant, if meant literally, and unhelpful if it is only an error of exposition.

It is implicit in the Moore and Kaldor position that banks are free to meet any demand for loans that are forthcoming at the going rate of interest. 'Commercial bank loan officers must ensure that loan requests meet the bank's income and collateral requirements. They must in general satisfy themselves as to the credit worthiness of the project and the character of the borrower' (Moore, 1988a, p. 24). Alternatively, 'modern commercialised banks are price setters and quantity takers in both their retail deposit and loan markets' (Moore, 1988a, p. xii). Indeed, rightly or wrongly, this is seen as an essential precondition of the horizontal money supply curve:

> The *accommodative* position . . . maintains that no effective quantity constraints exist on bank reserves. Individual banks can always obtain additional reserves,

at the market price, so long as lender confidence in their solvency . . . is preserved. As a result, solvent banks are never quantity-constrained for reserves. *The credit money supply function is horizontal in the market period*, at an interest rate that depends on the central bank's marginal supply price of reserves. (Moore, 1991a, p. 404, second emphasis added)

This is not to suggest that Central Bank interest rates are fixed forever. Central Banks will adjust this rate from time to time having regard to other policy objectives and their freedom of manoeuvre – itself likely to depend on size and openness of the economy. In Lavoie (1994) reference is made to the role of the 'political class and the financial lobby' in the setting of rates, a role that would surely merit more investigation. At one point, Kaldor (1983) suggests that 'the supply of money is represented . . . by a horizontal line or a set of horizontal lines, representing different stances of monetary policy' (p. 22). But, *given* the level of officially-determined rates (for what one might call the 'market-period', Moore, 1991a, p. 406) the supply of loans for all who are creditworthy, will be perfectly elastic at the going rate of interest, equal to the official rediscount rate plus a mark-up.

The question of creditworthiness has been a problem for those who wish to argue that the supply of credit is perfectly elastic at the going rate of interest. The fact that lending is constrained by banks' collateral requirements is widely recognized in the horizontalist literature (see for example Kaldor, 1981, p. 15; Moore, 1988a, p. 24; Lavoie, 1994, p. 13). Most recently Moore has pointed out that saying that banks are price setters and quantity takers in retail markets:

> is not to deny that many small borrowers are effectively credit constrained. New businesses and poor households, in particular, do not possess the income, assets and credit records that banks require in order to make profitable and financially sound loans (the banks' three C's: credit, collateral and character). (Moore, 1994, p. 123)

Furthermore, it is generally recognized in the same sources that the criteria for the identification of sound borrowers will not be constant but will vary with circumstances. The question is, how is this to be represented in terms which relate to the rate charged on loans? One possibility, threatening from the horizontalist point of view, is that banks respond by raising the mark-up when confronted by borrowers of diminishing creditworthiness. It is easy to see how this could then be linked to volumes (but of stocks or flows?) in order to suggest that the credit supply curve is upward-sloping beyond a certain point. Naturally, this is rejected by horizontalists. In Lavoie's paper it is rejected on the grounds that expansion does not necessarily lead to less creditworthy borrowers (we return to this in a moment)

and on the grounds that bankers do not anyway discriminate between customers by marginal variations in mark-ups. The criteria are absolute.
Customers meet them or they do not. The appropriate representation of
changes in bankers' perception of the creditworthiness of borrowers.
Lavoie argues, citing earlier practice by Davidson (1972) and Arestis and
Eichner (1988) is by the incorporation of shift variables in the demand for
credit. If collateral requirements get tighter, the demand curve shifts to the
left. It is the 'solvent' demand curve that matters.

Minsky (1975, p. 112) is often credited with being the first to argue that
banks would raise lending rates at the peak of the cycle as they became
increasingly concerned about firms' solvency regardless of the degree of
accommodation by the Central Bank. A similar argument, appears in Wray
(1990):

> Eventually, however, financial institutions will come up against the maximum
> 'prudent' leverage ratio. Another innovation, or a revision of standards, will
> again allow expansion without a rise in interest rates. However, in the meantime,
> only a rise in the liquidity premium would induce banks to expand loans further.
> That is, *the money supply curve is upward-sloping relative to interest rates* in the
> absence of innovations or revisions of norms of behaviour, even though there is
> no strict quantity constraint on bank lending. (pp. 166–7, our emphasis)

By far the most perceptive representation of the ideas of cyclically varying
risk premia and perceptions of risk appear in Dow (1993, 1996; see also
Dow and Earl, 1982, p. 140). The supply curve is horizontal for some of its
length at an interest rate equal to the discount rate plus a mark-up. Beyond
a certain volume, the curve slopes upward as banks' perceptions of the risk
attaching to borrowers increases. Finally, the whole curve shifts with the
cycle, lying at a lower level in the expansionary phase (giving a larger
volume of credit) since mark-ups over official rates are smaller reflecting the
lower perception of risk. 'A rate structure is implicit in "the interest rate"
shown in horizontalist credit supply curves. Here it is being suggested that
there is a systematic movement within the structure over the cycle which
should be made explicit' (Dow, 1994. p. 10).

Horizontalists like Moore and Lavoie would presumably have little
problem with the idea that there is a rate 'structure' in the sense that
different classes of borrowers are charged different rates and would raise no
objection to the idea that this structure should shift around. Linking it to
different stages of the cycle is simply specifying one particular form of
Central Bank reaction function (or a specific set of preferences on the part
of the 'financial lobby'). But the suggestion that the structure turns upward
beyond a certain point (again, is the relevant magnitude a stock or a flow?)
runs up against Lavoie's argument that the data simply do not support an

association between deteriorating risk and expansion. The mechanism assumed to be at work (Minsky, 1975, chs. 5, 6) is a rising *aggregate* debt/equity ratio in the upswing of the cycle. That it is *inevitable* is contradicted by evidence that the debt/equity ratio of US firms fell in the upswing of the 1920s but did not fall in more recent recessions (Isenberg, 1988; Lavoie, 1994, p. 15). Nor does theory demand that it should do so. If firms borrow more in an upswing (*planning* to raise their debt equity ratio) they will experience higher profits, unless we introduce some systematic mechanism to prevent this, and the higher profits, leading to higher equity values, could leave the ratio higher as planned, unchanged or even diminished. Minsky's financial fragility hypothesis – that increased borrowing leads to higher debt/equity ratios – and Kalecki's (1937) principle of increasing risk which it much resembles, may be applicable in the case of the individual firm in isolation, but the aggregate outcome, when all firms are expanding, is simply uncertain.

The third, and final, strand in this argument is the structuralist one, that Central Banks, certainly in the present climate, cannot be relied upon to accommodate fully the demand for reserves. In these circumstances the banks own circumventory practices push up costs and this will be reflected in a rising mark-up over official rediscount rates – the credit supply curve will slope upward. In a non-accommodating situation banks will be forced to attract more time deposits (with lower reserve requirements) and will have to offer inducements to depositors, in the form of interest premia, to encourage them to make the switch.

As a source of rising cost of loans two points can be made about this argument. First, the question of whether Central Banks accommodate fully or not is an empirical one and one which is not easily demonstrated, as the responses (Moore, 1991a; Palley, 1991) to Pollin's (1991) tests show. However, if the Central Bank does not accommodate fully, interest rates are likely to rise. As regards the slope of the loan supply schedule there remains the question of how this is to be interpreted. Clearly if the Central Bank does not accommodate fully and rates rise, that is a decision of the Central Bank and it was never in dispute that the authorities could and would adjust rates according to policy or other pressures. The question is one of time and we are back to Moore's use of the term 'market-period'. Horizontalists might be tempted by Lavoie's (1994, fig. 1) argument that even in conditions of non-accommodation the loan supply schedule is horizontal in the market period. Banks make all the loans they can at the going rate of interest. As the (downward sloping) demand for loans curve shifts out beyond a certain point, however, the supply curve shift upward. *Over a longer period*, the series of intersections which are generated lie on a NE–SW diagonal and trace out an upward sloping 'dynamic supply curve'.

We are now deeply into questions of how endogeneity is best represented.

5.7.   IS THERE A HORIZONTAL MONEY SUPPLY CURVE?

We have seen enough in these pages to be fully aware that the ability to symbolize the endogeneity thesis by reference to a 'horizontal money supply curve' is highly cherished; so much so that attempts to give the curve an upward slope (by structuralists and others) are fiercely resisted. As we said at the beginning of the last section, however, there are many confusions. It is not always clear whether the magnitudes under discussion are stocks or flows; there is a tendency to assume that once the shape of a credit or loan supply curve is plausibly established the shape of the money supply curve is automatically established. (We offer this as a charitable explanation for the fact that 'the' curve whose shape is under discussion is inconsistently referred to as a *money* supply curve (Lavoie, 1985, p. 71; Kaldor, 1982, p. 24, 1983, p. 22; Moore, 1989, p. 66; Rousseas, 1986, p. 85; Wray, 1990, pp. 166–7) and a *credit* or *loan* supply curve (Palley, 1991, p. 398; Dow 1993, 1994 and Dow and Earl, 1982, p. 140)). In a paper by Lavoie we are even invited to 'examine the mechanisms that have been advanced to generate an upward-sloping credit *or* money supply curve' (Lavoie, 1994, p. 12, our emphasis).[13]

It is easy to see why the horizontal supply curve is such a potent symbol. It offers a direct confrontation to the exogenous, vertical money supply curve and produces a horizontal *LM* curve which for many is essential for the destruction of the neoclassical *IS/LM* apparatus.

In this section we want to suggest that what is referred to as a money supply curve intersecting the vertical (interest rate) axis in interest-money space is not a money supply curve at all. At best, it is an equilibrium curve tracing the locus of shifting money demand and supply curves.[14] Its shape will depend upon a number of issues raised in the last two sections (broadly speaking the terms on which banks are prepared to lend) but it also depends upon the demand for money, an issue on which the endogeneity thesis is curiously quiet, as we shall see in the next section. It follows from this, of course, that critical references to the 'horizontal money supply curve' (HMSC) throughout this section should be taken to refer to any curve described as a supply curve and intersecting the vertical axis. This embraces the quite literally horizontal money supply curve but also all its variants: upward sloping, upward sloping beyond a certain point and so on.

We begin by taking statements like this at face value:

> Now, in the case of credit money the proper representation should be a *horizontal* 'supply curve' of money not a vertical one. Monetary policy is represented *not* by a given quantity of money stock but by a *given rate of interest*; and the amount of money in existence will be demand-determined. (Kaldor, 1982, p. 24, emphasis in the original)

> The credit money stock is credit-driven and demand-determined. Both the base and the money stock are endogenous. The money supply function is horizontal in interest-money space. The supply and demand for credit money are interdependent, and interest rates are exogenous. (Moore, 1989, p. 66)

That is to say, that references to an HMSC (or its variants, let us remember) are intended as references to a *stock* curve drawn in the familiar space of money quantity on the horizontal axis and interest rate on the vertical. To understand the conditions strictly necessary for such a phenomenon, we can usefully think back to Section 5.2, where we distinguished between interest-endogeniety and base-endogeneity.

The first of these, we can recall, referred to the fact that the multiplier linking the monetary base to broad money showed some positive elasticity with respect to r_b, the bond rate, on the vertical axis. Specifically, this elasticity arose from the behaviour of the banks' reserve ratio, β. Higher bond rates proxy higher rates of return on all non-money assets and therefore indicate a higher opportunity cost to banks of holding (zero-interest) reserves in their balance sheet. Higher bond rates entail smaller reserve ratios and a larger money multiplier. The degree of elasticity (and the positive slope of the M_s curve) depends upon the size of the coefficient on β. For a perfectly elastic money supply curve, this coefficient must be equal to infinity.

This we can prove formally by differentiating equation (5.2) with respect to the bond rate. Likewise, we could show that the same, horizontal, result would follow if the coefficient on α, the public's cash ratio, were infinite. The interpretation here is that the higher return on non-money assets, the greater the incentive for the public to economize on the holding of cash balances and the greater the quantity of a *given* quantity of base that is available to banks to hold as reserves.

With neither of these coefficients equal to infinity, the money supply curve has only a positive slope and a continuous expansion of the money stock (on a given base) requires a continuous increase in r_b Hence, as we noted in Section 5.2, interest-endogeneity scarcely captures the essence of an endogenous money supply which is that expansion is the norm, *at going interest rates*. This situation is consistent only with a continued expansion of the base. (Persisting with mathematical analogies, we can show that the supply curve becomes horizontal if we set $\delta B/\delta r_b = \infty$).

To summarize, we can say that a HMSC requires one or more of the cash and reserve ratios, α and β, *or* the supply of monetary base B, to be perfectly elastic with respect to the bond rate, r_b. Neither of the first two conditions is seriously argued in the post-Keynesian literature. Accommodationists (like Moore) argue that horizontality results from the central bank's passive acquiescence in increasing the monetary base. Structuralists (like Pollin) come part way toward the condition by arguing that as interest rates rise, innovative activity by banks enables them to operate with a smaller reserve ratio. In effect, β becomes elastic with respect to some appropriate measure of interest rates. But there is no suggestion that the elasticity is *infinite*. (It seems almost trivial to point out that the condition of infinite elasticity requires that α and β collapse to zero as soon as interest rates rise – but it needs to be remembered.) Indeed, as we saw in Section 5.4, the structuralists are only too keen to interpret their position as meaning that the 'HMSC' is upward-sloping. We repeat there is no argument for horizontality emanating from the behaviour of α and β.

If the idea of a HMSC is to be taken seriously, it must follow from the accommodationist line of argument. Here (again as we saw in Section 5.4) the central bank supplies reserves on demand, for reasons which vary from defending the structure of the financial system, to political expediency. The question is, can this argument be tightened up and formalized in such a way that supports the condition of infinite elasticity of reserve supply with respect to the bond rate. (Note that the condition requires not only perfect elasticity, but also with respect to the *bond rate*, since no other rate can appear on the vertical axis for reasons we discuss immediately below.) This amounts to saying that the central bank operates with a very strict feedback rule. Strict in the sense that it specifies a change in interest rates as the sole determinant of reserve supply and strict also in specifying the bond rate as the sole relevant rate. It is not sufficient for horizontality simply to believe that *one* of the factors which enters central bank decision making is *often* the behaviour of *some unspecified* set of interest rates. In fact it seems quite plausible, and in the UK the *Financial Times* daily money market report seems to confirm, that the Bank of England bases its daily operations to adjust the supply of reserves to some degree upon what is happening to market rates. But interest rates are only part of the decision and the rates in question are 7-day money market rates. This is not at all the same thing as *infinitely elastic with respect to the bond rate*.

If the assumption of infinite (negative) interest-elasticities of demand for cash (by the public) and reserves (by banks) or infinite (positive) interest-elasticities of reserve supply are necessary conditions for an HMSC, the framework seems already indefensible. There are further difficulties, however, and while they may be redundant in the light of the foregoing argument, they are nonetheless interesting – not least from the point of view of our later argument in Section 5.8 that the endogeneity thesis has been rather cavalier in its treatment of the demand for money.

In interest-money space, consider the interest rate and its function carefully. The function of the interest rate on the vertical axis is to represent the opportunity cost of holding money. In a simple world where money does not pay interest, the cost is usually represented by the bond rate, r_b, proxying for the rate on non-money assets as a whole (see Section 5.2, above). The reason for this lies in the reason for drawing the original money supply function in interest-money space, which is to explore the nature of money market equilibrium. Even if we ignore the demand side, and concentrate only on the behaviour of supply, we are still led back to the bond rate on the vertical axis since, as we were at pains to stress in Section 5.2, supporters of exogenous money have never argued that the 'vertical' money supply curve was literally so, but that it was positively inclined as a result of the credit multiplier having a positive interest elasticity. That in turn (see equations (5.2)–(5.6) is due to banks' economizing on reserves as the return on other assets increases. The rate on the vertical axis must be r_b.

By contrast, the endogeneity thesis has it that the money supply curve, turned through (slightly less than) 90 degrees intersects the vertical axis *at the discount rate set by the Central Bank*. If we were to put r_d (with or without mark-up) on the vertical axis (to suit the HMSC), then the exogenous ('vertical') money supply curve with which the HMSC is being contrasted would have to be negatively sloped (equation (5.6)). The only way out of this dilemma would be to assume that the $r_b - r_d$ spread is constant so that changes in r_b can proxy for changes in r_d. As well as being empirically absurd, this would cause a host of theoretical difficulties elsewhere.[15]

We suggested in the previous section and at the beginning of this that there was some confusion about whether the HMSC depicted stocks or flows or for that matter whether it strictly depicted the supply of money or of credit. To appreciate that these confusions spring from the fundamental inability of any such curve to capture the essence of endogeneity, let us imagine (just for the sake of exploration) that we were to ignore the problem of 'which interest rate?' and draw a horizontal curve in interest-money space. The exact shape of such a curve, we know from the arguments of the last section, is determined by the price of bank loans. It must be a *credit* supply curve. But is it a stock curve? The extracts in Section 5.4 certainly could be read to refer to stocks and the quotations at the beginning of this section make it absolutely clear that what is intended in depicting endogeneity by means of a 'horizontal' curve is a contrast with the stock curve of exogenous money. Let us suppose next (we shall query the supposition in a moment and argue directly against it in the next section) that

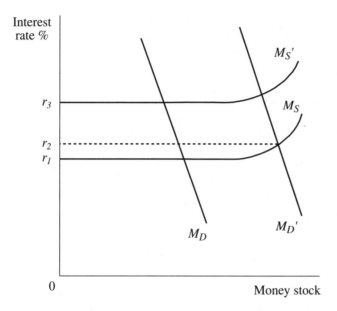

Figure 5.3   Shifts in the demand for and supply of money

there is no problem in translating directly from a credit (stock) supply curve
to a money stock supply curve. What would be the point of so doing?
Would it be possible, for example, to cast the debates of the last section in
this framework? According to one group of arguments, there comes a point
in the expansion of bank lending at which the cost of loans rises. Imagine
dealing with this if what we have is a stock curve. We are invited to believe
that at some given volume, the equilibrium credit stock will correspond to
an interest rate, r_1, corresponding (let us assume) to the horizontal section
of the credit supply curve. While at a larger volume of credit (larger banks'
balance sheets) the demand curve cuts the upward sloping portion of the
supply curve and the interest rate is r_2 ($r_2 > r_1$).

This is shown in Figure 5.3. The question we raised in the introduction
applies. Why are we concerned with stock equilibria? In a world of endogenous money, there is a continuous *flow* of net new bank lending and our
interest lies (or should lie) in rates of change of stocks. How do we cope
with that here? We can easily imagine the demand curve shifting to the right
but then so too must the supply curve if we are not to have continuously
rising interest rates. For the supply curve to shift, the central bank must
supply reserves at the going discount rate (which the Bank of England does
on a daily basis) and banks must periodically increase their capital base,
which they do. If we wish, then, to focus on the 'normal' case where the

stock of credit is expanding we can do it using a stock diagram by allowing both curves to shift continuously outward, changing the supply curve
intercept as required by changes in discount rates, but it is very cumbersome.

Now consider some disturbances, the effects of which one might well
wish to analyse, using this framework. Suppose that banks run up against
limited supplies of base. The central bank is unwilling to discount the
volume of bills offered at the going rate of interest. Notice that in this case
the supply curve must *shift* upward since the official discount rate rises (the
mark-up assumed constant). The central bank cannot limit available
reserves without this effect. We may already be in the upward sloping
portion of the supply curve, but the shortage of reserves does not move us
further up it or make it steeper (a rise in the mark-up over a given discount
rate); the reserve shortage causes a rise in the official rate. With higher bank
borrowing costs (relative to non-bank finance) and eventually a depressing
effect on real activity, the demand curve shifts to the right more slowly and
the central bank continues discounting bills in just the volume (at just the
discount rate) necessary to maintain the reduced rate of lending growth.
The rate of shift of the demand curve, in other words, is dependent upon
the shape of the supply curve and the rate charged on bank lending at the
point where the two stock curves intersect.

The same complication arises if we imagine the transition from the boom
to recession phase of the cycle. We begin with the two stock curves intersecting (for simplicity) in the horizontal section of the supply curve at a
lending rate, r_1. There is a net flow demand for new bank loans and these
are being met at this rate of interest: both stock curves are thus shifting to
the right. The economy then enters the downturn. Collateral values and the
prospective returns on investment fall. Banks increase their mark-up. In the
former case, the supply curve shifts up (to r_3 in Figure 5.3) and cuts the
demand curve at a lower stock equilibrium. But this is of little interest.
What really matters is that the rise in bank lending rates causes a reduction
in the *flow* demand for net new lending. The upward shift of the supply
curve causes a slowdown in the rightward shift of the demand curve. Once
again, the position of the supply curve influences the shift behaviour of the
demand curve. This is extremely cumbersome and in its complexity this
framework threatens to obscure the central feature of the endogeneity
approach – the preeminence of flows.

Finally, consider how the HMSC framework would deal with a change
in what might be called the 'underlying conditions of endogeneity'.
Suppose, for example, that the demand for bank lending became more
interest-sensitive.

The consequence of this change, naturally, is that a change in the rate

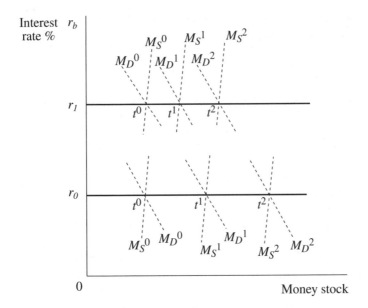

Figure 5.4   Shifting demand and supply schedules

charged on bank lending (a change in r_d or a change in the mark-up) causes a larger reduction in the flow of lending than it would previously have done. But the HMSC can show nothing relevant to the elasticity of demand for bank lending, never mind anything of relevance to *changes in* elasticity. One obvious context in which one might wish to discuss such changes is that of monetary control where a rise, for example, in r_d is now more effective in slowing the rate of monetary expansion. Ignoring the problem of wrong interest rate on the vertical axis, all one can do in interest–money (stock) space is shift the HMSC upward.

If we insist on using interest-*money* space however, Figure 5.4 shows what happens rather more realistically. At the original rate of interest r_0, the (stock) supply curve is shifting to the right by a given amount per period of time. But this raises another difficulty. The expanding money stock must be held by non-banks. The supply curve is shifting to the right as a result of a demand for net new lending but banks' balance sheet identity and the formal definition of monetary assets both require a consistency between credit-driven money supply expansion and demand for the resulting deposits. This is easily overlooked, partly as a result of careless talk about the endogenous money supply being demand-determined. In the circumstances, it is tempting to think of the demand and supply of money being 'equal and identical' (we return to this in the next section). But, as we said earlier, it is the demand for *credit* to which banks respond, not a demand for money. Exactly how the demand for the resulting deposits is reconciled with the demand for loans is a source of some controversy (Cottrell, 1986; Moore, 1985b; Palley, 1991, 1994; Arestis and Howells, 1996). Our own preference, argued elsewhere, is for changes in relative interest rates. Whatever the mechanism, however, our rightward shift in money supply curve must be accompanied by a demand curve.

All of this is shown, in Figure 5.4 by the position of M_s at $t_0, t_1, t_2, \ldots$ If the central bank raises the official discount rate to r_1 then, assuming *some* interest-sensitivity in the demand for lending, M_s shifts to the right more slowly. This much we can show in Figure 5.4 by shifting the *locus* from r_0 to r_1. But the effect of a change in the sensitivity itself we can show only by repeating our steps but then showing M_s shifting by a rather smaller amount per time interval. Once again, if we ignore the question of which particular rate of interest is on the vertical axis and why the demand curve should be shifting in each case by exactly the amount required to maintain the *locus* horizontal at that rate, we can show something of what we wish but it is so complex as to add nothing in clarity to a purely verbal description of the process.

Consider another difficulty, Equation (5.6) tells us the determinants of the (exogenous) money supply. What is it amongst the terms in equation (5.6) that allows a *continuous* expansion of the money stock, as envisaged in the endogenous case? Since interest rates cannot be *continuously* rising (or falling) and since the reserve ratio (RR) has a lower bound of zero, clearly continuous expansion requires a continuous expansion of the base. And indeed the fact that reserves can always be found somehow is universally recognized in the endogeneity literature as we saw in Section 5.3. From equation (5.6), therefore, it is clear that an expansion of the money stock accompanied by an expansion of the base requires a *shift* in the conventional stock curve. This is just another way of bringing us to the conclusion that we reached earlier in this section, in our discussion of elasticities. We have either to assume an infinite elasticity condition with respect to r_b for the banks' reserve ratio or public's cash ratio (the interest-endogeneity case that we ruled out as totally implausible) or we must assume the same elasticity condition with respect to the base. This indeed is what the endogeneity literature overwhelmingly does. But this condition, continuous changes in the base, *requires a continuous shift* of the money supply curve, not a rotation through (slightly less than) 90 degrees.

What is referred to as a horizontal money supply curve can now be seen for what it is if taken literally – a *locus* of the intersections of an expanding demand for money with a money stock increasing at a rate driven by the demand for credit. (Notice that even then horizontality is at best a stylized fact, since it has the wrong interest rate on the vertical axis.) There seems no reason to suppose that the rate of expansion of both demand and supply should be continuously equal in the short run. It seems reasonable to argue that disparities will result in changes in interest rates, including the non-money rate, r_b, (or differential, $r_b - r_m$) which is on the vertical axis. For simplicity, the credit-driven supply and the demand for the resulting deposits are assumed to grow at the same rate in Figure 5.4, and there is no change in the r_b or $(r_b - r_m)$ rate on the vertical axis, but this need not be the case. In these conditions, we have a horizontal trace but it is not a money supply curve and we have r_b and not r_d on the vertical axis. The first and last sentences of the following quotation capture the situation rather well:

> The use of the term horizontalism is a second-best solution. We reject the use of supply and demand, for money or for credit. As a graphical representation, it is limited for two important reasons. First, one can never really distinguish between supply and demand. Second. such a graphical analysis is appropriate to study stocks, whereas the relevant aspect of money is how it flows responding to the needs of trade. While rejecting the use of the graph, however, we still like the expression since it does conjure up immediately the divergence between the exogenous and endogenous money approaches. (Rochon and Vernengo, 2000, p. 9)

More briefly: in an endogenous money regime, the money supply may behave as if there were a horizontal money supply curve. We turn now to the question of what is happening to the demand for money, while the demand for credit is causing changes in the supply.

5.8.   THE DEMAND FOR ENDOGENOUS MONEY

In the last section we argued that a more satisfactory alternative to the 'vertical' supply curve of exogenous money, is a money supply curve which shifts continually to the right, and not a 'horizontal' one drawn in the same interest-money space. As we have just seen, this highlights the issue (which also confronts the HMSC, and indeed any analysis of money supply determination which focuses upon the flow of funds[16]) of the behaviour of the demand for money – the shifting supply curve must be accompanied by a shifting demand curve. In fact, it raises the question of what it is that co-ordinates the growing supply of deposits (resulting from the demand for net new loans) with the willingness to hold the expanding stock of deposits which is being created. This question has exercised a number of scholars in the endogeneity tradition (Arestis and Howells, 1996; Chick, 1986: Palley, 1991, p. 397, 1994; Moore, 1991b, 1997; Goodhart, 1989b, 1991; Kaldor and Trevithick, 1981; Howells, 1995, 1997) though some have found it more troublesome than others. The origin of the problem lies in the fact that the demand for loans and the demand for the resulting deposits involves different groups of people with different motives. The demand for the loans which create the deposits has its origins in the desire of deficit units to spend in excess of income. It is an income–expenditure decision. Furthermore, it is a decision made by a subset of the community since not everyone is involved in increasing their indebtedness to banks. (Indeed, it is not even the case that everyone holds (a stock of) bank debt. We return to this point later.) By contrast, the decision to hold the newly-created deposits is a portfolio decision and those involved are 'the community as whole'. Put like this, it would seem an extraordinary coincidence if the *ex ante* preferences of deficit units for more bank debt matched the *ex ante* preferences of the whole community to hold the resulting additional deposits with the precision and continuity required to maintain banks' balance sheet identity.

Let us not overstate the scale of the problem. Many of the factors which make the net expansion of bank credit the normal state of affairs, are also responsible for increases in the demand for money. To understand this, and to get a better grasp of the problem as well, it is useful to consider a sequence. Let us assume that a firm increases its bank borrowing. There must, obviously, be some reason for this and, if we assume that interest relativities (the relative prices of credit) are given, then it is reasonable to suppose that the extra credit is required to finance an increase in nominal output. Nominal GDP and bank credit have increased and so too, *usefully*, has the money supply. However, the money supply has expanded one-for-one with output and, velocity being greater than one, this is more than is required. All is not lost, however, this increase in nominal spending by our firm will facilitate increased spending by others, through the familiar multiplier process. But there is nothing to guarantee that multiplier-induced expansions of income will occur in a magnitude and in such a space of time as to make the increase in the demand for money match the increase in the loan-generated supply. Remember, too, that this example abstracts from the some institutional complexities. Bank lending to firms may increase only because banks buy existing debt. Firms (and households) might spend the loans on the purchase of financial assets – giving rise to capital gains rather than to multiplier-assisted increases in income (Chick, 1992, p. 110). Clearly, the path of income changes following an expansion of lending is very uncertain.

The best we can say is that lending (money supply) and the demand for money will *tend* in the same direction. The bank lending and money supply functions will both contain income, price and interest rate variables. But it is most unlikely that both sets of variables will be identical ('animal spirits' appearing in the loan demand function but not in the demand for money?) and quite implausible that the common terms will appear with the same coefficients. In the long run, the demand for credit and the demand for money will assuredly move in the same direction. But the fact remains that so long as we are dealing with two groups of agents, with differing motives, an *ex ante* coincidence of preferences is quite implausible. The question, then, is how are these *ex ante* preferences to be reconciled, *ex post*?

There are several possible responses to our question.[17] The first two, neither of which are seriously promoted by post-Keynesian economists involve an appeal to buffer stock notions of the demand for money and to the liquidity trap. In the latter, the demand for money is infinitely elastic and interest rates are very low. Consequently, with expectations that the next movement in rates must be upward, wealthholders fear a capital loss would result from holding non-money assets. But the mere possibility of liquidity trap conditions is insufficient for our purpose. We want to know how it is that the demand for deposits adjusts *continually* to the loan-induced supply. And there is no serious suggestion in any money demand literature that the liquidity trap is a permanent and universal phenomenon.[18] In the buffer stock case, the demand for money is infinitely elastic but only over a range. Wealthholders do not continually adjust their money holdings but do so only when such balances reach upper or lower limits (Laidler, 1984). When those limits are reached, our question reappears.

Another possibility appears in Kaldor and Trevithick's 1981 paper. Their main target was the naive monetarism of the first UK Thatcher government. Their interest in the supply of money, therefore, was to show that it could never be in excess supply in a way that threatened the stability of the price level. After all, if it were possible for the demand for credit to result in a stream of new deposits which were in some sense 'excessive' in relation to demand. then this opened the troublesome possibility that the desire to run down these deposits would result in an increased demand for goods and services and the whole monetarist sequence could re-emerge. Thus the purpose was an attack on the Quantity Theory and all its works rather than a thorough discussion of the dilemma we have posed here. The mechanism that they envisaged for the reconciliation of deposit creation with money demand was the *automatic* application of excess receipts of money to the repayment of overdrafts. Thus, the individual actions of borrowers taking out new loans (or extending existing ones) could threaten an 'excess' creation of deposits *ex ante*, but the actions of other (existing) borrowers in repaying some of their debt would mean that the net deposits which resulted *ex post* would be only what people wished to hold.

'Automatically' is the keyword. It is a reasonable assumption that those with overdrafts who have receipts in excess of payments will use the excess to reduce their debt and this will ('automatically') reduce the quantity of new deposits that are actually created. The problem is not everyone has an overdraft, an observation made by Cottrell (1986) and by Chick (1992, p. 205). And it is not sufficient to argue that some people somewhere (for example virtually all firms) do have overdrafts. Once it is accepted that the first round recipients of 'new' money may not wish to hold it, then the genie threatens to leave the bottle. The question remains: how are the 'excess' balances to be disposed of?

The most dramatic response is probably Moore's concept of 'convenience lending'. In so far as it involves the rejection of an equilibrium demand for money it has echoes of the buffer-stock notion, though we shall see that it is more far-reaching in denying the existence of even outer limits to desired money balances.

The basis for this rejection of an independent money demand curve lies in the rejection of the idea of equilibrium in general. 'In the real world there is *no* unique "general equilibrium position" toward which the economy is tending' (Moore, 1991, p. 128). Moore's argument is that since there *is* money, there must be uncertainty; if there is uncertainty, then there is no general equilibrium; if there is no general equilibrium '*there is no meaning to the notion of an "ultimate equilibrium" stock of money demanded*' (Moore, 1991, p. 130, emphasis in the original). In the context of monetary theory, this is a far-reaching as well as an extreme position (though not necessarily an isolated one – see the quotation from Rochon and Vernengo, above). If there is no demand curve, there can be no 'excess' supply. Changes in the (credit-driven) quantity of money are limited to financing the additional demand which gave rise to the loans and have no further impacts on demand, output or prices.[19]

But does the rejection of *general* equilibrium, a proposition, it might be added, which would attract much support in post-Keynesian circles, really solve the problem of how the quantity of loan-created deposits just matches the change in the demand for money? There are certainly two problems with the argument as advanced by Moore.

First, there is a question mark over the meaning that Moore seems to attach to the 'demand for money'. For Moore, the ready (and limitless) acceptance of money appears to rely heavily upon money's acceptability in exchange. 'I cannot agree . . . with Goodhart's central criticism, that the *acceptance* of money in exchange does not supplant the *underlying demand relationship*' (Moore, 1991, p. 127, emphasis in the original). But the fact that money is always acceptable as a means of payment is not, surely, saying a great deal. When buyers buy goods or services (or even financial assets) with the proceeds of a loan, sellers readily accept the deposits because deposits are generally acceptable. That is not in dispute. As Palley and

Chick put it the question is what happens *after* it has been accepted. Identifying 'acceptability in exchange' with the 'demand for money' is surely introducing a novel meaning for the latter as Goodhart points out in the extract below.

The extract raises a second question. This is whether the rejection of 'general equilibrium' entails rejecting all idea that people have preferences to which they will seek to give expression. Moore's contention had been that Goodhart would hardly refuse a gift from his aunt and since he would not refuse it then he must have a demand for it.

> Moore is, of course, absolutely correct that I will *accept* $10,000 . . . but I do not necessarily want to *hold* that sum as a money balance indefinitely. Given the *existing* pattern of expectations, prices, my wealth (now happily increased by $10,000), I do have an underlying *partial* equilibrium demand for money balances that does differ from the amount with which I have just been supplied, and that difference will cause me to rearrange my whole portfolio. (Goodhart, 1991, pp. 134–5, original emphases)

It is easy to think of variations on this theme. We would not expect, for example, that traders who find business better than they originally expected at the beginning of the week start to refuse deposits for payment on Thursday say, because their money balances were bigger than they desired. It is at the end of the week that the 'demand for money' becomes relevant. It is the demand for money which determines whether the unplanned additions to deposits continue to be held (as they might be in a buffer stock scenario) or whether, unless other variables change, decisions are made to switch out of money and into other assets until the unplanned level of money balances reaches its original planned proportion of the portfolio.

Clearly, the idea that people have a perfectly elastic demand for any good is something of a novelty. To make such behaviour plausible, Moore describes the action of sellers who passively accumulate the 'new' deposits created by lending, as 'convenience lending'. The idea is that all the deposits are held (for reasons we shall see in a moment) as a matter of 'convenience' because no special inducement is required to get people to accept them in exchange. Acquiring them involves no sacrifice. No consumption is deferred and no liquidity is surrendered. The new deposits act like a windfall. The 'lending' refers to the status of deposits as loans to the bank.

But it is difficult to see how the fact that people receive 'windfalls' entails no *subsequent* effect on behaviour. The fact that something is acquired in greater quantity than was planned is surely likely to induce a reaction, regardless of whether or not effort was exerted in its acquisition. It still seems implausible that the unsolicited deposits will not at some point be exchanged for some other form of wealth. Indeed, Moore concedes, and this is significant in the light of what is to follow, that *individuals* may hold these deposits only for so long as it takes them to decide on future consumption and investment patterns but then crucially he says 'For the economy as a whole . . . such [convenience] lending is long term' (Moore, 1988b, p. 298). By this, of course, Moore means that *individuals* may decide periodically to sweep their growing deposits into higher earning non-bank liabilities but this only shuffles the ownership of the deposits, it does not change the quantity. (As we accepted in the last paragraph, the newly-created deposits *are* held.) Only actions which cause *repayment* of loans cause a reduction in deposits.

There are echoes of Kaldor and Trevithick in the last sentence, but what goes before is more significant. First, it is incontestable that individuals trading money balances has no effect on the aggregate unless loans are repaid or net payments are made to the public sector. *However*, the trading may very well affect other variables as Moore seems to recognize.

Consider now the following passage:

> Suppose all wealthholders were to . . . have their transactions balances swept into higher-interest-earning, nonbank liabilities. The issuers of these liabilities would then find themselves with higher money balances, and the distribution of deposit ownership would change. *But so long as these economic units did not use their sweeping proceeds in turn to repay bank loans, or turn them in for cash, there would be no change in the total quantity of deposits.* (Moore, 1991, p. 130, emphasis added)

All of this seems to us only to be restating in a rather cumbersome way, a standard textbook account of money market equilibrium. (Usually illustrated in such books by the use of a vertical (exogenous) money supply curve.) The argument above, and in such texts, is that an increase in the quantity of money must be held. Individuals may endeavour to run down excess money balances but this only shuffles the ownership. In the aggregate the new money stays held in customers' bank accounts. We can call this convenience lending if we so choose. But the crucial point in such textbook accounts is that something (quite important) has happened as a byproduct of these individual efforts to reduce money holdings. In the reshuffling process something has been bought. In a Keynesian world, it is predominantly financial assets whose prices rise and whose yields fall. In other traditions, it may be goods and services with consequences for output and possibly prices.

This suggests a rather obvious mechanism whereby the loan-induced supply of deposits is reconciled with the demand for them. Let us continue with the case where loan demand (perhaps because of 'animal spirits') creates new deposits in excess of those demanded in present circumstances. Agents, individually, attempt to run down deposits by buying assets. Collectively, this is self-defeating – causing only a redistribution of deposits. However, the redistribution is accompanied by a rise in asset prices and a fall in their yields. Crucially, as agents move their wealth into non-money assets, yields on these latter must fall relative to rates *on bank lending* and relative to the rate *paid on deposits*. The change in this second relative rate is the well-known mechanism traditionally cited in the textbook account of how changes in money supply are reconciled with demand. Its effect is relevant here, in so far as a fall in the rate on non-money assets moves us down the money demand curve and yields a one-off increase in the demand for our excessively growing deposits. It is the first differential though that is crucial here, however, since it acts upon continuing flows. Non-money assets are the liabilities of non-banks. They are liabilities issued by non-banks as a means of raising funds. To a large extent, therefore, they are substitutes for bank loans. As the rates on corporate bonds and short-term paper (for example) fall relative to the rate charged on bank lending so there is a fall in the price at which the economic units whose liabilities these are can raise new funds. If the yield on existing corporate bonds falls, new bonds can be issued with these lower yields and bond finance becomes cheaper, at the margin at least, relative to bank finance. With the cheapening of a partial substitute for bank finance, the demand curve for bank lending shifts inward. It is this change in relative interest rates that brings the *ex post* demand for bank lending (and the ongoing *flow* of new deposits) into line with the community's increasing demand for money.

5.9. CONCLUSION

The core of the endogeneity thesis is that the money supply is determined by banks' quantity-taking behaviour in the market for loans and this, in turn, is determined by the 'state of trade'. One might add, given the confusion which has arisen at various points over stocks and flows that it *should* also be central to the endogeneity argument that expansion of the money stock is the norm and that the focus of attention should be upon *flows*. The direction of causality, from lending to money and reserves, has some empirical support (from the US) and in the UK is so widely recognized, by banking practitioners and by the customary 'flow of funds' analysis of the money supply, as to be almost taken for granted. Nonetheless, there is scope for further confirmation, in other regimes, and one particularly interesting line of enquiry would be to test for endogeneity across monetary regimes at different stages of evolution. This would shed further light on the causes of endogeneity and would offer an oblique empirical test of the 'stages of banking' thesis.

Beyond this widespread agreement that the demand for bank lending is the key to money creation, there lies much controversy. There is disagreement over the passivity with which banks respond to the demand for loans and the passivity (or otherwise) with which central banks supply reserves. Both of these have become connected with what is probably a misguided discussion about whether the money supply curve is truly horizontal. The question of how banks respond to demand, in their mark-up policy for example, is both interesting and important but it needs to be separated from arguments about the shape of any alleged money supply curve. This is also an area in which there is much potential for empirical work. The difficulty will be obtaining appropriate data on bank lending rates.

The other major issue is the reconciliation of the supply of loan-created deposits with the demand for money. This too is an obvious area for further empirical work. In principle, it should not be difficult to establish or reject a role for relative interest rates. In practice, this too will be hampered by the paucity of data on lending rates. If indeed there is widespread agreement on the importance of bank lending, and this extends beyond the theme of endogeneity, then a case could be made for a research project devoted to improving our knowledge and understanding of bank lending rates.

NOTES

1. The author is grateful to Philip Arestis and Malcolm Sawyer for comments and advice in the preparation of this chapter, and to colleagues, most of whom are mentioned in the references, for their contribution to the ideas and arguments expressed here, whether they agree with them or not. Errors and omissions are his own responsibility.
2. For a survey of post-Keynesian monetary theory as a whole see Arestis (1992) and Cottrell (1994).
3. It may be the scale of the stakes that is responsible for the crusading tone of Basil Moore's *Horizontalists and Verticalists* (1988a). It is certainly present in Lavoie's (1994, p. 2) insistence that post-Keynesians must never contemplate the slightest upward-slope to the money supply curve on the grounds that this reprieves the IS/LM model.
4. In Section 5.7 we shall suggest that this enthusiasm has led to number of errors of exposition. Furthermore, while trying to carry through the contrast to the shape of the supply curve may look like a dramatic way of stating the differences between endogenous and exogenous money regimes, it actually leads to an understatement of the fundamental differences of the two approaches.
5. 'M4 private sector' (or sometimes M4PS) denotes the 'non-bank non-building society private sector'. This clumsy expression reflects the extension that was necessary to the earlier and more familiar 'non-bank private sector' when the UK broad money aggregate switched from M3 to M4 in 1989 and incorporated building society deposits. The underlying idea fortunately remains simple. Money is defined as a specific set of assets held by the general public. 'General public' excludes the public sector and also those institutions whose liabilities these assets are.
6. An increase in the number of cash machines helping agents to economise on holdings of

cash, for example, a trend which could be reversed by banks charging for their use – a possible development given much attention in the early months of 2000.

7. 'Regulation Q' had its origin in the bank crashes of the US great depression where competitive payment of interest on deposits had been blamed for alleged weaknesses in the US banking structure. It imposed zero interest rates on checking deposits and gave the Fed power to set ceilings for rates on time and savings deposits. As a general rule, the ceilings rose with the term to maturity, banks thus having more freedom to set rates on longer-term deposits. The illiquidity of such deposits, however, made them unattractive to depositors until banks began the practice of issuing certificates (of ownership) of such deposits and a market developed for the trading of those certificates. With an active market for CDs, depositors could have the advantage of the higher interest rate on a longer-term time deposit with the knowledge that they could raise cash instantly if necessary. Banks had the advantage that this attraction enabled them to pay slightly lower rates on a deposit with certificate than on a corresponding time deposit with no certificate.

8. Such episodes provide example of the 'inflation bias' in policy making which has led some economists to argue for greater independence for central banks in recent years (see for example King, 1995).

9. Notice that this discussion assumes either that Central Banks are non-independent (of government) or that they themselves have multiple objectives which include full employment and/or growth. The former assumption would cover the position of the Bank of England, at least until 1997 while the latter assumption is relevant in the cases of the US Federal Reserve and the Bank of Canada.

10. Or, indeed, from a tightening of monetary policy itself. Assume that this leads to a rise in price, increase in collateral requirements, and reduction in supply of credit from non-bank sources. The inevitable consequence will be a jump in overdraft utilization and the liquidity problems described here unless the Central Bank relieves the shortage.

11. This illustration also draws attention to an asymmetry in the loan/deposit creation process. Central Banks can initiate a monetary expansion, through open market operations and expansion of the base; they cannot (at tolerable cost) initiate a reduction by reversing the process (see Moore, 1986, 1988b).

12. Supporters of the accommodationist approach include Minsky (1982, 1986), Rousseas (1986), Pollin (1991) and Dow (1993, 1994). Niggle (1991) points out that the degree of accommodation (and the possibilities for reserve-economizing innovation) will depend upon institutional features of the regime.

13. Though it should be acknowledged that the discussion throughout the text is aimed at the credit supply curve and in all the figures in the paper the supply curve is consistently identified as a *credit* supply curve.

14. This argument was first advanced in Arestis and Howells (1996).

15. At the very least this would require that the term structure be invariant over time.

16. See for example Cuthbertson, 1985, p. 173.

17. A longer list and more detailed examination of possible responses is in Howells (1995).

18. Readers who find the idea of the demand for money being permanently infinitely elastic mildly amusing, should remember that just these conditions are implied by Basil Moore's 'convenience lending' mechanism which we examine in a moment.

19. Implicit in this particular claim is the assumption either that velocity is one, or that multiplier changes in income always act in such a way as to maintain velocity at its greater than one level. See Chick's observation earlier in this section.

REFERENCES

Anderson, R.G. (1993), 'The effect of mortgage refinancing on money demand and the monetary aggregates', *Federal Reserve Bank of St Louis Review*, **75** (4), 49–63.

Arestis, P. (1992), *The Post Keynesian Approach to Economics*, Aldershot: Edward Elgar.

Arestis, P. and Eichner, A.S. (1988), 'The Post Keynesian and Institutionalist Theory of Money and Credit', *Journal of Economic Issues*, **22**, 1003–22.

Arestis, P. and Howells, P.G.A. (1996), 'Theoretical issues in endogenous money: the problem with "Convenience Lending"', *Cambridge Journal of Economics*, **20** (5), 539–51.

Chick, V. (1986), 'The evolution of the banking system and the theory of saving, investment and interest', *Économies et Sociétés* (Série M P no.3).

Chick, V. (1992), 'Keynesians, Monetarists and Keynes', in P. Arestis and S.C. Dow (eds), *On Money, Method and Keynes: Selected Essays*, London: Macmillan.

Chick, V. (1993), 'The Evolution of the Banking System and the Theory of Monetary Policy', in S.F. Frowen (ed.), *Monetary Theory and Monetary Policy: New Trends for the 1990s*, London: Macmillan.

Cottrell, A. (1986), 'The Endogeneity of Money and Money-Income Causality', *Scottish Journal of Political Economy*, **33** (1), 2–27.

Cottrell, A. (1994), 'Post-Keynesian monetary economics', *Cambridge Journal of Economics*, **18** (6), 587–606.

Cuthbertson, K. (1985), *The Supply and Demand for Money*, Oxford: Blackwell.

Davidson, P. (1972), *Money and the Real World*, London: Macmillan.

Davidson, P. (1988), 'Endogenous money, the production process and inflation analysis', *Economie Appliquée*, **XLI** (1), 151–69.

Davidson, P. and Weintraub, S. (1973), 'Money as cause and effect', *Economic Journal*, **83** (332), 1117–32.

Dow, S.C. (1993), *Money and the Economic Process*, Aldershot: Edward Elgar

Dow S.C. (1996), 'Horizontalism: a critique', *Cambridge Journal of Economics,* **20** (4), 497–508.

Dow, S.C. and Earl, P. (1982), *Money Matters*, Oxford: Martin Robertson.

Earley, J. and Evans, G. (1982), 'The problem is bank liability management', *Challenge*, Jan/Feb, 54–6.

Goodhart,C.A.E (1984), *The Theory and Practice of Money*, London: Macmillan.

Goodhart, C.A.E. (1989a), 'The conduct of monetary policy', *Economic Journal*, **99**, June, 293–346

Goodhart, C.A.E. (1989b), 'Has Moore become too horizontal?', *Journal of Post Keynesian Economics*, **12** (1), 29–34.

Goodhart, C.A.E. (1991), 'Is the concept of an equilibrium demand for money meaningful?', *Journal of Post Keynesian Economics*, **14** (1), 134–6.

Goodhart, C.A.E. (1994), 'What should central banks do? What should be their macroeconomic objectives and operations?', *Economic Journal*, **104**, 1424–236.

Hicks, J.R. (1967), *Critical Essays in Monetary Theory*, Oxford: Oxford University Press.

Howells, P.G.A. (1995), 'The demand for endogenous money', *Journal of Post Keynesian Economics*, **18** (1), Fall, 89–106.

Howells, P.G.A. (1997), 'The demand for endogenous money: a rejoinder', *Journal of Post Keynesian Economics*, **19** (3), 429–34.

Howells, P.G.A. and Hussein, K.A. (1997), 'The demand for money in the UK: transactions as the scale variable', *Economics Letters*, **55**, 371–7.

Howells, P.G.A. and Hussein, K.A. (1999), 'The demand for bank loans and the "state of trade"', *Journal of Post Keynesian Economics*, **21** (3), 441–54.

Isenberg, D.L. (1988), 'Is there a case for Minsky's financial fragility hypothesis in the 1920's?', *Journal of Economic Issues*, **22** (4), 1045–69.

Kaldor, N. (1970), 'The new monetarism', *Lloyds Bank Review*, July, 1–18.

Kaldor, N. (1982), *The Scourge of Monetarism*, Oxford: Oxford University Press.

Kaldor, N. (1983), 'Keynesian Economics after Fifty Years', in D. Worswick and J. Trevithick (eds), *Keynes and the Modern World*, Cambridge: Cambridge University Press.

Kaldor, N. (1985), 'How monetarism failed', *Challenge*, **28** (2), 4–13.

Kaldor, N. and Trevithick, J. (1981), 'A Keynesian perspective on money', *Lloyds Bank Review*, January.

King, M. (1994), 'The transmission mechanism of monetary policy', *Bank of England Quarterly Bulletin*, August, 261–7.

King, M. (1995), 'Credibility and monetary policy: theory and evidence', *Scottish Journal of Political Economy*, **42** (1), 1–19.

Laidler, D. (1984), 'The buffer stock notion in monetary economics', *Conference Proceedings: Supplement to the Economic Journal*, **94**, 17–34.

Lavoie, M. (1984), 'The endogenous credit flow and the Post Keynesian theory of money', *Journal of Economic Issues*, **16** (3), 771–97.

Lavoie, M. (1985), 'Credit and Money: The Dynamic Circuit, Overdraft Economics and Post Keynesian Economics', in M. Jarsulic (ed.), *Money and Macro Policy*, Boston: Kluwer-Nijhoff.

Lavoie, M. (1994), 'Horizontalism, liquidity preference and the principle of increasing risk', University of Ottawa, mimeo.

Minsky, H.P. (1975), *John Maynard Keynes*, New York: Columbia University Press.

Minsky, H.P. (1982), *Can it Happen Again? Essays on Instability and Finance*, Armonk NY: M. E. Sharpe.

Minsky, H. (1986), *Stabilizing an Unstable Economy*, New Haven, CT: Yale University Press.

Moore, B.J. (1979), 'The endogenous money stock', *Journal of Keynesian Economics*, **2** (1), 49–70.

Moore, B.J. (1985a), 'Wages, Bank Lending and the Endogeneity of Credit Money', in M. Jarsulic (ed.), *Money and Macro Policy*, Boston: Kluwer-Nijhoff.

Moore, B.J. (1985b), 'Contemporaneous reserve accounting: can reserves be quantity constrained?', *Journal of Post Keynesian Economics*, **7** (1).

Moore, B.J. (1986), 'How credit drives the money supply: the significance of institutional developments', *Journal of Economic Issues*, **XX** (2) 443–52.

Moore, B.J. (1988a), *Horizontalists and Verticalists*, Cambridge: Cambridge University Press.

Moore, B.J. (1988b), 'The endogenous money supply', *Journal of Post Keynesian Economics*, **X** (3), 372–85.

Moore, B,J, (1988c), 'The endogeneity of money: A comment', *Scottish Journal of Political Economy*, **35** (3), 291–4.

Moore, B.J. (1989), 'A simple model of bank intermediation', *Journal of Post Keynesian Economics*, **12** (1).

Moore, B.J. (1991), 'Money supply endogeneity', *Journal of Post Keynesian Economics,* **13** (3), 404–13.

Moore, B.J. (1991b), 'Has the demand for money been mislaid?', *Journal of Post Keynesian Economics*, **14** (1), 125–33.

Moore, B.J. (1994), 'The demise of the Keynesian multiplier: a reply to Cottrell', *Journal of Post Keynesian Economics*, **17** (1), 121–33.

Moore, B.J. (1997), 'Reconciliation of the supply and demand for endogenous money', *Journal of Post Keynesian Economics*, **19** (3), 423–35.
Moore, B.J. and Threadgold, A.R. (1985), 'Corporate bank borrowing in the UK, 1965–81', *Economica*, **52**, 65–78.
Myrdal, G. (1939), *Monetary Equilibrium*, London: William Hodge and Co.
Niggle, C.J. (1990), 'The evolution of money, financial institutions, and monetary economics', *Journal of Economic Issues*, **XXIV**, 443–50.
Niggle, C.J. (1991), 'The endogenous money supply theory: an institutionalist appraisal', *Journal of Economic Issues*, **25**(1), 137–51.
Palley, T. (1991), 'The endogenous money supply: consensus and disagreement', *Journal of Post Keynesian Economics*, **13** (3), 397–403.
Palley, T.I. (1994), 'Competing views of the money supply process: theory and evidence', *Metroeconomica*, **45** (1), 67–88.
Palley, T.I. (1995), 'The demand for money and non-GDP transactions', *Economics Letters*, **48**, 145–54.
Pollin, R. (1991), 'Two theories of money supply endogeneity: some empirical evidence', *Journal of Post Keynesian Economics*, **13** (3), 366–96.
Pollin, R. and Schaberg, M. (1998), 'Asset exchanges, financial market trading and the M1 income velocity puzzle', *Journal of Post Keynesian Economies*, **21** (1), 135–62.
Rochon, P. and Vernengo, M. (2000), *Credit, Interest Rates and the Open Economy: Essays on Horizontalism*, Cheltenham: Edward Elgar.
Rousseas, S. (1986), *Post Keynesian Monetary Economics*, London: Macmillan.
Seccareccia, M. (1988), 'Systemic viability and credit crunches – an examination of recent Canadian cyclical fluctuations', *Journal of Economic Issues*, **22** (1), 49–77.
Sims, S.A. (1972), 'Money, income and causality', *American Economic Review*, **63** (2), 540–52.
Weintraub, S. (1978), *Keynes, Keynesians and Monetarists*, Philadelphia: University of Philadelphia Press.
Wray, L.R. (1990), *Money and Credit in Capitalist Economies*, Aldershot: Edward Elgar.

6. Political economy of central banks: agents of stability or sources of instability?

Costas Lapavitsas

6.1. INTRODUCTION

Central banks have long been the object of the reformist zeal of credit practitioners and political radicals. They have also been subjected to withering criticism by those who think that instability in capitalist economies either originates in money and finance, or that it is exacerbated by the operations of central banks. In recent years there has been a proliferation of theoretical and empirical interest in central bank independence. This work has contributed, even if partially, to an actual trend toward greater independence for central banks. Similarly, free banking arguments, advocating the abolition of central banks and the instigation of freely issued bank money with a view to eradicating financial and monetary instability, have also become increasingly prominent.

It is claimed in this chapter that the recent theoretical emphasis on the role of the central bank in the financial system significantly overstates its significance. There are narrow limits to the effectiveness of central bank financial and monetary operations, determined by the demands and requirements of capitalist accumulation. That is not to deny that conscious policymaking by central banks can be partially successful in its aims. However, the tendency to financial and other instability, which is characteristic of capitalist economies, cannot be abolished by central banking, regardless of the experience of the central bankers and the erudition of their economic advisers. In this light, though in different ways, both the theory of central bank independence and that of free banking are misplaced.

Section 6.2 analyses the central bank as an economic institution by utilizing insights from Marxist political economy and concentrating on its functions as bank of banks, bank of the state, and holder of the reserve of a nation's international money. Section 6.3 considers the analytical issues posed by the central bank's activities in operating monetary policy, overseeing the credit system and acting as lender of last resort. Both sections 6.2 and 6.3 pay attention to the historical development of central banks (particularly the Bank of England), and examine closely the links between logical and historical analysis of central banking. On this basis, Sections 6.4 and 6.5 turn to recent theories of central bank reform and advance, respectively, critiques of central bank independence and free banking.

6.2.   WHAT IS A CENTRAL BANK?

6.2.1.   Bank of Banks

The character and role of the central bank are inseparable from the structure of the credit system of a capitalist economy. The view adopted in this chapter is that the capitalist credit system has a pyramid-like structure comprising (in three successive layers and from the top downwards): money market relations, individual bank credit relations, and spontaneously emerging inter-firm commercial credit relations (Itoh and Lapavitsas, 1999, ch. 4). The pyramid of the credit system rests upon relations of capitalist accumulation undertaken by industrial and commercial capitals.

Banks that have regular and easy access to the money market can raise their efficiency and flexibility in handling credit transactions and settling payments among themselves by depositing a part of their reserves with a single bank, subsequently using its liabilities (originally its bank notes) for payments. The economies and elasticities arising from this practice are analogous to those that emerge when individual industrial and commercial capitals choose to hold their reserves with a local bank. A central bank emerges spontaneously through the actions of money market banks. It emerges as a private bank with a definite and limited capital size; it fulfils the function of holding the central reserve of the banking system; it can also fail or be replaced by another bank. The pyramid of the capitalist credit system is complete when the central bank emerges at its apex.

It is important to note in this connection that the liabilities of an emergent central bank are typically used as means of settlement among banks in the money market but also in large-scale commercial transactions. Its banknote liabilities are, from very early on, 'the coin of wholesale trade' (Marx, [1894] 1981, p. 529), and their use naturally spreads to commercial and credit transactions between and within local areas closely related to the commercial centre in which the central bank is usually based. The interpenetrating of commercial and credit transactions that are completed with central bank liabilities sustains (both logically and historically) the role of these liabilities as national money. However, as long as the central bank remains a private bank with limited capital and circumscribed business activities, central bank liabilities (particularly its bank notes) are unlikely to become a country's generally used money. At the very least, issuing and handling bank notes of small face value is unlikely to be as profitable for the bank of banks as similar operations with large notes undertaken among banks.

Consequently, and as the pattern of historical development is broadly confirmed by the spontaneous emergence of a central bank as the apex of the credit system leaves considerable room for continued use of commodity money. Historically, activities such as the payment of wages and the settlement of commercial and credit transactions between geographical areas relatively remote from the central bank and the money market persist in the use of commodity money. In these geographical areas, local banks that issue their own banknotes can continue to function as efficient providers of banking credit to capitalist accumulation. As long as the state does not consciously ban the use of commodity money, the latter retains its importance in a capitalist economy (both domestically and internationally), alongside credit money issued by private banks and the central bank.[1] It follows from the persistence of commodity money in domestic transactions (and more so in international ones) that the reserves of a spontaneously emerging central bank largely comprise commodity money: they become the central commodity money (gold) hoard of a capitalist economy.

The gradual exclusion of commodity money (gold) from international payments among capitalist countries during the twentieth century has significantly changed the functions of the central bank and of its bank notes, as will be discussed in more detail below. World War I was an obvious threshold, past which the political decision to spare gold money in domestic and international transactions signalled the strengthening of the regulatory role of the state in the capitalist economy. However, to minimize the risk of theoretical confusion, the fundamental principles of the operations of central banks are best derived by first abstracting from the conscious intervention of the state in the sphere of money and finance. For this reason, much of our subsequent analysis is undertaken on the assumption that commodity money is used concurrently with credit money (convertible into each other) as means of circulation, payment and bank reserve element. The implications of the abolition of the monetary role of commodity money (and the emergence of inconvertible credit money) will be briefly considered subsequently.

Thus, in its most elementary function, a central bank is a bank of banks, as manifested by its holding of a centralized reserve for the banking system as a whole. Given the existence of a centralized reserve, individual banks can systematically turn their own reserves from accumulations of commodity money into accumulations of claims on others (above all, on the central bank). This process, however, cannot become complete as long as commodity money continues to be in use: individual banks must hold some quantity of gold in reserve to meet local and immediate requirements. Nevertheless, if convertibility into gold prevails, it is evidently cheaper for banks to hold central bank liabilities, other things equal. It is thus possible for the largest part of a country's hoarded monetary gold to become the reserve of the central bank, access to it being provided by the liabilities of the central bank. Analogously, it is possible for the gold hoard of the central bank slowly to assume a national character, to become the national hoard of a capitalist economy.[2]

Given that it possesses the centralized banking reserve, the relationship maintained by the central bank between its own liabilities and reserves is of critical importance for the operations of the banking system as a whole. Broadly speaking, the reserve requirements of individual banks are determined empirically and have an elastic relationship with the banks' lending operations (Itoh and Lapavitsas, 1999, ch. 4). Insofar as ordinary bank reserves are claims on the central bank's gold hoard (that is, they are liabilities of the central bank), the size of the central bank's reserve inevitably exercises a significant influence on the ability of individual banks to secure reserves and so expand their lending business. Concern about the size of its gold reserve, on the other hand, constrains the ability of the central bank to provide its own liabilities to individual banks. By the same token, it also constrains the ability of the private banks to provide their own liabilities to industrial and commercial capitalists.

Historical evidence that the relationship between reserves and liabilities begins spontaneously to influence the central bank's operations is provided by the so-called Palmer rule, which guided the Bank of England already by the early 1830s.[3] This rule required that the Bank should keep no more than two-thirds of its assets in the form of securities (the last third taken up by gold) against the whole of its liabilities (bank notes and deposits). As Clapham (1944, vol. II, p. 125) observed, in propounding this rule 'Palmer and Norman were describing the fair weather practice of a single decade, not promulgating a dogma'. The Palmer rule was the precursor of the much better-known Bank Act of 1844. This Act, however, removed whatever flexibility Palmer's rule possessed, and forced onto the Bank a rigid quantitative relationship between its gold hoard and its banknote liabilities.[4]

A closer look is necessary here at the relationship between the central bank's reserve of commodity money and the ability of individual banks to extend credit. The balance between the demand and supply of loanable money capital across the economy translates, in the final instance, into changes in the proportion between the gold reserve and the liabilities of the central bank.[5] More specifically, the flows of debt repayment, security purchases, loans, and new deposits, which take place between the banking system and capitalists involved in real accumulation, are ultimately reflected in the proportion of the central bank's gold reserve to its liabilities. Consequently, the central bank's gold reserve acts as both pivot and reflection of the movement of banking credit. This allows the price at which the central bank provides its own liabilities (mostly the rate of commercial bill rediscount and the rate of short-term lending to banks) to become the benchmark rate for the money market rate of interest.

There is no reason to expect a stable relationship between the total quantity of credit money created by ordinary banks and the liabilities of the central bank, regardless of whether the latter are convertible into gold or not. For the operations of the banks what matters is an empirically ascertained minimum below which their reserve ratios should preferably not fall. The actual levels of bank reserve ratios, meanwhile, vary with the stage of the business cycle; they further depend on the particular institutional arrangements of both the credit system and real accumulation. If, for example, new borrowing instruments make it easier for banks to borrow funds in the money market, bank reserve ratios are driven downwards. Put differently, insofar as a money multiplier exists, that is, an algebraic relationship between the total quantity of credit money and the reserves held by ordinary banks at the central bank, it is an unstable magnitude that depends on the phase of the business cycle and the particular institutional framework to hand.

Since they are the main means of access to the national gold hoard, the liabilities of the central bank can become the preeminent form of a country's credit money. To sustain the generation and flows of commercial credit among firms, and to facilitate the use of individual bank liabilities as credit money, a generalized system of clearing various credit claims against each other is essential. By settling claims against each other, banks can economize on their reserves, rely less on gold for payments, and secure a more rapid and smoother circulation of banknotes and deposits. The most important means of payment in the clearing process, hence the preeminent form of credit money, comprises the liabilities of the central bank. As has already been argued, however, for central bank liabilities (banknotes) to become legal tender, that is, a means of payment with obligatory acceptability, action is required on the part of the state. Naturally, the state confers its own legitimacy onto money that is already critically important for the operations of large-scale trade and the credit system. For complete disappearance of commodity money from advanced capitalist exchange, further emergency action by the state is required.[6]

6.2.2. Bank of the State

The thorny analytical problems of the nature of the state and its relationship to capitalist accumulation do not come within the ambit of this chapter. Suffice it simply to assume that, in advanced industrial capitalism, a national state necessarily emerges that taxes, spends, borrows and provides a national character to money. Unlike the feudal state, which could directly command labour and products, the bourgeois state uses money to employ people and generally perform its operations. Bourgeois state finance emerges slowly, with much trial and error, based on the following three prerequisites. First, a system of national taxation, applicable to both foreign trade and the annual revenue of the economy, incorporating direct and indirect taxes, operating with a degree of predictability and formed subject to the bourgeois democratic process. Second, systematic calculation in advance of state expenditure on salaries and wages, on the standing army, on the purchase of commodities, on subsidies to capitalists and on welfare transfer payments to certain sections of the community. Third, existence of a mechanism for bridging the gap between income and expenditure through borrowing.

Both the projected and the sudden and extraordinary borrowing needs of the state impinge upon the supply of loanable money capital. The state can borrow directly from the banks, and it can also seek recourse to the open market, thus creating the national debt. For one financial institution to assume a pivotal role in dealing with the borrowing needs of the state, two conditions are necessary: first, the existence of regular tax receipts and equally regular state expenditure;[7] second, sudden bursts of expenditure, typically induced by war. Although it is not inevitable, a bank with regular and easy access to the money market is favourably placed to become the manager of the borrowing needs of the state. The bank that possesses the main reserve of the banking system is best able to marshal the available credit in the money market and place it at the disposal of the state (as well as lend on its own account).

Central banking is from its inception connected with the financial needs of the bourgeois state, particularly in time of war. Lending directly to the state and managing the issuing of its short-term borrowing instruments in the money market are central banking functions on an equal footing with holding the aggregate reserve of the banking system. State debt provides depth and fluidity to the money market. Moreover, since the central bank manages the accounts of the state, collects tax receipts and disburses some expenditure, it has available to it temporarily idle money that belongs to the state. This allows the central bank more easily and flexibly to intervene in the money market. Consequently, the bank in charge of state finance is in a stronger position to dominate the money market and to lend directly to other banks. The national character of the central bank is further strengthened when the state proclaims its banknotes to be legal tender.

For the Bank of England (paradigmatic for central bank emergence), the connection with the state was more evident than its role as bank of banks during the first century of its existence. The Bank was formed by (mostly) London merchants in 1694 as a joint-stock company to provide the new king of England with war finance:

> The establishment of the Bank of England can be treated like many historical events both great and small, either as curiously accidental or as all but inevitable. Had the country not been at war in 1694, the government would hardly have been disposed to offer a favourable charter to a corporation which proposed to lend it money. (Clapham, 1944, I, p. 1)[8]

The Bank of England remained technically a private concern for two and a half centuries, and had substantial private banking interests until well into the nineteenth century. In the characteristic English manner in which institutions are never abolished but become something entirely different in the course of their existence, the Bank became the bank of banks as well as of the state through the gradual loss of some functions and the accretion of others.[9]

Its public character gives to the central bank a role and a position in the economic reproduction of society that can partially transcend the narrow confines of capitalist accumulation. Capitalist credit involves the formation of expectations about uncertain future returns and some attempt at rational analysis of economic decisions. For the central bank, these requirements apply at the aggregate level. To intervene centrally in the money market, the central bank must estimate the borrowing needs of the various market participants, as well as possess data on past behaviour, the performance of the market as a whole, and the operations of the financial institutions. The central bank must also form projections about the state's borrowing needs and pattern of debt repayment, in the context of the overall cyclical and secular movement of capitalist accumulation. The naturally pivotal role of the central bank in the supply of credit to real accumulation has historically engendered very diverse reactions. Social reformers have aimed at the transformation of capitalism through the operations of a nationalized central bank, while others concerned with economic instability have advocated the reform or even the abolition of central banks. In the rest of this chapter it is shown that the operations of central banks are severely limited by the anarchical nature of capitalist production and trade, though they can also enjoy a measure of success in influencing the direction and the pace of capitalist accumulation.

6.2.3. Holder of International Money

The bank of banks and bank of the state becomes a nation's central bank when it also emerges as the guardian of the nation's hoard of international money. The capitalist world market comprises units of capital that compete internationally in several commodity and financial markets, but within a system of national states. These states impose their own character on laws, tariffs, subsidies, work practices and money. A precondition for an individual capital to enter and compete in the world market is to have access to a hoard of internationally acceptable means of payment. Each national bourgeoisie seeks to secure its own position in the international division of labour and to defend its own national interests in the world market. These interests include the ability to import and export key commodities for the operations of industry and for the needs of the population. They also include the ability to borrow and lend in the global financial markets. Possession of a hoard of internationally acceptable means of payment is a precondition for the successful defence of national bourgeois interests in the world market. At the same time, diplomacy, bribery, coercion, piracy and war are also perfectly plausible methods of defending the national interest. To deploy such non-economic policies of defending the national interests in the world market, the national bourgeoisie again needs to possess a hoard of internationally acceptable means of payment, 'the sinews of war'.[10]

Under conditions of competitive industrial capitalism, which include extensive domestic circulation of commodity money, the internationally acceptable means of payment is gold: a country needs to possess a hoard of gold in order to participate in the world market (Itoh and Lapavitsas, 1999, chs 4, 6). Thus, the hoard held by the central bank for domestic purposes naturally begins to acquire an international role. Persistent or acute balance of payments deficits, sudden needs for purchases abroad, pressures of war, and so on, are reflected in the fluctuations of a country's gold hoard held by the central bank (though borrowing abroad can lessen the pressure on the hoard). The hoard continues all the while to reflect the domestic relationship between loanable money capital and real accumulation, and to support the movement of domestically circulating gold.

> The function of the metal reserve held by a so-called national bank . . . is three-fold: (i) a reserve fund for international payments, i.e. a reserve fund of world

money; (ii) a reserve fund for the alternately expanding and contracting domestic metallic circulation; (iii) (and this is connected with the banking function and has nothing to do with the function of money as simple money) a reserve fund for the payment of deposits and the convertibility of notes . . . If notes are issued to replace metal money in domestic circulation . . . the second function of the reserve fund disappears. (Marx, [1894] 1981, pp. 701–2)

In a simple and concrete way, the central bank's hoard of gold stands for the innumerable links between a national economy and the world market. To protect the hoard becomes an overriding concern of the central bank since it amounts to defending both the ability of the national bourgeoisie to participate in the international division of labour and the foundation of the domestic credit system. If the domestic monetary system exhibits diminishing reliance on commodity money (without completely extricating itself from gold), the domestic function of the gold hoard becomes weaker. As a result, fluctuations in the central bank's hoard reflect mostly the movement of the balance of trade and of loanable capital across the nation's borders. The fluctuations of the hoard are accompanied by corresponding exchange rate movements, though the latter are necessarily very narrow as long as credit money is freely exchangeable into gold.

A balance of payments deficit, whatever its cause, often leads to increased pressure to deliver payments abroad, a tendency of the exchange rate of the domestic currency relative to foreign ones to fall, and a drain of international money from the central bank. Under pressure to pay abroad, capitalists seek central bank liabilities by urgently selling securities or attempting to borrow from the central bank in order to obtain access to gold. In such a situation, the central bank typically finds itself acquiring securities and other loan assets, while losing reserve assets. To defend its reserves the central bank can adopt a number of policies that can also be used in combination. One is altogether to suspend the convertibility of its liabilities into the international means of payment. A less drastic option is rationing of either its loans or of access to the international means of payment. A further option is to raise the price at which it lends, leading to a general domestic rise in the rate of interest. If conditions allow in the world financial markets, higher interest rates encourage the inflow of loanable capital and so lessen the scarcity of means of payment. Yet another option is for the central bank directly to borrow abroad from other central banks or financial institutions.

Protecting the hoard of international means of payment tends to constrain the ability of ordinary banks to find reserves, and limits the provision of fresh loans to industry and trade. In the course of the business cycle, if a pressing need to settle a balance of payments deficit coincides with the emergence of a commercial and industrial crisis, a fully-fledged monetary crisis results. Compounding domestic with international pressure for means of payment might result in usurious rates of interest, even though the actual sums of international money flowing abroad might be very small relative to total output.

> [the gold drain] has this effect because it intervenes in circumstances where any-thing extra on one side or the other is sufficient to tip the scales . . . But it is pre-cisely the development of the credit and banking system which on the one hand seeks to press all money capital into the service of production . . . while on the other hand it reduces the metal reserve in a given phase of the cycle to a minimum, at which it can no longer perform the functions ascribed to it – it is this elaborate credit and banking system that makes the entire organism over-sensitive. (Marx, [1894] 1981, p. 706)

Historically, it takes a long time for the third function of the central bank to emerge fully. The Bank of England, for instance, had neither the capa-bility nor the technical knowledge successfully to defend its hoard through interest rate operations until the middle of the nineteenth century. During the Napoleonic Wars, the Bank had come under sustained criticism from bullionist writers, among whom Ricardo was the most coherent and out-spoken, to the effect that the 'overissue' of its banknotes had caused falls in the exchange rate and rises in the price of gold (a proxy for inflation). That made the Bank extremely reluctant to accept that its credit money bore any systematic relation to either exchange rates or the price of gold bullion. The Usury Laws, furthermore, imposed a 5 per cent ceiling on its discounts until 1833. By the 1830s, however, the Bank certainly took the exchange rate into account in deciding its discount policy. This fact, together with the existence of Palmer's rule, mentioned above, created a more propitious background allowing the Bank Act of 1844 to establish a rigid connection between Bank of England note liabilities and its gold assets that was explicitly dependent on the movement of the exchange rate.

Bank Rate policy, that is, the raising of the Bank's interest rate in order to attract gold from abroad and so relieve pressure on sterling, dominated the second half of the century and until the outbreak of World War I. The ability successfully to undertake Bank Rate policy depended critically on London being the commercial and financial heart of the British Empire, and the greatest repository of loanable capital in the world. Only after the 1870s could Britain rely on attracting the necessary foreign inflows of gold by means of raising the rate of interest (Sayers, 1957, pp. 14–15). By the end of the century British financiers and bureaucrats were confident that Bank Rate policy would always be able to face up to extraordinary pressure on the Bank's hoard. How ill-advised they were, and how institutionally-specific the effectiveness of interest rate protection is for the hoard of the central bank, was revealed at the outbreak of World War I. The sudden upsurge in foreign and domestic demand for the Bank's gold reserves could not be tackled even with a 10 per cent Bank Rate (Hawtrey, 1938, ch. IV). After World War I and the collapse of convertibility of credit money into gold, Bank Rate policy never again recovered the significance it had had in the second half of the nineteenth century. In the twentieth century, protecting the hoard of means of international payments has acquired a more complex meaning, some aspects of which are discussed in the rest of this chapter.

6.3. OPERATOR OF MONETARY POLICY, OVERSEER OF THE CREDIT SYSTEM, AND LENDER OF LAST RESORT

6.3.1. Monetary policy

Its position in the credit system allows the central bank to undertake 'monetary policy'. In the first instance, the central bank can enter the money market as buyer or seller of bills and other securities, respectively lowering or raising the market rate of interest, other things equal. Evidently, when the central bank buys securities, the banks acquire central bank liabilities, and when the central bank sells securities, the banks lose central bank liabilities. The induced movements of the market rate of interest express, respectively, easier and tighter conditions under which the banks can supply credit to real accumulation. Such open market operations are an indirect way of affecting the availability of credit to accumulation. The central bank can also employ a more direct way of achieving the same result by altering the terms on which it is prepared to lend directly to banks. By making its liabilities less or more easily available to banks the central bank can, respectively, raise or lower the rate of interest.

How effective the central bank is in influencing the rate of interest depends on the stage of the business cycle.[11] During the recession phase, loanable capital is abundant but lending opportunities are few and the rate of interest tends to be low: the central bank would find it difficult to raise the rate of interest in the unlikely event that it would wish to do so. Toward the end of the upswing, on the other hand, the rate of interest tends to rise as the supply of credit is stretched: the central bank would find it easier to raise the rate of interest. When accumulation reaches crisis, credit dries up as the demand for means of payment soars: the central bank must increase its own rate of interest, forcing the market rate to rise.[12]

The ability of the central bank to influence the market rate of interest also depends on the relationship between its reserves and its liabilities within a given institutional framework. When gold circulates domestically and is used to pay internationally, discretionary manipulation of the rate of interest has to be reconciled with fluctuations of the central bank's gold hoard that reflect both domestic and international forces. The overriding need to defend the international hoard, for instance, severely limits the ability of the central bank to pursue a low interest rate policy, even when domestic conditions allow it. A large and growing hoard, on the other hand, significantly increases the freedom of movement of the central bank. At all events, fluctuations of the central bank's reserve set objective limits to the central bank's discretionary powers over interest rates.

Attenuation of the role of gold, both domestically and internationally, heightens the ability of central banks to influence market interest rates. Under the Bretton Woods system, for instance, whereby the US dollar was convertible into gold at the fixed rate of $35 to the ounce in transactions among central banks, dollars formed a substantial part of the international reserves of central banks, thus limiting their ability to adopt discretionary domestic policies. On the other hand, as long as the liabilities of the US Federal Reserve System were internationally accepted as means of payment, the federal Reserve's own ability to adopt discretionary domestic policies was increased. The tenuous link with gold, however, provided some external discipline on the Federal Reserve, given that persistent balance of payments deficits exercised downward pressure on the dollar exchange rate and the US tended to lose gold reserves.

When the link between credit money and gold breaks down completely, as has happened since the collapse of the Bretton Woods system, the ability of the main central banks in the world market to exercise discretionary power over the rate of interest increases greatly.[13] Monetary policy has assumed its present historical significance because of the attenuation, or complete absence, of reserve discipline on the main central banks. The rate of interest has become partly an instrument of public economic policy, and a multitude of often contradictory demands are placed on central banks regarding its manipulation. These demands typically include price stability (the stability of the value of money), a satisfactory level of economic activity (perhaps also a low rate of unemployment), and a state of the balance of payments compatible with high growth and employment. Collapse of the Keynesian ideology of full employment characteristic of the post-World War II long boom and emergence of bouts of rapid inflation since the early 1970s have elevated price stability into the primary objective of the main central banks. Raising the rate of interest, and correspondingly tightening the conditions for the advance of credit, has emerged as the main instrument for controlling price inflation. However, as is more fully analysed in the discussion of central bank independence below, the same conditions that have raised monetary policy to such prominence have also exacerbated the anarchical nature of the international monetary system. Exchange rate instability, price inflation, and financial speculation set narrow limits within which monetary policy can be pursued.

6.3.2. Overseer of the Credit System and Lender of Last Resort

Analysis of the overseer and lender of last resort functions of central banks require prior discussion of instability in the capitalist economy. In this connection, the analytical approach matters greatly. For classical and neoclassical economics, the capitalist economy represents a natural and harmonious social order. In contrast, for Marxist political economy, the capitalist economy is inherently unstable and its instability incorporates several monetary and financial aspects. The following three levels can be identified in Marx's analysis of monetary and financial instability.

First, in an economy that contains simple processes of commodity exchange, the possibility of economic instability arises purely from the social functions of money. According to Marx ([1867] 1976, p. 209), the functioning of money as means of circulation inevitably implies that, 'No one can sell unless someone else purchases. But no one directly needs to purchase because he has just sold.' The crude form of Say's law, which asserts that the supply of commodities always generates an equal demand – on the implicit assumption of direct exchangeability among commodities – is simply incorrect for a monetary economy. Indeed, in a monetary economy, the antithetical form of sale and purchase themselves 'imply the possibility of crises'. Moreover, the functioning of money as means of payment – particularly in settling outstanding obligations generated in the course of simple exchange – also gives rise to the possibility of monetary crises. Interconnected series of promises to pay, as well as the 'artificial system for settling them', can break down when particular payment failures lead to a chain reaction and cause 'a general disturbance of the mechanism, no matter what its cause' (Marx [1867] 1976, p. 236). On such occasions, commodities have to be sold at 'sacrifice' prices in order to obtain money as means of payment. For the commodity owner these are trying times: 'As the hart pants after fresh water, so pants his soul after money, the only wealth' (Marx, ibid.). The tribulations of the commodity markets are essentially due to the 'sudden transformation of the credit system into a monetary system' (ibid.).

Second, in an economy with a developed process of exchange backed by advanced credit and finance, monetary crises of quite a different order of magnitude and complexity become possible. Monetary crises might be

caused by sudden breaks in the chains of industrial and commercial transactions prevalent in a particular country. Monetary crises might also be
intensified by shocks to the chains of credit, which run through industry
and trade.

Third, in a specifically capitalist economy, monetary crises inevitably
result from the essential motion of capitalist accumulation itself (Marx,
[1895] 1981, Pt. V). For our purposes, the most important point in this connection is that in a monetary economy founded on industrial capitalist
accumulation the inherent, but abstract, possibility of monetary crisis
becomes a regularly observed reality. The tendency to monetary crisis is
particularly manifested in the cyclical crises that characterize capitalist
accumulation.

In a note on the functioning of money as means of payment, Marx
([1867] 1976, p. 236) remarked that:

> The monetary crisis, defined in the text as a particular phase of every general
> industrial and commercial crisis, must be clearly distinguished from the special
> sort of crisis, also called a monetary crisis, which may appear independently of
> the rest, and only affects industry and commerce by its backwash. The centre of
> movement of these crises is to be found in money capital, and their immediate
> sphere is therefore banking, the stock exchanges and finance.[14]

Thus, Marx's note distinguishes between two kinds of monetary crisis:
those that form a particular phase of a general industrial and commercial
crisis (which we might call type I), and those which appear independently
of a general industrial and commercial crisis (which we might call type II).
According to the note, the analysis of the relationship between means of
payment and monetary crisis 'in the text' of *Capital* referred specifically to
type I crises. However, a close reading of 'the text' reveals no reason why
the analysis is inapplicable to type II crises (the later inclusion of the note
in *Capital* is an implicit acknowledgement of this). After all, and as already
quoted above, the text claims that a disturbance to the chain of promises to
pay 'no matter what its cause' can lead to a monetary crisis. Our analysis of
the role of central banks in confronting monetary instability is founded on
the distinction between monetary crises that are an integral part of the
broader periodic industrial and commercial crises of a capitalist economy
(type I) and those that arise purely as a result of the operations of the credit
system (type II).

Neither monetary instability arising purely from the social functions of
money (that is, the first layer in Marx's analysis of monetary crisis) nor type
II monetary crises are specific to the capitalist economy. Any significant disturbance of the process of debt repayment and loan renewal within an
economy that contains extensive credit mechanisms might give rise to

financial instability. Nevertheless, in a specifically capitalist economy the operations of the credit system could exacerbate the instability that is inherent to accumulation, as well as provide a natural breeding ground for speculation, rule-bending and outright fraud. The reason is that the advance of credit at once involves the formation of expectations about the future and influences the reallocation of the spare resources of society.

Goodhart's (1985) theory of the origin of central banking is relevant in this context. According to Goodhart (ibid., ch. 5), banks know more about each other than the public knows about banks, and it is too expensive for the public to collect information about the creditworthiness of individual banks. Banks that are not prudent, therefore, get a free ride on the efforts of the other banks to maintain a public image of uprightness. Further, banks as financial intermediaries issue liabilities (deposits) of fixed monetary value with which they buy assets (loans), also of fixed monetary value. This difference between financial assets occurs because lenders know less than borrowers about the projects on which their money is lent. Hence, the contract between lenders and borrowers cannot have a variable value, contingent on the actual outcome of the project (Goodhart, 1987). Despite their nominally-fixed value, however, bank assets in practice have variable and market-determined value. Since the market-determined value of deposits is expected to match their fixed monetary value, there arises scope for instability. Depositors worried about retrieving the full monetary value of bank liabilities they hold – and not able to distinguish among banks – might precipitate contagious bank runs that threaten the stability of the credit system. Therefore, the banks spontaneously assign the role of overseer to a 'good' bank among themselves. The overseer bank cannot continue with its private operations for long since its position induces conflicts between its public and its private interests. Eventually the overseer bank becomes a public non-profit central bank (Goodhart, 1985, ch. 8). In order to protect the value of the depositors' assets, the central bank provides lender of last resort facilities, that is, it lends flexibly to banks when bank runs materialize.

Goodhart's stress on the spontaneous emergence of central banks is intuitively appealing, and his argument that the public cannot normally tell a 'good' bank from a 'bad' one is persuasive. It is important, however, more sharply to distinguish between the general overseeing of the banking system and the function of lender of last resort. Goodhart essentially interprets all instances of acute financial instability as type II crises, that is, as crises arising purely from the processes of credit. However, type I monetary crises do not originate in the imprudent decisions of some banks but in the interaction of the banking system with real accumulation, as that is typically observed in the course of the business cycle. By this token, type I monetary crises reflect and exacerbate, but do not cause, the instability of capitalist accumulation. Such crises are likely to threaten the stability of the credit system as a whole since they are combined with commercial and industrial crises. The central bank, as the possessor of the central reserve of the banking system and banker to the state, is the natural source of the requisite means of payment when type I crises materialize.[15]

By policing the credit system the central bank can indeed reduce the danger of type II crises arising from rule-bending and the inevitably precarious structure of promises and counterpromises that constitutes credit. But the danger of type II crises due to the activities of rogue banks, plain rumour or natural disasters cannot be fully eliminated. When such crises materialize, the central bank is still called upon to provide the requisite means of payment in order to avoid wholesale bankruptcies and the collapse of the credit system as a whole. Nevertheless, the historical importance of the lender of last resort is due to credit crises of type I rather than II. Type I crises are not merely, or even primarily, a result of banking activities. Ultimately, they result from the inability of merchant and industrial capitalists to continue producing and selling at the same levels as before, thereby becoming unable to honour their past debts. The resultant credit crisis exacerbates the underlying commercial and industrial crisis.

Central banks are certainly concerned with the stability of the credit system as a whole, and so attempt to weed out 'bad' banks. More than this, however, central banking rests on the ability to provide means of payment when full-blown capitalist crises materialize. Effectively to function as lender of last resort the central bank relies on holding the national reserve of money (domestic and international) and on having access to the credit of the state. Moreover, the central bank is not always able to protect its reserve against external pressure and at the same time act as the lender of last resort: the institutional and historical conditions under which this action is possible have to be specified in advance. Bagehot (1873, p. 79) famously argued that:

> What is wanted and what is necessary to stop a panic is to diffuse the impression that though money may be dear, still money is to be had. If people could be really convinced that they could have money if they wait a day or two, and that utter ruin is not coming, most likely they will cease to run in such a mad way for money. Either shut the Bank at once, and say that it will not lend more than it commonly lends, or lend freely, boldly, and so that the public may feel you mean to go on lending.

The context for his argument, however, was provided by the classical industrial, mercantile and monetary crisis of laissez-faire capitalism:

> The problem of managing a panic must not be thought of as mainly a 'banking' problem. It is primarily a mercantile one. All merchants are under liabilities; they have bills to meet soon, and they can only pay those bills by discounting bills on other merchants. In other words, all merchants are dependent on borrowing money, and large merchants are dependent on borrowing much money . . . If the bankers gratify the merchants, they must lend largely when they like it least; if they do not gratify them, there is a panic. (Bagehot, 1873, p. 73)

The ability of the Bank of England to satisfy the pressing need for money on such occasions, and so rescue not only bankers but also merchants and eventually industrialists, derived from its possession of the ultimate banking reserve and its access to the credit of the state. Nonetheless, for the Bank effectively to apply Bagehot's prescription more was required than possession of the centralized reserve, access to state credit, and the accumulation of experience. As Bagehot (ibid., p. 75) himself pointed out, the practice of lender of last resort often contradicted the need simultaneously to defend the Bank's gold hoard against external pressure. Only after the establishment of the City of London as the centre of the financial mechanism of the British Empire was the Bank of England able successfully to undertake last resort lending in crisis. These conditions were not present during the first two-thirds of the nineteenth century.

To be sure, Bagehot (ibid., p. 80) also argued that the centralization of the reserve was 'anomalous' but, like a practical Englishman, he proposed to make use of what existed rather than aim at some 'natural or many reserve system of banking' (ibid., p. 80). Bagehot's treatment of the centralized reserve as 'abnormal' is often quoted by the advocates of free banking, who prefer to consider as 'natural' a system of decentralized, individually held bank reserves (Smith, 1936, 133–44). It is, however, a rather peculiar view of reality which treats what actually exists as abnormal and reserves the term 'natural' for the models theorists construct in the quiet of their study.

6.4. CENTRAL BANK INDEPENDENCE AND FREE BANKING

The heightened importance of central banking operations in the post-Bretton Woods world has led to intense theoretical debate regarding the role of central banks in a capitalist economy. In this debate, the antithetical proposals for central bank independence and for free banking have commanded much attention. A critical analysis of these proposals is undertaken below, informed by the preceding theoretical exposition of the character of the central bank.

6.4.1. Mainstream Theoretical Analysis of Central Bank Independence

Central bank independence appears to be 'an idea whose time has come' (Goodhart, 1994). A large body of theoretical and empirical work purports to have established the welfare improvements and the superior inflation performance resulting from central bank independence. It will be shown below that this literature suffers from conceptual weaknesses that decisively limit its persuasiveness. The roots of these weaknesses can be found in the inappropriate treatment of the central bank as a monetary planner in command of the supply of fiat money in a capitalist economy, rather than as an institution embedded in the financial system and sustaining the supply of credit money. The actual trend toward central bank independence, on the other hand, though partly resulting from the considerable influence of the theory, calls for analysis of financial and monetary instability in the post-Bretton Woods world.

The theoretical literature has its origins in Kydland and Prescott's (1977) influential analysis of rules versus discretion, further developed by Barro and Gordon (1983a, 1983b). Systematic presentations of the theory can be found in Blanchard and Fischer (1989) and Cukierman (1992) (with several extensions). Analysis commences with the decision making of the government (policymaker), assumed to minimize the following loss function:

$$L(\pi_t) = \pi_t^2 + \alpha \, (y_t - y^*)^2 \qquad \alpha > 0, y^* = ky_n, k > 1 \qquad (6.1)$$

Where π_t, is the current rate of inflation, and y_t, y^*, y_n are, respectively, current, desired and 'natural' output. Current output is determined according to:

$$(y_t - y_n) = \beta \, (\pi_t - \pi_t^e) + u_t \qquad \beta > 0, u_t \sim N \, (0, \sigma_u^2) \qquad (6.2)$$

Where π_t^e is the expected rate of inflation. This is a simple market-clearing model in which divergences between current and natural output are usually explained in terms of nominal wage contracts set at the beginning of each period. Thus, a difference between current and expected inflation results in a change in real wages which alters output and employment. Equilibrium hinges on the assumption that output cannot permanently diverge from its natural rate.

The rate of inflation is assumed to depend on the rate of growth of the money supply, m_t, which is the policymaker's instrument. To keep the mathematics simple, we will not include a stochastic element in the relationship of money to inflation (for instance, to account for velocity shocks), and assume instead that all external shocks enter through (6.2). Thus:

$$\pi_t = m_t \tag{6.3}$$

Given these three relationships, the government's problem is to choose π_t such that L is minimized subject to (6.2). This results in the following first order condition:

$$\pi_t = \frac{\alpha\beta(k-1)y_n}{1+\alpha\beta^2} + \frac{\alpha\beta^2}{1+\alpha\beta^2}\pi_t^e - \frac{\alpha\beta}{1+\alpha\beta^2}u_t \tag{6.4}$$

The solution thus depends on inflation expectations. Under rational expectations, π_t^e, equals the expected value of the right-hand side of (6.4), hence equilibrium inflation is given by:

$$\pi_t = \alpha\beta\,(k-1)y_n - \frac{\alpha\beta}{1+\alpha\beta^2}u_t \tag{6.5}$$

The first element represents a positive inflationary bias, and the second represents inflation resulting from stabilizing policy dealing with output shocks. Clearly this outcome is less socially desirable than equilibrium with $\pi_t^e = 0$, also taking into account that output cannot ultimately diverge from the 'natural' rate. Thus, in the first-best solution, monetary policy plays a purely stabilizing role resulting in inflation equal to:

$$\pi_t = -\frac{\alpha\beta}{1+\alpha\beta^2}u_t \tag{6.6}$$

The reason why the first-best solution does not prevail and a positive inflationary bias is present is the 'time or dynamic inconsistency' inherent to all 'rules'-based monetary policy. Since L is minimized given the expectations of inflation, the government has an incentive to cheat on the rules, thus creating inflation and temporarily raising output above the natural rate. One possible explanation for such action by the government is that natural output is below desired output due to 'distortions', such as trade unions. The precise manner in which distortions result in this discrepancy is not usually specified. More broadly, the government could seek recourse to monetary policy because fiscal policy has reached a limit in expanding output and employment (Alesina and Tabellini, 1987). Finally, the government might simply be bribing the electorate by generating unexpected inflation, a process that can generate a 'political business cycle'. Be that as it may, after a few repetitions of the government's action, people cease to be fooled. To prevent the government from lowering their real wages (which is the effectual cause of the rise in employment), agents adjust their inflation expectations upwards until they reach the level of the first component of (6.5) at which point they are equal with current inflation. Thus, it becomes impossible for the government to generate temporary gains in employment. 'Discretion' in monetary policy leads to social welfare lower than that under enforceable rules.

Into this framework Rogoff (1985, 1989) incorporated the 'conservative' central bank, an institution (frequently personified by its governor) which assigns a relatively greater weight to inflation than the government (for reasons not explained theoretically). The 'conservative' central bank thus minimizes:

$$L^{CB}(\pi_t) = (\gamma\pi_t^2 + \alpha(y_t + y^*)^2 \qquad \gamma > 1 \qquad (6.7)$$

Evidently the first order condition remains as in (6.4) except that the denominator now is $\gamma + \alpha\beta^2$. Consequently, equilibrium inflation is given by:

$$\pi_t = \frac{\alpha\beta(k-1)y_n}{\gamma} - \frac{\alpha\beta}{\gamma + \alpha\beta^2}u_t \qquad (6.7')$$

It follows immediately that inflationary bias at equilibrium is smaller, resulting in a gain in social welfare. It is also clear that the stabilizing interventions of the conservative central bank are smaller than analogous ones made by the government. This implies that the variability of output under a conservative central bank is greater. The reason for these results is clearly the greater weight attached to the 'bad' of inflation by the central bank. which makes its inflationary interventions smaller, thus leading to a smaller upward adjustment of inflationary expectations.

An important issue in this connection is whether the policymaker (government or central bank) can become committed to a particular monetary policy rule (inflation or money supply) prior to the decision-making period. From the structure of the loss function it is clear that a commitment policy which is not dynamically consistent is not credible (credibility being measured by the difference between actual and expected inflation).[16] If, however, information about shocks to output (or to the demand and supply of money, when a random element is inserted) is asymmetrically distributed, the all-or-nothing aspect of credibility disappears. If the central bank possesses more information about these economic processes than the public, and signals it to the latter through the actual rate of inflation (hence imparting uncertainty), there are gradations to credibility (Canzoneri, 1985).

The central bank's private information gives it room to undertake stabilization and expansionary policy but the policymaker must avoid severely disturbing inflationary expectations lest credibility is considerably reduced. Loss of credibility reduces the effectiveness of future policy since people's inflationary expectations adjust appropriately in advance of the policymaking period. Concern about credibility is the closest that society comes to ensuring commitment of policymakers to particular monetary policies (though no mechanism exists which can enforce such commitment). It is generally assumed that a conservative central bank whose decision-making powers have been rendered independent of the government is better able to increase its credibility (improve its reputation).

Finally, a more recent extension of the literature (partly spurred by the experience of New Zealand) has been to devise optimal contracts that make central banks follow the first-best rule given by (6.6). This is basically a principal–agent approach, developed by Persson and Tabellini (1993) and (mainly) Walsh (1995), based on the notion that the central bank's receipt of transfer payments from the government (budgetary allowances, salaries, and so on) should be made conditional on the actual rate of inflation, $t(\pi_t)$. This results in a utility function for the central bank of the following type:

$$U^{CB} = t\,(\pi_t) - \{\pi_t^2 + \alpha\,(y_t - y^*)^2\} \tag{6.8}$$

The first-order condition for the maximization of which is:

$$\pi_t = \alpha\beta\,(k-1)y_n - \frac{\alpha\beta}{1+\alpha\beta^2}u_t + \frac{1}{2}\frac{dt}{d\pi_t} \tag{6.9}$$

Consequently, the first-best result for inflation ('rules') can be obtained by designing a contract which sets the transfer payments to the central bank depending on the observed value of inflation alone, and according to the following rule:

$$\frac{1}{2}\frac{dt}{d\pi_t} = -\alpha\beta\,(k-1)y_n \Rightarrow t = -2\alpha\beta\,(k-1)y_n\pi_t + c \tag{6.10}$$

Where c is the constant of integration.

The contract appears to eliminate the inflationary bias of discretionary policy in (6.5), while also allowing for an optimal response to output shocks determined by the second term of (6.9).

6.4.2. Is this a Central Bank?

It is a remarkable aspect of this literature that the central bank to which it copiously refers has no banking functions at all. The theoretical framework contains no financial system and there is no borrowing and lending. Money in these models is purely state fiat money created at the whim of the policymaker. In equations (6.2) and (6.3) the central bank is simply a monopolist controlling the supply of legal tender, ultimately determining (passively or actively) the rate of price inflation, but with no ability to influence output and employment in the long run.[17]

However, modern money is largely credit money created through the complex interaction of factors that include the loan demands emanating from the process of output production, lending operations of the financial institutions and generation of financial institution reserves. The distinctive analysis of modern money as credit (rather than fiat) money, which underpins our earlier analysis of central banking, has deep classical roots, including Steuart, the banking school and Marx, and has been revived in recent years by post-Keynesianism.[18] For this approach, to posit the central bank as simply a monopolist of fiat money is weak and misleading theory. The central bank's controlling operations over the supply of credit money are inseparable from its organic role in the financial system of a capitalist country as the bank of banks, the bank of the state and the holder of international money.

In this light, a moment's reflection shows that the concept of central bank independence' is a lot less clear than appears at first sight. The decision making of the central bank cannot be 'independent' of the rest of the credit system since the central bank is the bank of banks, regularly and extensively intervening in the money market. Stable and long-existing markets are characterized by a dense web of relations, such as professional, informational, training, and even personal ones, all of which are very pronounced in financial markets. Similarly, the central bank's decision-making cannot be 'independent' of the mechanisms of industrial production and trade, though it is naturally more remote from these than from the financial system. The central bank is regularly exposed to influence by the institutions and personnel of industry and trade, since it ultimately underpins the supply of credit to them and can substantially influence their performance. In short, the central bank might possess the mantle of a public institution, but remains a spontaneously arising economic entity the range, type, and manner of operations of which are determined by its underlying character as a bank. It is a creature of the financial system in terms of its personnel and much of its activities. Analogously, the bank of the state, even when it does not itself lend directly to the latter, necessarily becomes entangled with state personnel that oversees and plans revenue collection, expenditure and borrowing. Finally, but no less significantly, the central bank can scarcely become independent of other state mechanisms in taking decisions regarding the reserves of international money, given the importance of the latter for the defence of the international interests of the national bourgeoisie.

It is apparent that the 'independent central bank' of the theoretical literature is not a central bank at all. It is, rather, a social planner armed with a single instrument of economic policy, fiat money, in pursuit of one aim, price stability. With this in mind, independence acquires meaning: it is, above all, independence of the social planner from the executive branch of the state, the periodically elected government. Since the theory considers governments to be inherently mendacious and untrustworthy, it concludes that social welfare would be greater if the monetary planner achieved greater independence from the electoral process. Thus, judging by price stability alone, economic theory proposes appointment of a benevolent monetary dictator. In view of this, the following four related but separate points are important.

First, the internal consistency of the theoretical work on central bank independence is problematic, as McCallum (1995, 1997) has already claimed. The argument is simple and telling: if the independent central bank is indeed concerned about inflation and realizes, as it must, that monetary policy cannot shift long-run employment away from the natural rate, why should it accept the inferior outcome of (6.5′) and not aim for the first-best of (6.6)? Analogously, if no means exist of forcing the elected government to adopt the optimal monetary policy (the lack of such means being, presumably, the root of the problem), who is going to enforce the 'optimal contract' between the government and the central bank? McCallum considers this argument as offering support to central bank independence, despite pointing out the analytical problems of the theory, since he also accepts the impossibility of shifting output away from the natural rate by means of monetary policy. He interprets his argument as implying that outcomes could be enforced which are even better for society than those achieved by Rogoff's conservative central bank. However, if McCallum's argument supports the theory, it does so by pointing out that, since the theory inherently treats central banks as monetary dictators, they might as well act dictatorially.

Second, it is deeply paradoxical for theorists within the neoclassical tradition, who typically proclaim the welfare and efficiency optimality of free markets, to advocate assigning absolute control over money to a planner. If systematic disharmony and disequilibrium at the macro level originate in the misuse of monopoly over legal tender by central banks at the behest of politicians, it seems more consistent to demand the abolition of this monopoly and the determination of the supply of credit money via the competitive issue of liabilities among banks. That such a proposal might not be practicable under present political conditions is not a decisive consideration in the realm of theory.[19] If, as equation (6.2) claims, systematic disturbances to equilibrium output are caused by inflationary shocks emanating from the misuse of monopoly of legal tender, it appears more congruent with neoclassical analysis to demand market freedom in the realm of money rather than a benevolent social planner with dictatorial powers over money.

Third, if indeed society is to have a planner in command of monetary policy and the issuing of money, why should the planner's remit be limited to price stability? The view that it is impossible to effect permanent shifts in output by means of demand management is merely an assumption, despite its overwhelming popularity in contemporary economics. A social planner, who has complete control of money and significant influence over the generation and allocation of credit, possesses considerable powers to promote capitalist accumulation in certain areas and restrict it in others. There is no *a priori* reason for the planner to abdicate the power over capitalist accumulation afforded by command over money and credit. At the very least, and even if it were accepted that production and accumulation should be left alone, there is no reason why the planner should not attempt to influence the distribution of income through preferential rate loans, consumption-smoothing advances, housing credit advances, and the like. If the creation of a public institution with monopoly powers over money and credit is advocated, there is no reason why this institution should not avail itself of these opportunities for policy.

Fourth, the appointment and democratic accountability of such a planner are considerably more complex issues than allowed for in the literature. As we have seen, the literature posits central bank independence largely as a matter of making the planner independent of the elected executive, given that to win elections governments have to placate, bribe and deceive the electorate. Monetary policy is best left in the hands of experts with sufficient stability of tenure and freedom to pursue what is 'optimal' for society. Here we have a clear example of what Marxists call the 'reification' of economic activity. The economy is not a set of social relations based on the reproduction of material life over which humanity ought to be able to exercise conscious control in its own interest. Rather, it is a mechanism that obeys its own logic and movement over which democratic processes exert a disturbing influence. Hence the planner ought to be independent of electoral expressions of popular will. That is a remarkably narrow view of economic activity in general and of monetary policy in particular. Monetary policy is a powerful instrument that can influence production and distribution: why refuse society the opportunity to employ it consciously and in its own democratically ascertained interests? There is no *a priori* reason why a monetary planner could not be subject to mechanisms of election and accountability in which broad swathes of people can participate.

6.4.3.   The Actual Trend Toward Central Bank Independence

Irrespective of the theoretical problems inherent to the concept of central bank independence, in recent years, several countries have instigated legal and institutional changes aiming at greater independence for their central banks, having the US Federal Reserve and the German Bundesbank as ostensible prototypes. In Europe, agreement in 1990 regarding the European System of Central Banks (ESCB) commenced the process of establishing a European Central Bank (ECB), eventually deciding to seat the latter in Frankfurt. The ECB is run by a council comprising the governors of all the constituent central banks of the ESCB and an appointed executive committee of five, including the governor whose tenure is for eight years. Decisions are reached on the basis of one person-one vote, but the existence of the executive and the casting vote of the governor give a decisive advantage to the permanent officials. The ECB will manage the common currency, the euro, with the overriding aim of price stability. A condition for member central banks to participate in the ESCB is that they should themselves achieve independence in their respective countries, eventually becoming plain branches of the ECB. The influence of the Bundesbank and the German government are apparent in the design and the location of the ECB.

In the UK, changes introduced by the Labour government of 1997 have granted a substantial measure of independence to the Bank of England. The trend toward greater independence for the Bank was started soon after the exit of sterling from the European Monetary System in 1992 with regular meetings between the Chancellor of the Exchequer and the Governor. Under the Tory government, however, there was never any doubt that the Chancellor held ultimate power over interest rates. Under current arrangements, the Bank of England is run by a committee of government appointees, rather than the traditional group of influential and well-connected financiers, traders, and industrialists. The present constitution of the committee appears to lean toward 'monetary experts' rather than overtly political appointees. The committee has operational independence, that is, it can set interest rates, but the government determines its goals.[20] This amounts to the government setting a target range for price inflation and the Bank of England using its own discretion to achieve it. As part of the institutional changes, moreover, the Bank of England has transferred many of its supervisory functions over the financial system to a new and separate overseer.

In Japan, with effect from 1998, the Bank of Japan (BoJ) has acquired greater independence from the Ministry of Finance (MoF). Since the end of World War II the balance of power over the Japanese financial system has decisively favoured the MoF. Monetary policy has been operated by the BoJ but the presence of MoF officials on the BoJ's executive board, and the appointment of an MoF official as BoJ governor every other turn, secured a decisive advantage for the government in the setting of interest rates. The enormous supervisory powers of the MoF over the financial system, including the issuing of new bank licenses and permits for the opening of new branches, have further skewed the balance against the BoJ. Under the new arrangements, the MoF has lost the right to appoint one of its officials as governor but kept two non-voting members on the BoJ policy committee. The BoJ has operational independence on the setting of interest rates and its goal is price stability. However, there are no clear inflation or other targets given to it, and it is required that its policy must not contradict the general macroeconomic policy of the government. Finally, the MoF transferred a significant part of its supervisory functions to a separate body.

These real-world trends partly reflect the considerable influence exercised by the theory of independent central banking, despite its conceptual weaknesses. In particular, the empirical offshoots of the theory, which have proliferated in the 1990s, have proved quite influential. Typically these studies construct indices of central bank independence and econometrically test their relationship to price inflation. Grilli et al. (1991), for instance, find that for a group of developed industrialized countries there is a significant negative relationship between the two for certain periods. Similarly, Alesina and Summers (1993) find that a clear downward sloping relationship exists for industrialized countries. Not only this but, contrary to (6.5'), Alesina and Summers cannot identify a positive relationship between output variability and central bank independence. Instead of treating this result as problematic for theory, however, the literature typically welcomes it as an unexpected bonus: independent central banks somehow deliver lower inflation and stable output.

The validity of the empirical studies is deeply problematic. Construction of indices of independence is an *ad hoc* exercise fraught with profound difficulties (Cukierman, 1992, ch. 18). In constructing the indices, the literature distinguishes, as it must, between legal (or formal) and actual independence. The former is mostly a matter of the law governing the operations of the central bank (its statutes). The latter is a matter of informal arrangements between the central banks and the government, as well as other centres of economic decision making. Actual independence also depends on the analytical capabilities of the central bank, and even its governor's personality. The necessity of making this distinction in empirical work is particularly apparent in light of our earlier discussion. An actual central bank, as opposed to the monetary planner assumed by theory, is inevitably embedded in a set of social and economic relations. Consequently, it is practically impossible to assign concrete content to the concept of central bank independence. As a result, in empirical work, economists avoid indices of actual independence in preference to those of legal independence. Since indices of legal independence are based on interpreting the statutes of central banks and little else, they are deeply flawed for purposes of testing the theory. It is no exaggeration to claim that the empirical literature on central bank independence is largely worthless (Forder, 1996).

To pursue the issue a little further, at which point do legal restrictions on the influence of government over policy render a nominally independent central bank actually independent? When there are no government officials on the policy committee? When there is complete goal independence? When the elected authority legally abrogates all powers to intervene in monetary policy in all contingencies? It is impossible precisely to resolve these issues – and measure actual independence in practice – because of the qualitative difference between an actual central bank and the monetary planner assumed by theory. The problems of measurement of independence, in other words, do not spring from the inevitable difficulty of translating theoretical concepts into empirically testable ones (though this might also exist), but from the weakness of the theoretical concept of independence itself. Consequently, empirical work resorts to grossly unsatisfactory expedients, such as using the actual turnover of governors or the ratio between actual and legal tenure of governors, as proxies for the disparity between actual and legal independence. Even worse, empirical work often relies on questionnaires that basically ask central bankers how independent they feel at a particular moment in time. The problem with the latter is apparent: when inflationary performance is good, governors are likely to feel that they face no serious problems of political interference.

To make matters worse, Cukierman (1992, ch. 20) has stressed that the vaunted negative econometric relationship between inflation and central bank independence for industrialized countries becomes positive when the sample expands to developing countries. That is, perhaps, not surprising when one bears in mind the relative absence of deep and fluid money markets in several developing countries. In such situations, and given the weaknesses of revenue collection characteristic of the tax systems of several developing countries, direct lending by the central bank (often a bank found to be independent according to legal indices) is essential to balancing the government budget. The concept of central bank independence once again appears to lack meaning in practice.

Last, but not least, even for the group of industrialized countries for which a negative relationship is shown to exist for significant periods of time in the postwar era, causation is by no means demonstrated. It is plausible that broader factors account for satisfactory inflation performance as well as for the particular institutional outlook of the central bank. The historical experience of hyperinflation together with the system of collective bargaining, for instance, might have made counter-inflationary policy more acceptable to German society regardless of the relatively high degree of Bundesbank independence. Similarly, rapid increases in productivity, the nationwide system of collective bargaining, and the relatively small claim of the state on national income, might have limited the effect of inflationary pressures in Japan, despite the relative lack of independence for BoJ.

At a deeper level, the trend toward actual central bank independence in recent years may be interpreted as a policy reaction to the increase in financial and monetary instability in the post-Bretton Woods world.[21] When the centralized reserve of the financial system comprises a produced commodity with its own value (typically gold) it is evident that the central bank (and by extension the constituent banks of the financial system) faces a rigidly determined limit in extending its liabilities at any moment in time. Even if the national reserves comprise mostly foreign exchange, typically US dollars, considerable reserve discipline continues to apply across the financial system, provided that convertibility into the money commodity is maintained. The most evident mechanism through which reserve discipline operates under conditions of convertibility into gold is the inevitable fixity of exchange rates among convertible currencies. In so far as fixed exchange rates have to be defended, the international role of the centralized reserve of the banking system attains overwhelming preponderance over its domestic role. In such a context, monetary policy (that is, the manipulation of central bank liabilities through market-based processes with the aim of influencing interest rates and the generation of credit money by individual banks) is severely circumscribed by the need to defend the national reserve in the face of international pressures.

Abolition of convertibility into gold has introduced flexible exchange rates and simultaneously removed the formal link between gold reserves and liabilities of the central bank. An immediate consequence has been the relaxation of reserve discipline on the main central banks of the international economy, above all on the US Federal Reserve, the main issuer of the internationally acceptable means of payment.[22] This development has increased greatly the ability of several central banks (particularly those of large developed countries) to exercise discretionary influence over interest rates, and has accorded to monetary policy its historically extraordinary current significance.

Freed from reserve discipline imposed by convertibility into the money commodity, central banks (especially the US Federal Reserve) have been able to treat the rate of interest entirely as an instrument of public policy, thereby attempting to meet several, often conflicting, aims. Complete collapse of the Keynesian ideology of full employment, coupled with repeated bouts of rapid inflation in the post-Bretton Woods world, have contributed to the elevation of price stability into the overriding aim of central banks.

Presumably, a central bank that is independent of the elected executive would be able to manipulate its liabilities in a manner which regulates the generation of credit money by other banks and restores stability to the price level. At the same time, the social discontent associated with counter-inflationary monetary policy, resulting from possible reductions in output and rises in unemployment, would be deflected from governments and attributed to unelected monetary experts.

Nevertheless, the following three factors set limits to the ability of central banks to operate monetary policy with the sole objective of price stability. First, attenuation of reserve discipline and the concurrent wave of financial innovation in the post-Bretton Woods world have increased the scope for credit money generation by financial institutions. The collapse of the apparent stability of the demand for money is only the most prominent of a host of important related developments. These include emergence of new forms of credit money issued by banks, and the possible emergence of credit money issued by non-bank financial firms, backed by fully market-able assets rather than central bank liabilities. It is not at all clear that the central bank (independent or not) is able to control the generation of such diverse forms of credit money (and their effect on commodity and asset prices) armed only by its influence on the rate of interest.

Second, removal of the link with gold and introduction of floating exchange rates have resulted in the emergence of exchange rate instability unprecedented in the history of capitalism. Driven by international move-ments of loanable money capital, the main exchange rates in the world market exhibit enormous fluctuations, which have significant effects on domestic production. Though there is no longer an immediate and press-ing need to defend international reserves of gold, no nation can remain indifferent to its currency's exchange rate for long periods of time. At present, exchange rate policy remains largely in the hands of elected governments rather than being relegated to an independent central bank. That is not particularly surprising since exchange rate policy affects directly the position of the national bourgeoisie in the international division of labour, and inevitably raises issues of political power and hegemony. It is not likely that such an inherently political area of economic decision making would be completely entrusted to technical experts. Consequently, the ability of the independent central bank to pursue monetary policy with the single aim of price stability will remain circumscribed by the lack of power over exchange rate policy. At the same time, counter-inflationary monetary policy, as previously explained, is likely to operate through raising the rate of interest, thus attracting international inflows of loanable capital and leading to exchange rate appreciation. The extent to which exchange rate appreciation (and the problems it inevitably causes for exporting industries) will be accepted by the national bourgeoisie as a price worth paying for lower inflation is not clear at the outset. For independent central banks this amounts to a profoundly contradictory position: on the one hand, interest rate policy inevitably has implications for exchange rates that affect inflation, on the other, central banks have no power to formulate exchange rate policy. In this context, major problems of policymaking would be avoided only through pure good fortune.

Third, the last two decades have witnessed the rapid growth of largely speculative financial activity associated with the markets for foreign exchange, stocks and shares, and real estate. This is a complex phenomenon requiring separate analysis, but it seems safe to assert that the loss of convertibility into gold has increased the autonomy of the financial sector relative to real capital accumulation. Financial bubbles, the burst of which results in considerable dislocation and disturbance for productive activity have regularly appeared during the last two decades. It is unlikely that an independent central bank will ever be able to determine monetary policy aiming at price stability alone. Achieving the latter will probably be tempered by the need to prevent, deflate, or manage the aftermath of speculative financial instability.

6.5. FREE BANKING

Free banking has a much more substantial theoretical pedigree than central bank independence, despite being much more tendentious as a practical proposition. In its present form the theory owes much to Hayek (1:976a, 1976b), though it can trace its ancestry at least to Parnell (1827, 1832). Free banking proponents essentially believe in the inherent harmony of capitalist markets, and seek to extend it to the realm of money. State control and monopoly rights over the issuing of money are, presumably, the ultimate cause of economic instability and crises:

> *The past instability of the market economy is the consequence of the exclusion of the most important regulator of the market mechanism, money, from itself being regulated by the market process.* (Hayek, 1976b, pp. 79–80, original emphasis)

In this light, emergence of central banks cannot be a spontaneous and natural development of the financial system. Rather, central banks are monopolies issuing legal tender, which are extremely useful in supplying the state with cheap finance. In providing such finance and by using their powerful monopoly position in the financial markets central banks become a source of economic instability in a capitalist economy:

A central bank is not a natural product of banking development. It is imposed from outside or comes into being as the result of Government favours. This factor is responsible for marked effects on the whole currency and credit structure which brings it into sharp contrast with what would happen under a system of free banking from which Government protection was absent. (Smith, 1936, p. 169)

It is important to note that, in the opinion of free banking supporters, mere convertibility of credit money into a commodity money is not enough to guarantee stability of prices, since, apparently, the role of central banks was also profoundly destabilizing throughout the nineteenth century when such convertibility prevailed. Consequently, to provide stability for the exchange value of money (indeed, for the whole of the market economy), a banking system with a central bank should be replaced by natural, free banking.[23] There should be no special regulations imposed on entrants to the banking business other than those which generally apply to all companies. Banks should be allowed to go bankrupt. A reserve asset should be designated, which could be gold but also a commodity bundle, and the liabilities of banks should be immediately convertible into it.[24] All banks should possess their own reserves of this asset, and a clearing system should be erected to allow for mutual settlement of claims among banks. No bank liabilities should be legal tender.

Under such conditions, free banking supporters believe that the process of competition would prevent over-issuing of liabilities by individual banks. Were an individual bank to overissue, it would rapidly lose reserves in the clearing process (White, 1984, ch. 1; Dowd, 1989, ch. 1). If the bank wished to maintain an excessive amount of outstanding liabilities it would face rising costs in securing reserves. To earn the competitive rate of profit, banks would have to issue liabilities prudently, thus also gaining and keeping the confidence of the public. The more the public became accustomed to the operations of a free banking system the more difficult it would be for individual banks to hoodwink their customers into keeping their liabilities away from the process of clearing. Competition and the profit motive, based on convertibility into an asset that cannot be created at will, would be sufficient to ensure stability in the value of credit money and would facilitate emergence of broader economic stability.

The theory of free banking rightly concentrates on the principles of self-regulation of bank-issued credit money, particularly regarding quantity and exchange value of credit money. In this respect, free banking has several elements in common with the tradition of Steuart, the banking school, and Marx, mentioned above. At the same time, however, free banking theory erroneously asserts that harmony can naturally prevail in determination of quantity and exchange value of credit money. The claim that central banks are the ultimate source of capitalist instability is an inversion of the historical and the logical process. On the contrary, and as discussed earlier, central banks are able to contribute to the amelioration of capitalist crises, and are forced to do so in the midst of anarchical credit operations that determine the quantity and exchange value of credit money. In this connection, three points are important with reference to free banking theory.

First, as argued above, the capitalist economy regularly generates monetary crises resulting from both the underlying instability of production and exchange itself (type I) and the independent operations of the credit system (type II). The view that credit processes fundamentally contribute to capitalist instability has at least as long an ancestry as free banking. Tooke (1840, vol. III, p. 206, emphasis in the original), the main exponent of the banking school, an arch free trader and defender of the concept of self-regulation of credit money, famously dismissed the idea of free banking: 'As to free banking, in the sense in which it is sometimes contended for, I agree with a writer in one of the American journals, who observes, that *free trade in banking is synonymous with free trade in swindling.*' The 'swindling' mentioned by Tooke relates to what we have called type II crisis. The banking school also recognized 'overbanking' as a source of crisis, that is, the overextension of banking credit characteristic of the last phase of the upswing of the classical business cycle.[25]

There can be no natural harmony in the relation of credit to real accumulation. Trade credit (inter-firm) has an objective foundation in the buying and selling activities of capitalist firms. But trade credit can also be tremendously expanded without the underlying transactions changing significantly in value. Similarly, banking credit has an objective foundation in the spare money that is systematically generated in the turnover of capital and becomes loanable capital when appropriated by the credit system. But banking credit still depends on anticipating future returns and its advance is extensively connected with the processes of trade credit (Itoh and Lapavitsas, 1999, ch. 4). No rigid controlling influence from real accumulation (that is, from technology, real wages, and the speed of capital turnover) exists over banking credit. Both trade and banking credit are inherently elastic, and that is why they can support and stretch real accumulation. The latter ultimately does set limits to the operations of credit, but such limits might well take the form of a sudden contraction of the overextended structure of claim and counterclaim. For banks, as well as industrial and commercial capitalists, the need for a central bank as a lender of last resort cannot be obviated in these circumstances.[26]

Second, centralization of bank reserves is a spontaneous process based on the economic benefits it brings to banks, since they can pursue their business more flexibly and cheaply by depositing their reserves with one institution. By holding a claim on a centralized hoard instead of a quantity of the reserve commodity, individual banks can economize on the size of their reserve, other things equal. The banking system as a whole, moreover, is able to maintain a smaller reserve of commodity money in order to sustain its operations. Centralization of reserves, a tendency accelerated by the existence of panics and the possibility of bank runs, is a condition for the further expansion of the credit system.

The international role of money also contributes to centralization of the national reserve of means of payment. To participate in the world market and in the international division of labour, a national bourgeoisie must possess a hoard of international means of payment. Whichever commodity bundle comprises the reserves of a free banking system, it would also have to be convertible into foreign money. Moreover, even if the national denominations of money were abolished, each national bourgeoisie would still have to possess a hoard of means of payment earmarked for its international transactions. Balance of payment crises, national emergencies, and wars, would contribute to concentration and centralized management of the national hoard. War has in practice proved the strongest force for concentration of the gold hoard in the history of capitalism. There is no reason to assume that a free banking system, constructed under present political conditions, would avoid the tendency toward centralization of the international means of payment.

Third, the argument that the quantity and exchange value of credit money can be stabilized by the process of bank competition and clearing is a contemporary version of what was called 'the law of the reflux' in classical political economy. This law – originally discovered by Steuart, given a particular form by Smith known as the 'real bills doctrine', and adopted by the banking school – essentially claimed that the quantity of bank-created money (bank liabilities) does not become excessive because of regular maturing of bank assets and inflow of deposited savings into banks (Itoh and Lapavitsas, 1999, ch. 1). Free banking supporters, on the whole, recognize the affinity between their own analysis and the law of the reflux, the latter treated as a broad statement about the behaviour of credit money (Glasner, 1989, ch. 3). If quantity of credit money is kept within limits, its exchange value cannot decline dramatically and price inflation can be avoided.

The putative effectiveness of competition and clearing in achieving stability of the exchange value of credit money is exaggerated by free banking supporters. The most that clearing among banks can do is ensure that banks issue liabilities in step with each other so that they avoid losing reserves. Even that is not certain, however, if certain banks can sustain a different pricing of their liabilities from that of their rivals for significant periods of time (Goodhart, 1985, p. 30). Assuming that banks do issue liabilities in step, the well-known and very old criticism of this approach to credit money immediately surfaces: competition and clearing by themselves cannot guarantee that the total quantity of credit money is not excessive. If banks collectively lowered the price of their liabilities they could continue to increase the total quantity of credit money, all be it in step with each other.[27]

For Selgin (1988, pp. 81–2), if banks continued to expand their issues in step, the variance of clearing of debits and credits would increase, exacerbating the need for banks to hold higher precautionary reserves and resulting in a self-correcting equilibrium. That is plain unwarranted assertion. More persuasively, though still cursorily, White (1984, pp. 17–18 and 1989, pp. 33–4) stated that, if overissue occurred, the country as a whole would lose reserves abroad and this would correct the problem. White (1989, pp. 140–41) pursued this analysis further:

> Contrary to what the headlines lead us to think, there is no cause for alarm at the international money flows or resulting trade 'deficits' and 'surpluses' in a world of purely metallic currency. Indeed, there is no special reason even to keep track of national aggregates. One might as well keep track of net money shipments from left-handed to right-handed persons. Money moves across national borders as easily and inconsequentially as it moves from one side of Main Street to the other. The concept of a national money supply is irrelevant, because the world's money is homogeneous.

If money had no national denominations the problem of exchange rates would indeed not exist. The national bourgeoisie, however, would still need to hold an international reserve to be able to buy and pay abroad as extraordinary needs arose. The movement of international money would never be as 'inconsequential' as moving cash among left-handed and right-handed persons. While national denominations persist, furthermore, the relation between the total quantity of domestic credit money and the external requirements for money cannot be simply dismissed but must be theorized explicitly. It is not at all clear that the free issue of credit money can be reconciled with protecting the national hoard and defending the exchange rate. On the contrary, the domestic role of credit money is much more likely to be in constant conflict with its international role.[28]

Competition and clearing by themselves, that is, a simple version of the law of the reflux, cannot harmoniously regulate the total quantity of credit money relative to real accumulation. To claim with any degree of persuasiveness that such harmony can prevail further arguments are necessary regarding the operations of banks in the course of capitalist accumulation.

In the course of history, theorists attracted to the notion that the domestic quantity of bank-created credit money could be automatically regulated through the operations of the credit system have regularly attempted to devise theories of bank behaviour that bear out this claim. The best known of these is the previously mentioned Real Bills Doctrine proposed by Adam Smith, that is, the suggestion that if banks lent short-term and in order to purchase assets that generate real returns, no overissue of credit money would be possible.[29] For that to hold, however, it is also necessary to show that the advance and the repayment of banking credit as a whole also possess a natural harmony relative to real accumulation. The Real Bills Doctrine is a fallacy for a variety of reasons, including the impossibility of banks adequately differentiating among assets and the fact that fluctuations in the rate of interest are likely to have a decisive influence on the assets offered to and purchased by banks. The fallacy, nonetheless, is not so much the result of poor theory-making but more of the objective absence of bank practices which could provide the much-desired natural harmony. It is true that, strictly speaking, the fallacy of Real Bills is not an argument in favour of central banking: the same lack of harmony in domestic determination of the total quantity of credit money also exists when the credit system possesses a central bank. The point, however, is especially problematic for free banking supporters, who believe that capitalist instability would vanish if central banks were abolished.

The law of the reflux and convertibility into gold could, perhaps, provide an anchor for the value of credit money, but that anchor would operate through complete lack of harmony. The experience of business cycles shows that capitalist credit is periodically overextended and contracted as real accumulation goes through its motion, and the exchange value of credit money falls and rises in consequence. Commodity money (gold) provides an anchor for these fluctuations, but only in the sense that overextended bank credit suddenly collapses as borrowers rush to obtain means of payment, thus inducing falls in commodity prices. The need to defend the national hoard and to protect exchange rates is also a decisive lever in inducing the sudden fluctuations of credit, in practice making gold the anchor of the value of credit money. In that context, the lender of last resort can ameliorate the worst side-effects of the violent readjustment of the value of credit money to the value of gold.

6.6. CONCLUSION

Independent central bank and free banking theories recognize that central banks possess some aggregate organizing capacity in the capitalist economy, but both theories are based on partial representations of capitalist reality. The credit system naturally tends to possess a centralized reserve of domestic and international means of payment, and so tends to give rise to a central bank, which underpins credit money. It is not surprising that this bank also tends to be the bank of the state, as long as the latter needs a bank. Nor is it unnatural for this bank to become manager of the hoard of the nation's international money. Its position leads the central bank to supervise the credit system, to lend in times of distress, and to protect the hoard of international money. However, there are limits to what central banks can do, imposed by the fact that credit is about forecasting the unknowable future, as well as by the anarchy of the underlying process of real capitalist accumulation.

Central bank independence, in particular, is a deeply problematic notion in theory and practice. The extensive body of theory dealing with the concept is, in reality, not at all concerned with central banks but with a social planner in charge of monetary policy. If society is to have such a powerful monetary institution, however, establishment of its instruments, goals, process of appointment and accountability ought to be undertaken in a suitably broad and socially aware context. The assumptions of continuous market clearing and natural rate of unemployment, and the narrow concern with inflation, provide a very poor framework for doing so. The actual movement toward greater central bank independence, on the other hand, suffers from considerable ambiguity on what is 'independence'. It was argued above that such ambiguity is inevitable: a central bank holds an organic position in the financial system, it is a private institution that has necessarily acquired the mantle of a public one. It cannot be independent either of the private sector or of the state. The actual trend toward central bank independence in the last two decades is rather a response to the monetary instability of the post-Bretton Woods world. In the absence of reserve discipline provided by the money commodity, and in the face of repeated bouts of inflation, a central bank with discretionary powers over monetary policy might be able to stabilize the domestic price level without significant influence from (or costs for) politicians. Nevertheless, continuous financial innovation in the generation of credit money, foreign exchange fluctuations, and financial speculation, set limits to the ability of the central bank to pursue price stability alone.

The historical experience since the collapse of the Bretton Woods system has revealed increasing confusion and anarchy in capitalist production and trade. The proposal for central bank independence, though not practically infeasible, aims at introducing harmony through the powers of the central bank. This strongly exaggerates what the central bank can do within the financial system. The proposal for free banking, on the other hand, aims at introducing harmony by abolishing the central bank, the presumed cause of disharmony. This proposal, apart from its doubtful practical feasibility, turns effect into cause. The central bank, though it cannot abolish instability, can at least ameliorate some of its worst aspects. Free banking would not only fail to introduce harmony in economic life but would probably result in more instability in capitalist trade and production.

NOTES

1. As Marx ([1894] 1981, p. 656) observed, in England and Wales in 1844 there were £8.63 million of local banknotes in circulation together with £21 million Bank of England notes. Independent issuing banks were also active in Scotland and Ireland. In 1857 the total circulation of banknotes in the UK was £39 million while gold circulation was £70 million.
2. It took the Bank of England, whose history provides the basis for our analysis, a century after its establishment in 1694 to emerge as the holder of the centralized reserve of the banking system. At the time of the Napoleonic Wars the Bank's notes were the most credible means of obtaining gold, as far as other banks were concerned. It took even longer for the Bank to establish its short-term lending rate as the benchmark rate of the money market. The Usury Laws, a relic of the Middle Ages, set a ceiling of 5 per cent on the Bank's discounts until 1833.
3. 'Between the end of the Restriction Period and the beginning of the "Currency" and "Banking" controversy there occurred, almost without notice, a great change in the attitude of the Bank directors towards the regulation of their issues' (Morgan, 1965, p. 100).
4. A rigid formal relationship between the Bank of England's reserves and liabilities was precisely what currency school authors, the chief supporters of the Bank Act of 1844, desired to put in the place of Palmer's rule (Viner, 1937, pp. 224–9).
5. For more on the concept of loanable money capital, its relationship to the rate of interest, and its place in Marx's economic analysis (see Itoh and Lapavitsas, 1999, chs 3, 4, and Lapavitsas 1997).
6. It is well-attested historically that gold does not spontaneously disappear from capitalist circulation, despite the continuing encroachments of credit money: 'During all this last Victorian era the nation's stock of coined money and notes remained extraordinarily uniform: nothing could better illustrate its insignificant function in daily business, in spite of the utility of that thin film of gold, on which a few notes and piles of cheques rested, in linking the currency of Britain with the world's other currencies' (Clapham, 1944, 11, p. 299). Gold disappeared from British domestic circulation when the outbreak of World War I imposed its own pressing requirements for national payments abroad in the money metal.
7. 'As the national debt is backed by the revenues of the state, which must cover the annual interest payments etc, the modern system of taxation was the necessary complement of the system of national loans' (Marx, [1867], 1976, p. 921).
8. See also Andreades ([1909] 1966, Pt 11, ch. 1), who argues that the regulation of the paper currency and the lowering of the rate of interest concomitant upon the establishment of a national bank, were perceived as needs of commerce.
9. The state connection of the Bank of England allowed it to secure privileges which increased its private profits. The most significant privilege was to be the only joint-stock bank allowed to issue notes in the vicinity of London, the commercial heart of the country. Thus, the Bank lent money to the state at a profit and issued its privileged promises to pay at a further profit. The Bank's profits continually generated complaints and calls for the nationalization of its public activities. The Bank fiercely resisted the establishment of other joint-stock banks in London until 1833, even though the latter did not

have the right to issue notes. One of its main weapons was to prevent the inclusion of these banks into the clearing mechanism. Joint-stock banks were not admitted into the mechanism until 1854 (Gilbert, [1834] 1922, vol. II, sec. XXXII).

10. The emphasis of the Classical school on the self-regulating properties of international economic relations, and its corresponding attack on Mercantilism, actually obscured the inherently antagonistic nature of capitalist state relations.

11. For a theoretical analysis of the business cycle from a Marxist standpoint see Itoh and Lapavitsas, 1999, ch. 6.

12. In addition to price-oriented methods of altering the supply of its liabilities to banks, the central bank might also directly ration the supply. This method evidently has drastic implications for the ability of banks to satisfy the credit requirements of their own customers, and is not something to which central banks easily or normally resort. Direct rationing might also apply to the reserves of the central bank, a policy often accompanied by direct quantity controls on the reserves and the lending activities of the banks themselves. Direct credit controls evidently limit the freedom of operation of the credit system.

13. It is worth stressing that the majority of the smaller central banks are still confronted with the need to defend their own reserves of international means of payment, even if these are simply foreign exchange.

14. This note first appeared in the third German edition of the first volume of *Capital*, prepared for publication by Engels a short while after Marx's death in 1883. Nevertheless, the note was actually written by Marx with the impending edition in mind, as subsequent German editions of *Capital* make clear. In the Penguin English translation of *Capital*, used throughout this work, it is mistakenly stated that the author of the quote was Engels and not Marx.

15. 'A central bank is a banker's bank. It affords to the other banks of the community, the competitive banks, the same facilities as they afford to their customers . . . These facilities being secured to them, the competitive banks are relieved form their responsibility for the provision of currency . . . The real reason for that is not, as is sometimes supposed, that the central bank is usually a bank of issue, with the power of creating currency in the form of its own notes . . . The Central Bank is the *lender of last resort*. That is the true source of its responsibility for the currency' (Hawtrey, [1932] 1962, pp. 116–17, emphasis in original).

16. In practice, credibility only indicates the extent to which financial markets accept a particular monetary policy. That credibility is usually empirically studied in terms of the divergence of the long-term from the short-term rate of interest is confirmation of this point.

17. The intellectual origins of this approach clearly lie in Lucas' (1979) reformulation of Say's Law for the modern era. While the underlying approach is fundamentally monetarist, the failed experiments of the late 1970s and financial innovation throughout the 1980s have left theorists with little doubt that the demand for money is unstable. Thus, the older monetarist suggestion of a 'rule' to regulate the rate of growth of the money supply is clearly unworkable. Consequently, faith is now placed in the hands of the 'conservative' monopolist of legal tender, which could regulate the supply of money and keep inflation in check, if freed from the influence of politicians.

18. This is not to suggest that there is unanimity among the writers of this tradition regarding the operations of the central bank. Among post-Keynesians, for instance, there are those who believe that the central bank has no option but to continue providing all the reserves required by the banking system, given that banks have already fully satisfied the demand for loans by the real sector. Hence, the supply of money is perfectly elastic and the central bank can only manipulate the rate of interest (Moore, 1988). Others maintain that the banking system can procure reserves by its own actions (that is, through financial innovation and liability management). Thus, the supply of credit money is upward sloping and it is possible for the central bank to limit the quantity of credit money (Pollin, 1991; Rousseas, 1986).

19. In this respect, the arguments of the free banking school, analysed below, seem to abide

more closely to the underlying assumptions of neoclassical economics regarding the welfare properties of free markets. This is regardless of the feasibility of its main proposal that free competitive issue of credit money should replace legal tender.

20. The distinction between goal independence and instrument (operational) independence for the central bank is discussed in more detail in Fischer (1994, 1995).

21. See Itoh and Lapavitsas (1999, chs 7, 8).

22. It should be stressed that considerable reserve discipline continues to operate on the majority of the smaller central banks, typically those of developing countries. The requirement to possess dollars in order to confront balance of payments crises might be less rigid than that of possessing gold but amounts to an external imposition on central banks nonetheless.

23. The historical absence of free banking regimes is acutely felt by theorists who wish to argue that such a system is somehow natural. Much has been made in this respect of the supposed free banking regime that prevailed in Scotland prior to the Act of 1844 (White, 1984, ch. 2). However, it was clearly understood at the time of the Act's introduction that Scottish banking could afford to operate with small and decentralized gold reserves mostly because the banks knew that they could ultimately obtain gold quite easily from the Bank of England (Checkland, 1975, pp. 432–3).

24. The ability of the reserve asset to function as a unit of account is a thorny issue, and not sufficiently discussed in the free banking literature. No matter what its past stability might have been, the relative value of the asset could always change as the productivity of labour changes, thus inducing price instability. Under such circumstances, the appropriate composition of the commodity bundle would be far from clear, and its ability to function as means of payment, that is, to settle past debt, would be perpetually in doubt.

25. In contemporary economic literature, the inherent instability of the structure of credit (a chain of promise and counterpromise) is widely accepted. A currently influential argument claims that panics and runs on banks might occur simply because of self-validating rumours about the solvency of particular banks (Diamond and Dybvig, 1983). Free banking advocates have devoted a lot of effort to refuting this widely held opinion, but without particular success (Dowd, 1993, ch. 6).

26. Timberlake (1984) has argued that prior to the establishment of the Federal Reserve in 1907 the clearing house acted as lender of last resort and created necessary money. In other words, there was a spontaneous tendency toward centralization of the bank reserve and a rational basis for use of this reserve within the clearing house. Timberlake (ibid., pp. 14–15) also argued that: 'The Federal Reserve alternative, however, was critically different from the clearinghouse system. It introduced a discretionary political element into the monetary decision making and thereby divorced the authority for determining the system's behaviour from those who had a self-interest in maintaining its integrity.' That might be so but theory needs to recognize that the centralized banking reserve is also the nation's main hoard, and this gives to it a role in domestic circulation and in international transactions. Rationality in that context has to have broader limits than 'the self-interest' of banks.

27. Hayek (1976a, pp. 64–5) skirted around the issue when he proclaimed 'the uselessness of the quantity theory', and seemed to think that there is no constant demand for money (as the quantity theory of money presumably argues) when the issue of money is free. However, whether the demand for money is constant or not, the possibility of having too much freely issued money relative to goods cannot be simply dismissed. Smith (1936, pp. 33–5, 73–6) also devoted considerable space to the question but without offering a clear answer.

28. Glasner (1989, ch. 11) seems to believe that stabilizing the domestic price level, by applying his proposal of competitive banking based on a labour/wage standard, would also solve the problem of unstable exchange rates. But the possible imbalances and conflicts between the total quantity of credit money and the international hoard of means of payment have to be analysed explicitly and cannot be ignored.

29. What Vera Smith (1936), called 'bankmaessige Deckung'.

REFERENCES

Alesina, A. and Tabellini, G. (1987), 'Rules and discretion with non-coordinated monetary and fiscal policies', *Economic Inquiry*, **25**.

Alesina, A. and Summers, L.H. (1993), 'Central bank independence and macroeconomic performance: some comparative evidence', *Journal of Money Credit and Banking*, **25** (2).

Andreades, A. ([1909] 1966), *History of the Bank of England*, 4th edn, London: Frank Cass.

Bagehot, W. (1873), 'Lombard Street', in N. St John-Stevas, (ed.) vol. 9 of *The Collected Works of Walter Bagehot*, 1978, London: *The Economist*.

Barro, R.J. and Gordon, D.B. (1983a), 'A positive theory of monetary policy in a natural rate model', *Journal of Political Economy*, August, **91** (4).

Barro, R.J. and Gordon, D.B. (1983b), 'Rules, discretion and reputation in a model of monetary policy', *Journal of Monetary Economics*, **XII**, July.

Blanchard, O.J. and Fischer, S. (1989), *Lectures on Macroeconomics*, Cambridge, MA: MIT Press.

Canzoneri, M.B. (1985), 'Monetary policy games and the role of private information', *American Economic Review*, December, **75** (5).

Checkland, S.G. (1975), *Scottish Banking: A History, 1695–1973*, Glasgow: Collins.

Clapham, J. (1944), *The Bank of England*, vols I, II, Cambridge: Cambridge University Press.

Cukierman, A. (1992), *Central Bank Strategy, Credibility, and Independence: Theory and Evidence*, Cambridge, MA: MIT Press.

Diamond, D. and Dybvig, P. (1983), 'Bank runs, deposit insurance, and liquidity', *Journal of Political Economy*, **91**.

Dowd, K. (1989), *The State and the Monetary System*, Hemel Hempstead: Philip Allan.

Dowd, K. (1993), *Laissez-faire in banking*, London & New York: Routledge.

Fischer, S. (1994), 'Modern Central Banking', in F. Capie, C. Goodhart, S. Fischer, and N. Schnadt (eds), *The Future of Central Banking*, Cambridge: Cambridge University Press.

Fischer, S. (1995), 'Central bank independence revisited', *American Economic Review, Papers and Proceedings*, **85**, 2.

Forder, J. (1996), 'On the assessment and implementation of institutional remedies', *Oxford Economic Papers*, **48**.

Gilbart, J.W. ([1834] 1922), 'The History, Principles, and Practice of Banking', vols I, II, published as *Gilbart on Banking*, in A. S. Michie, London: G. Bell.

Glasner, D. (1989), *Free Banking and Monetary Reform*, Cambridge: Cambridge University Press.

Goodhart, C.A.E. (1985), (1988), *The Evolution of Central Banks*, Cambridge, MA: MIT Press.

Goodhart, C.A.E. (1987), 'Why do banks need a central bank?', *Oxford Economic Papers*, **39**, also published in C.A.E. Goodhart, *The Central Bank and the Financial System*, Macmillan, 1995.

Grilli, V., Masciandaro, D. and Tabellini, G. (1991), 'Political and monetary institutions and public financial policies in the industrialised countries', *Economic Policy*, **13**.

Hawtrey, R. ([1932] 1962), *The Art of Central Banking*, London: Frank Cass.

Hawtrey, R. (1938), *A Century of Bank Rate*, London, New York, Toronto: Longmans, Green.

Hayek, F.A. (1976a), *Denationalisation of Money*, London: The Institute of Economic Affairs.

Hayek, F.A. (1976b), *Choice in Currency*, London: The Institute of Economic Affairs.

Itoh, M. and Lapavitsas, C. (1999), *Political Economy of Money and Finance*, London: Macmillan.

Kydland, F.E. and Prescott, E.C. (1977), 'Rules rather than discretion: the inconsistency of optimal plans', *Journal of Political Economy*, June, **85** (3).

Lapavitsas, C. (1997), 'Two approaches to the concept of interest-bearing capital', *International Journal of Political Economy*, **27**, (1), Spring.

Lucas, R. (1972), 'Expectations and the neutrality of money', *Journal of Economic Theory*, April, 4.

McCallum, B.T. (1995), 'Two fallacies concerning central bank independence', *American Economic Review, Papers and Proceedings*, **85**, 2.

McCallum, B.T. (1997), 'Crucial issues concerning central bank independence', *Journal of Monetary Economics*, **39**.

Marx, K. (1973), *Grundrisse*, London: Penguin/NLR.

Marx, K. ([1867] 1976), *Capital*, vol I, London: Penguin/NLR.

Marx, K. ([1894] 1981), *Capital*, vol III, London: Penguin/NLR.

Moore, B. (1988), *Horizontalists and Verticalists: The Macroeconomics of Credit Money*, Cambridge: Cambridge University Press.

Morgan, E.V. (1965), *The Theory and Practice of Central Banking, 1797–1913*, London: Frank Cass.

Parnell, H. (1827), *Observations on Paper Money, Banking, and Overtrading*, London: Ridgway.

Parnell, H. (1832), *A Plain Statement of the Power of the Bank of England and of the Use It Has Made of It*, London: Ridgway.

Persson, T. and Tabellini, G. (1993), 'Designing institutions for monetary stability', *Carnegie-Rochester Conference Series on Public Policy*, December, 39.

Pollin, R. (1991), 'Two theories of money supply endogeneity: some empirical evidence', *Journal of Post Keynesian Economics*, **13**, (3), Spring.

Rogoff, K. (1985), 'The optimal degree of commitment to an intermediate monetary target', *Quarterly Journal of Economics*, November, **100** (4).

Rogoff, K. (1989), 'Reputation, Coordination, and Monetary Policy' in R. Barro (ed.), *Modern Business Cycle Theory*, Oxford: Blackwell.

Rousseas, S. (1986), *Post-Keynesian Monetary Economics*, Armonk: ME Sharpe.

Sayers, R. (1957), *Central Banking After Bagehot*, Oxford: Clarendon Press.

Selgin, G. (1988), *The Theory of Free Banking*, Totowa, NJ: Cato Institute/Rowman & Littlefield.

Smith, V. ([1936] 1990), *The Rationale of Central Banking*, Indianapolis: Liberty Press.

Timberlake, R.H. (1984), 'The central banking role of clearinghouse associations', *Journal of Money, Credit, and Banking*, **16**, (1).

Tooke, T. (1840), *History of Prices 1838–39*, vol. III, London.

Viner, J. (1937), *Studies in the Theory of International Trade*, London: George Allen & Unwin.

Walsh, C. (1995), 'Optimal contracts for central bankers', *American Economic Review*, March, **85** (1).

White, L. (1984), *Free Banking in Britain*, Cambridge: Cambridge University Press.

White, L. (1989), *Competition and Currency*, New York and London: New York University Press.

7. The NAIRU: a critical appraisal

Malcolm Sawyer[1]

7.1. THE POLICY IMPORTANCE OF THE NAIRU

There can be little doubting the central role which has been played in macroeconomic theory and policy, first by the natural rate of unemployment (hereafter NRU) and more latterly the non-accelerating inflation rate of unemployment (hereafter NAIRU).[2] These concepts have conveyed the message that the level of unemployment is effectively determined on the supply side of the economy (and usually seen as the labour market). Its influence on policy has arisen from its apparent message that demand reflation can have, at best, short-lived beneficial effects on employment with longer-term inflationary consequences, and that supply-side measures may have some effect on the unemployment whereas demand side measures may have some short-term effects but not any long-term or long-lasting effects. The fear of inflation, especially of rising inflation moving into hyper-inflation, has then led to a reluctance (to put it mildly) to allow the level of unemployment to fall below the NAIRU.

The central thrust of this chapter is a critical analysis of the economic theories associated with the concept of the NAIRU (which is shortly discussed in some detail). In doing so. we are particularly concerned with the impact which the concept of the NAIRU has had on policy formulation. The transfer from the theoretical to the policy level leads to the following consideration. The estimates for the NAIRU are based on the econometric estimation of models of the economy. Particular models are used and particular interpretations are placed on the relationship between the variables which the model involves. Since the NAIRU can never be directly observed, resort has to be made to the econometric estimation of wage and price equations from which an equilibrium solution for unemployment is derived and labelled the NAIRU. It is therefore important to know how valid those models are and the estimates derived from those models. Whilst some have pointed to the unreliability of those estimates (for example, Setterfield et al., 1992) and others to the degree of uncertainty surrounding the estimates (for example, Madsen, 1998), others have put a great deal of faith in specific estimates: for example the 'Tightness in the labor market is measured by the excess of CBO's estimate of the non accelerating inflation rate of unemployment (NAIRU) over the actual unemployment rate. It is an indicator of future wage inflation' (Congressional Budget Office, 1994, p. 4), and that Office uses an estimate of 6 per cent for the NAIRU.

> The sustainable rate of unemployment, or NAIRU, is believed to have risen in the UK during the 1970s and 1980s, but there is broad agreement that this increase has been partly reversed since the late 1980s. Although the magnitude of any fall is very difficult to estimate, most estimates of the current level of the NAIRU lie in the range of 6 to 8 per cent on the LFS measure of unemployment. However, considerably lower levels should be achievable in the long run through re-integrating the long-term unemployed back into the labour market, upgrading skills, and reforming the tax and benefit systems to promote work incentives. (Treasury, 1997, p. 82).

The instability of the estimates of the NAIRU can be illustrated by the following findings. Nickell (1990) estimates the equilibrium rate of unemployment (equivalent to the NAIRU) in the UK as having risen as follows (with actual rates of unemployment given in parenthesis): 1956–59: 2.2 per cent (2.24 per cent); 1960–68: 2.5 per cent (2.62 per cent); 1969–73: 3.6 per cent (3.39 per cent); 1974–80: 7.3 per cent (5.23 per cent); 1981–87: 8.7 per cent (11.11 per cent); 1988–90: 8.7 per cent (7.27 per cent).

Layard et al. (1991, p. 436) report actual and equilibrium unemployment for 19 countries for each of three decades and an essentially similar pattern is provided. namely the two types of unemployment move together. Lombard (1995) reports three estimates for the NAIRU in France for the early 1980s (when the actual unemployment rate averaged 8.3 per cent) of 9.0 per cent, 7.7 per cent and 6.9 per cent which suggest a high level of NAIRU and some sensitivity to methods of estimation. Some further estimates covering a wide range of countries is given OECD (1994, p. 22) and a similar picture is given in figures reported in ECE (1992, Table 5.7, and summarized in UNCTAD, 1995, p. 170).

Some further estimates covering a wide range of countries is given in Table 7.1, where the NAWRU is the non-accelerating wage inflation rate of unemployment which is clearly closely related to the NAIRU. The tendency of the NAWRU to mimic the actual level of unemployment over time is clear from that table. A similar picture is given in figures reported in ECE (1992, Table 5.7, and summarized in UNCTAD, 1995, p. 170). Setterfield, Gordon and Osberg (1992).

> suggest that estimates of the NAIRU [for Canada] are extremely sensitive to model specification, the definition of variables and the sample period used. [Further] . . . the final range of all NAIRU estimates . . . is about 5.5 percentage points. Indeed, the size of this range is so great that it covers virtually the entire range of male unemployment rates in Canada since 1956.

Table 7.1   Unemployment rates and NAWRU averages

	1970–79	1980–89	1990–93	1994
Non-European countries				
– unemployment rates	4.6	5.9	5.6	5.7
– NAWRU	4.8	5.8	5.4	5.5
Four major European countries				
– uemployment rates	4.3	8.7	8.8	10.2
– NAWRU	4.3	8.4	9.0	9.4
Small EC countries				
– unemployment rates	4.7	13.4	12.9	16.7
– NAWRU	4.6	12.5	14.1	15.0
Other European countries				
– unemployment rates	1.3	2.1	3.8	5.8
– NAWRU	1.3	2.1	3.5	5.1

Note: NAWRU is non-acceleratng wage inflation rates of unemployment.

Source: OECD (1994, p. 22).

The Directorate-General for Economic and Financial Affairs of the European Commission concluded that the concept of the NAIRU is 'unusable operationally' because

> empirical studies on both sides of the Atlantic have shown that large variations in NAIRU may be caused by apparently small differences in sample, retained explanatory variables and analytical formulation. Furthermore, the confidence interval around these estimates is so large that it generally contains the whole historical range of unemployment rates observed in the last 15 to 20 years.[3]

But as UNCTAD (1995, p. 172) observes 'natural rate estimates are still used to assess and guide macroeconomic policy, thereby contributing to rising unemployment'.

One expression of the belief in the NAIRU is given by Stiglitz when he writes that

> I have become convinced that the NAIRU is a useful analytic concept. It is useful as a theory to understand the causes of inflation. It is useful as an empirical basis for predicting changes in the inflation rate. And it is useful as a general guideline for thinking about macroeconomic policy. (Stiglitz, 1997, p. 3)

Another expression is by Willem Buiter, an independent member of the UK Monetary Policy Committee, where referring to the economic theory of a 'natural rate' of unemployment, Buiter said 'I can't live without [the theory], but no one knows what the natural rate is' (reported in *Financial Times* 19.3.99).

The focus of this chapter is not on the econometric estimation of the NAIRU or on the extent to which estimates have been derived which are reliable (for policy purposes) and/or which are constant over time. The focus is rather to evaluate the theoretical foundations of the models from which the estimates of the NAIRU have been derived. There are two particular purposes in doing this. First, if the theoretical foundations are judged unsatisfactory (on some relevant criteria), then it casts some doubts on the usefulness of the NAIRU concept. Second, if there is some inflationary barrier to the achievement of full employment (as suggested by the NAIRU), then it is highly relevant to know the nature of that barrier. Numerical estimates cannot tell us about the nature of any such barrier.

In the next section, we discuss what is meant by the notion of the NAIRU, and what could be considered the essential characteristics of the NAIRU. This is followed by a section in which we reflect on the relationship between economic models and reality. Section 7.4 provides a detailed critique of two approaches to the NAIRU which have been particularly influential, one more so in the United States (that of Gordon) and the other more in Europe (Layard et al., 1991). Following from that we argue that the mechanisms by which an economy would reach any NAIRU have been inadequately specified and can be subject to much criticism. The next section argues that the models underlying the derivation of a NAIRU have not only ignored the role of aggregate demand but have also (implicitly) invoked Say's Law that 'supply creates its own demand'. Section 7.7 provides a more formal treatment of the role of aggregate demand. In the next section, consideration is given to alternative views on how real wages are settled. Section 7.9 provides a discussion of the (lack of) implications of the NAIRU for the regional distribution of unemployment, and the last substantive section, we reflect on the reasons why it has often been observed that the estimates of the NAIRU track actual unemployment (albeit with some lag).

7.2.   DEFINING THE NAIRU

At one level, the definition of a NAIRU is (almost) self-evident, namely that, within the context of a particular model, the NAIRU is the equilibrium solution (for unemployment) arising from the imposition of the condition that the rate of inflation is constant[4] (and the conditions usually also include that expectations are fulfilled). There are, though, a range of models from which such an equilibrium rate of unemployment could be derived, and the question arises as to whether all such models (and hence all derived NAIRUs) would be usually included under the general heading of a NAIRU.

There are common themes which enables us to say that the concept of the NAIRU conforms to the following:

(i)   The NAIRU is an equilibrium rate of unemployment[5] which is based on what may be seen as supply-side consideration only. In those models from which a NAIRU is derived in which there appears to be some role for aggregate demand (or more generally demand-side consideration), then the structure of the model is such that the level of aggregate demand does not affect the NAIRU. This means that there is an essential separation of the supply-side and the demand-side (akin to the classical dichotomy) and the operation of some form of Say's Law (further discussed below). 'Thus the natural rate hypothesis applies the classical proposition of monetary neutrality to unemployment, and in doing so yields the policy ineffectiveness proposition that aggregate demand policy measures cannot change the sustainable or equilibrium rate of unemployment' (Cross, 1995, p. 181: note that Cross uses the term 'natural rate' more broadly than this paper does and as a synonym for NAIRU).

(ii)   The NAIRU is not path dependent. This does not mean that the short-term NAIRU is the same as the long-term one for there can be effects of changes in unemployment on the pace of (wage) inflation (cf. Cross, 1995). But it does require that there is some effect of the level of unemployment on (wage) inflation and that there are no persistent effects arising from, for example, the level of aggregate demand and its effects on investment, capacity and labour force participation.

The term hysteresis is often used to refer to cases where there is some prolonged effect from, say, current unemployment but where the effect gradually wears off, and hence where there are no persistent long-term effects. Apart from matters of accuracy in the use of words (noting that hysteresis in its application in the area of physics does involve persistent effects), it is important to note that the concept of the NAIRU precludes persistent effects arising from the path of aggregate demand.

(iii) The NAIRU is treated as a unique equilibrium. This is not an intrinsic feature of the NAIRU and indeed models can be readily developed in which there are multiple equilibria and where those equilibria can be viewed as NAIRUs (for example, Manning, 1992). But the estimation of the underlying equations and the general discussion on the NAIRU proceed in a manner consistent with a unique equilibrium. The treatment of the NAIRU as a unique equilibrium has significant policy implications. Simply, if there are multiple equilibria, the questions arise as to the relative merits of the different equilibria and what determines around which of those equilibria the economy actually operates (assuming that the model is a reasonable representation of the economy).

There are three other key aspects of the NAIRU which are worth noting. The first is that the NAIRU is usually be seen as a 'strong attractor' for the actual rate of unemployment (Phelps, 1995), that is the actual rate of unemployment is pulled towards the NAIRU, and hence the NAIRU becomes relevant for the actual experience of unemployment. The mechanism through which the NAIRU could be a strong attractor (and more generally the stability and adjustment properties of NAIRU models) is discussed below.

However, others have adopted a rather different perspective; for example, Blanchard (1995) remarks that 'the natural rate is at best a weak attractor' and that 'the natural rate is often as much an attractee as it is an attractor' (p. xiii). If that were the case, the NAIRU loses most of its power as a concept for explaining the evolution of unemployment, even if it in some sense described an equilibrium outcome. Clearly if the NAIRU were a weak attractor (because, for example, the level of aggregate demand determined a quite different level of employment) and/or if it were an attractee (because, for example, the path of the economy influences investment which creates the level of capacity which in turn effectively determines the NAIRU),[6] then its operational power would be rather limited.

In a similar vein, as de Vroey (1997) argues, Keynes could have readily agreed with Friedman on the definition of the 'natural rate of unemployment' (as in the quote given below) as corresponding to full employment (taking into account frictional and search unemployment) but differed in the major respect as to whether there was a strong feedback mechanism leading actual unemployment to the natural rate. Keynes would view the forces leading the actual rate of unemployment towards the natural rate as weak, and the achievement of the natural rate would require a high level of aggregate demand. In contrast, Friedman would view the adjustment of real wages in the face of the excess supply of labour as the mechanism by which the unemployment moved rapidly to the natural rate.

There is, though, a strong suggestion in the usual presentation of the NAIRU that actual unemployment is strongly influenced by the NAIRU (though this may come about through policy responses to divergences of unemployment from the perceived NAIRU). There is little hint in the discussion on the NAIRU of what would prevent actual unemployment veering towards the NAIRU. Specifically, and as further discussed below, this entails the assumption that aggregate demand will readily adjust to a level appropriate for the NAIRU. It also presupposes that there are not other constraints on an economy reaching the NAIRU, and one which comes readily to mind is a balance of trade constraint. In other words, the NAIRU is generally privileged over other possible determinants of unemployment (whether actual or equilibrium level of unemployment).

The second aspect is that the NAIRU can be viewed as an equilibrium level of unemployment with 'knife edge' properties in that any significant and prolonged deviation of actual unemployment from the NAIRU will involve continuously rising or falling inflation. Since the NAIRU is presented as a unique point (rather than, say, a plateau), this knife edge property appears to rule out even the smallest of deviations from the NAIRU. Any slight fall of unemployment below the NAIRU would then be viewed as leading to rising inflation, and the dangers of hyperinflation.

However, the rate of acceleration may not be that rapid: take, for example, the coefficients estimated by Layard et al. (1991) (hereafter LNJ) for the United States. Their figures suggest that for each 1 per cent unemployment is below the NAIRU, price inflation will rise by 1.4 per cent.[7] Hence at the end of five years with unemployment 1 percentage point below the estimated NAIRU, inflation would be just over 7 per cent higher: according to the model it would, of course, continue to rise. Gordon (1997) suggests that the rate of acceleration would be rather small, and postulates that unemployment 1 per cent lower than the NAIRU for a period starting at the end of 1997 through to 2005 would lead to inflation being 5.3 per cent higher at the end of the period. These orders of magnitude lead Stiglitz to state that 'Contrary to the accelerationist view, not only does the economy not stand on a precipice – with a slight dose of inflation leading to ever-increasing levels of inflation – but the magnitude by which inflation rises does not increase when the unemployment rate is held down for a prolonged period of time' (Stiglitz, 1997, p. 9). He estimates that inflation rises by 0.3 to 0.6 per cent for each 1 per cent unemployment is below the NAIRU.

The third aspect is that the NRU is identified with a competitive equilibrium following the well-known definition of Friedman for the NRU as

> the level that would be ground out by the Walrasian system of general equilibrium equations, provided there is embedded in them the actual structural characteristics of the labour and commodity markers, including market imperfections, stochastic variability in demands and supplies, the cost of gathering information about job vacancies and labour availabilities, the costs of mobility, and so on. (Friedman, 1968, p. 8)

As Pesaran and Smith (1995) observe

> according to this definition, the natural rate of unemployment is not a constant or immutable rate, but is determined by a host of market and non-market

factors. . . . Friedman's primary reason for introducing this concept . . . was an attempt to 'separate the real forces from the monetary forces' that impinge on the market rate of unemployment. (p. 203)

The view can be taken that the NAIRU is the general concept of which the NRU is a particular case when there is perfect, rather than imperfect, competition. This is then suggestive of the notion that unemployment above the natural rate can be ascribed to imperfect competition: the 'imperfectionist approach' (Eatwell and Milgate, 1983). There are a variety of ways, though, in which the NRU (and the associated framework) differs from the imperfectionist NAIRU, and two are highlighted here. First, the role of unemployment is essentially different. In the case of the NRU, unemployment is viewed as essentially search unemployment, and there is more or less unemployment than the 'natural rate' according to whether people (on average) spend more or less time on searching for improved wage offers.

The appropriate measure of unemployment is, then, one which matches up with search unemployment. In the case of the NAIRU, equilibrium unemployment is viewed as whatever is required to hold inflation in check, and does not carry any connotation of involving full employment or of arising from search. Unemployment is essentially a proxy for the factors which bear down on wage claims and measures of unemployment have to be considered in that light. The relationship between the level of unemployment and the factors bearing down on wage claims may change over time and this is reflected in a recent statement by Alan Greenspan, when he stated that 'heightened job insecurity explains a significant part of the restraint on compensation and the consequent muted price inflation' (Greenspan, 1997) and cites a survey which found that while in the recession year of 1991, 25 per cent of workers feared being laid off, this rose to 46 per cent in the relatively low unemployment year of 1996. The NRU can be seen as an essentially microeconomic phenomenon in the sense that it is based on individual decision making on search behaviour. Given the structure of the distribution of wage offers, there is an optimal degree of search for the individual. This leads to the unemployment experience of the individual, and then adding together the behaviour of individuals leads to the natural rate of unemployment. In some contrast, the NAIRU has a macroeconomic element. As will be seen below, there are microeconomic components as the price and wage behaviour is developed, but the equilibrium condition imposes the macroeconomic requirement that inflation is constant. The NAIRU is, then, not based on the choices of individuals (except in the sense that institutional arrangements which give rise to the NAIRU could be seen as having been collectively chosen). If the NAIRU does exist, it does so at the macro or systemic level, and there is no counterpart for the NAIRU at the microeconomic or individual level. It is not possible to observe mini-NAIRUs for each individual and to obtain the NAIRU through summation.[8] It is ironic that the concept of the NAIRU should have become so central to mainstream economics which is otherwise based on methodological individualism.

7.3.   ON MODELS AND REALITY

Most, perhaps all, concepts in economic theory (and more generally in the social sciences) are not directly observable or measurable. These concepts can be seen as ideal types in the sense of Weber. However, for many concepts, there is a correspondence between the theoretical concept and statistical measures which bear the same or similar name: in the realm of macroeconomics concepts such as money, income and unemployment fall into this category. But the correspondence is not an exact one: for example, the concept of money is often deemed in terms of a medium of exchange, store of value and unit of account, but any statistical measure of money such as, say, M1, does not fully reflect all three of those functions. Further, there are differences as to how the concept is characterized by different authors or paradigms. and questions as to the degree to which the statistical measure conforms to the theoretical construct bearing the same name. There are also a range of concepts (including utility and value) which are not expected to be directly observable[9] but which are thought to be useful in undertaking economic analysis (leaving aside the question of how usefulness is to be defined).

This situation is not unique to the social sciences, and there are many examples in the physical sciences of the use of concepts which were postulated to exist but which could not be directly observed. An example of this would be the notion of the existence of the planet Pluto which was postulated to exist because of the movement of other planets before Pluto itself was observed. Even here the question could be posed as to whether the observed Pluto conformed to the concept Pluto: for example, the concept may have been given a particular mass and volume which may not have corresponded precisely with the observed Pluto and then there are clearly measurement problems. It has recently been reported that there is to be a vote in the scientific community as to whether Pluto is indeed a planet: this came to my attention sometime after the Pluto example had been used in an earlier draft. But for many of the examples derived from the natural sciences it has been eventually possible to observe the postulated concept and confirm its actual existence.

It is argued here that the concept of the NAIRU falls into the category of concepts which are drawn upon because they are deemed to be a useful aid to analysis but by their nature can never be directly observed. The underlying concept may or may not actually exist, and to some degree the users of the concept may not be too concerned as to whether the concept does actually exist, though they would be concerned that the events in the real world conformed to the predictions derived from that concept. The NAIRU can never be observed directly, though it may be possible to observe whether events in the real world (in this case the rate of inflation) do or do not conform to the predictions based on the NAIRU. Even if there is observational conformity between the real world and the NAIRU concept (which is little more than inflation rises when unemployment is below a particular level and falls when unemployment is above that level), this would not permit us to conclude anything about the nature of the NAIRU (and this leaves aside the well-known difficulties in establishing whether or not there is conformity of the real world with the NAIRU). In particular, it could not be concluded that the level of unemployment for which inflation is constant is a NAIRU (which we take here to be supply-side determined).

The situation in the case of the NAIRU is further complicated by the following considerations. First, whilst there may be general agreement on the broad nature of the NAIRU (which we have sought to summarize in the previous section), there are a variety of different concepts of NAIRU. It has already been remarked that the natural rate of unemployment (NRU) could be treated as a sub-species of the NAIRU (in the sense that both correspond to non-accelerating inflation and constant labour share) but that the NRU is based on competitive markets whereas the NAIRU is generally not. The NRU is generally calculated as an equilibrium solution of the expectations-augmented Phillips' curve. I have. though, argued elsewhere (Sawyer, 1987) that the Phillips' curve itself has at least four interpretations, and hence any NRU calculated from a Phillips' curve has similarly different interpretations which can be attached.[10] More generally, any precise definition of a NAIRU depends on a particular economic model (or perhaps more accurately sub-model) along with the notion of equilibrium which is imposed (usually that expectations are fulfilled and that real wage grows in line with labour productivity).

Second, not only have estimates of the value of the NAIRU for any particular country varied according to the precise model specification which has been used, but estimates have (especially for most European countries) proved to vary over time. Indeed a number of authors who are favourably disposed to the NAIRU (for example, Gordon, 1997; Giorno et al., 1995) have produced time-varying estimates of the NAIRU. Whilst it is clearly possible that the parameters of the model from which the NAIRU has been derived change over time, and hence that the NAIRU changes, this would be a matter of faith (or assumption) which would need to be reinforced by good reasons as to why the underlying parameters had changed.

The fact that a concept cannot in its nature ever be observed does not mean that such a concept is wrong or useless. Whilst I would doubt the benefits which have come from the application of the concept of the NAIRU, I cannot doubt that it has been useful to policy makers (in the sense that they appear to have responded to the concept, though whether it has been useful for the health of the economy is a quite separate issue). It does mean, though, that care must be exercised in the use of that concept, and the assumptions and argument which lie behind the generation of that concept must be considered. In this regard, the NAIRU generally builds in two sets of assumptions, namely that the underlying equilibrium is supply-side determined and that the appropriate equilibrium conditions include expectations being fulfilled and wages rising in line with prices after adjustment for productivity changes.

The NAIRU appears to be a concept which can never be directly observed or measured. Estimates of the NAIRU can only be indirectly derived from the estimation of econometric models and the solution of those models under certain conditions (for example, inflation constant). The estimation itself may conflict with basic assumptions of the NAIRU approach (for example, wages respond to prices in a one-for-one manner). But any estimates which are derived from the estimation of econometric models are only as reliable as the models themselves.

7.4. A CRITIQUE OF THE MODELS: PRICE AND WAGE EQUATIONS

Different authors have proposed different models of the NAIRU. This itself is significant in that the models are often substantially different (rather than differing say in whether the economy is treated as open or closed, the degree to which government activity is included). Thus what can be said of one model may not be true of another. In this section the focus is on two models which have been influential and which are broadly representative of other models. The first model considered is that of LNJ (1991) (which is a development of Layard and Nickell, 1985, 1986), as that has been probably the most fully articulated (and is similar to the one which underlies the model of the Federal Reserve and the Bank of England).[11] In this discussion the closed economy version is used since consideration of an open economy complicates but does not basically alter the points we wish to make. The second one examined is the one which underlies the work of Robert Gordon (for example, Gordon, 1982).

7.4.1. Model of Layard, Nickell and Jackman

In the LNJ (1991) model (as reflected in the equations which they estimate and in their discussion in Chapter 7[12]), the NAIRU is derived from the interaction of price and wage determination. The price equation is generally based on profit maximization under conditions of imperfect competition, and yields the well-known relationship that price is equal to a mark-up over marginal costs where the mark-up depends on the elasticity of demand facing the firm. This can be rewritten as real wage is equal to marginal revenue product of labour. This is often, though erroneously, described as a demand for labour curve (cf. Hahn, 1995, p. 46; Sawyer, 1992).[13] It is not a demand for labour curve in two ways. First, the real (product) wage is not parametric for the enterprise but rather, since the price is set by the enterprise, it is endogenous at the enterprise level. Second, the profit maximization calculations would generate a point outcome (that is a unique level of output, employment, real product wage and so on). Different levels of real product wage and employment would only result if some variables exogenous to the enterprise change, and two notable ones here would be the level of aggregate demand and the competitors' prices (cf. Sawyer, 1992).

The equation based on the decisions of the firm on output and price which relates wage, relative to price, with employment offered is generally drawn as having a negative slope, even though

> Under imperfect competition there is no compelling reason to suppose that the 'demand' for labour is negatively sloped nor is there any reason to suppose that it has only one intersection with the 'supply' curve. Increasing returns are quite sufficient to give us what we want here ... Of course if there are multiple equilibria then even if we can be sure of convergent dynamic processes, initial conditions ('history') will play an important role in which equilibrium is eventually established. (Hahn, 1995, p. 47)

The price equation which LNJ (1991) initially derive (their equation 10 p. 364) postulates that price relative to wage depends on expected demand for output relative to the level of output based on full utilization of resources, and on planned output relative to the capital stock (reflecting effect of demand on mark-up and of output on marginal costs respectively). At a later stage. unemployment is taken as (negatively) related with expected demand for output relative to output based on full utilization of resources, and thereby price (relative to expected wages) becomes dependent on unemployment.

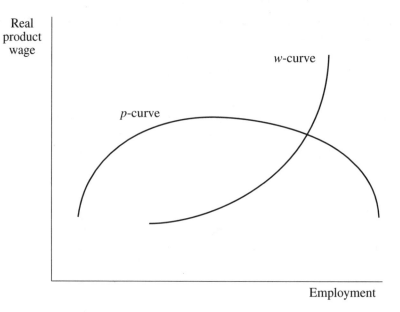

Figure 7.1   p- and *w-*curves

From these pricing considerations, an equation can be derived which relates the price relative to wage (the inverse of the real product wage) to the level of (un)employment (and a range of other factors). This is sketched for the real wage as a function of employment in Figure 7.1 as the *p*-curve. The positively sloped section is possible under imperfect competition, and gives rise to the possibility of multiple equilibria and complicates consideration of stability.

Two other approaches on the wage side lead to a relationship between the real wage and (un)employment, though the interpretation to be placed on the resulting equilibrium level of unemployment would be rather different.

The first possibility is the use of the aggregate supply of labour curve. It is widely recognized that placing a supply of labour curve alongside the price curve (which as we have argued is not a demand for labour curve but a locus of offers of real wage and employment) the resulting equilibrium level of unemployment is one of full employment (which follows from the definition of full employment as corresponding to workers being on their supply of labour curve). It is also recognized that such an equilibrium will involve less employment than an otherwise comparable position of perfect competition, and that there may be multiple equilibria which may be ranked.[14] However, whilst this approach has featured in the literature on imperfect competition, it has not, as far as we are aware, featured in the NAIRU literature. and hence is not further considered here.

The second possibility is a wage equation which is derived from the aspirations of workers and in that way is independent of enterprises pricing considerations. An example of this comes from Sawyer (1982) (and that was based on the wage equation estimated in Henry et al. 1976) where the wage change equation is of the general form:

$$Dw = a_0 + a_1 Dp + a_2 U + a_3 (w - p - T) \qquad (7.1)$$

where D is the difference operator, w log of money wage, p log of price level, U the rate of unemployment, and T a target real wage. With the condition of $a_1 = 1$ (that is, wages changes fully adjust to prices changes), the equilibrium condition of $Dw = Dp$ (assuming for convenience that labour productivity growth is zero) gives:

$$w - p = (a_0 + a_2 U - a_3 T)/a_3 \qquad (7.2)$$

which is a negative relationship between real wage and unemployment and hence a positive one between real wage and employment. The relationship here between the real wage and employment is drawn as the w-curve in Figure 7.1. The intersection of the two curves in Figure 7.1 provides an equilibrium level of unemployment which corresponds to a NAIRU.

7.4.2. Model of Gordon

The approach of Gordon (1982, 1997) is rather different, and is concerned to derive a reduced form equation linking price inflation with unemployment. He argues that

> the earlier fixation on wages was a mistake. The relation of prices to wages has changed over time . . . The Fed's goal is to control inflation, not wage growth, and models with separate wage growth and price mark-up equations do not perform as well as the equation above [reported as equation (7.5) below], in which wages are only implicit.' (Gordon, 1997, p. 17)

Apart from an unease arising from the idea that reliance should be placed on a reduced form which in some sense works better than the underlying structural equations, it also means overlooking the implicit assumptions which are being made to arrive at the reduced form. Gordon (1982) begins with a wage change equation of the form (where his notation has been adapted to that used in this chapter):

$$Dw_t = a_0 + a_1(Dp_{t-1} + \lambda_t) + a_2 X_t + a_3 x_t + a_4 z_{wt} + e_{wt} \qquad (7.3)$$

where X is real demand variable, x rate of change of X, Zw other factors influences wage changes and λ the 'equilibrium' growth of real wages.

The price change equation is similar and of the form:

$$Dp_t = \beta_0 + \beta_1 (D_{wt} - \sigma_t) + \beta_2 X_t + \beta_3 X_t + \beta_4 z_{pt} + e_{pt} \qquad (7.4)$$

what is σ is the trend productivity growth (and hence $w - \sigma$ the change in 'standard unit labour cost').

Substituting out for Dw leads to:

$$\begin{aligned}
Dp_t = \beta_0 + \beta_1\alpha_0 + \beta_1\alpha_1 Dp_{t-1} + \beta_1 (\alpha_1\lambda_t - \sigma_t) + (\beta_2 + \beta_1\alpha_2)X_t \\
+ (\beta_3 + \beta_1\alpha_3)x_t + \beta_4 z_{pt} + \beta_1\alpha_4 z_{wt} + e_{pt} + \beta_1 e_{wt}
\end{aligned} \qquad (7.5)$$

It can be seen that the demand variables which influence wages are treated as the same as those which influence prices, whereas it might be expected that demand in the labour market (perhaps negatively proxied by unemployment) would influence wage determination and demand in the output market (perhaps proxied by capacity utilization) would influence price determination. The third term on the right-hand side relates to the difference between trend growth of real wages (when α_1 is assumed equal to unity) and the trend productivity growth. Gordon (1982, p. 108) argues that this can be proxied by the deviation of productivity from trend.

The equation which is actually estimated by Gordon (1982) is price change as a function of lagged inflation (up to 20 quarters are included), weighted unemployment rate, and changes in that rate, productivity deviation (from trend), and a number of other variables which are not directly relevant here. The derivation of equation (7.5) which forms the basis of the estimated equation requires a number of assumptions, and we highlight the following:

(a) stability of the relationship between unemployment and capacity utilization and also one between changes in unemployment and capacity utilization;
(b) the absence of error correction mechanisms from both equations;
(c) (although not self evident from the above equations) the assumption that the price index relevant for wage settlements is the same price index relevant for price determination equations.

Further, changes in unemployment are often dropped from the estimated equation (as in many of the equations reports in Gordon, 1982, and more generally in Gordon, 1997).

We would argue that there is reason to cast doubt on each of these assumptions and note that many wage equations have found a role for changes in unemployment and for error correction mechanisms (that is an adjustment to the difference between actual real wages and some norm or target real wage).[15]

It is possible to argue, as Gordon (1997) does and as illustrated in the quote given above, that what matters is the reduced form relationship between inflation and unemployment since it is inflation which the Federal Reserve (and others such as the European Central Bank and the Bank of England) targets, and unemployment is used as the indicator of future inflation from which the Fed and others can make decisions on interest rates (assumed to influence aggregate demand and thereby the rate of inflation). However, that argument requires that the 'equilibrium' rate of unemployment which is calculated from the equivalent of equation (7.5) above provides an accurate estimate of the NAIRU, and as we have argued in order to arrive at equation (7.5), it is necessary to make a range of subsidiary assumptions, which may or may not be valid. The purpose of this section has been to expose some of the weaknesses of two main approaches to the estimation of the NAIRU. We have done this in light of the arguments in the preceding section on the nature of the NAIRU concept. Briefly expressed, this is that since the NAIRU can never be directly observed, the estimation of the NAIRU (and associated belief in its existence) is only as good as the underlying model from which the NAIRU is derived. If those models leave out some significant considerations, then the corresponding estimates will be misleading. This would lead us to concur with Frank Hahn when he writes that 'theories of the natural rate are amongst the class of shaky and vastly incomplete theories' (Hahn, 1995, p. 54).

7.5. EQUILIBRIUM, STABILITY AND ADJUSTMENT MECHANISMS

In this section we address the question of whether there are reasons to believe that the actual level of unemployment would tend towards the NAIRU (assuming it exists): in other words what are the adjustment mechanisms involved.

It is usual for an investigator to produce a single estimate of the NAIRU (and it should be noted that such an estimate is usually produced as a point estimate without any accompanying estimates of the standard errors or confidence intervals of such an estimate). In doing so, two assumptions are being made. First, the levels of the exogenous variables are being set at some (often unspecified) level: for example in the model derived from

Gordon (1982), some assumption has to be made about the rate of productivity growth. Second, and of more significance here, is that the assumption is made that the model provides a unique equilibrium outcome, and this assumption is generally introduced through the linearization (in levels or logs) of the relevant variables. Even within the confines of a supply-side model (and so leaving aside questions of the role of aggregate demand and of hysteresis), the presumption of a unique equilibrium must be questioned. Let us first note that models have been presented which encompass the essential notion of a NAIRU (in terms of the interaction of wage and price setting behaviour) and which generate multiple equilibrium (for example, Sawyer, 1982; Manning, 1992). This arises in effect from the nature of the price equation whereby (inverse of) the real product wage is a non-monotonic function of capacity utilization and thereby of unemployment, and in particular the real wage may rise with capacity utilization and employment over some range and fall over other ranges. This can simply be a reflection of a u-shaped cost curve and that under imperfect competition enterprises may be operating on the downward portion of that curve. This could not arise under perfect competition as the second order optimization conditions requires that the marginal product of labour is declining. Further, in models such as that of LNJ (1991) outlined above, imperfect competition in the product market is assumed, and the single aggregate price equation is intended to summarize the many enterprise or industry level price equations. There is rarely, if ever, any discussion of the problems of aggregation which would be entailed, bearing in mind that the material inputs of one enterprise are the outputs of other enterprises, whereas vertical integration is in effect assumed in the aggregate price equation. We are not concerned here with issues on the use of aggregate price equations (though it can be noted that price equations estimated at lower levels of aggregation suggest that the pattern of price formation varies between industries: cf. Sawyer, 1983). There is, though, a lack of any theoretical (since this is a theoretical matter) arguments as to the uniqueness of any equilibrium based on imperfect competition. Indeed the new Keynesian literature, which could be seen to have some overlap with the NAIRU, places some emphasis on possible multiple equilibria.

LNJ (1991, p. 370) argue that

> of course, in this context, a unique equilibrium is ensured by the linearity of the model. However, there is nothing sacrosanct about linearity, and as soon as we recognize that the impact of unemployment on the price mark-up on wages . . . can go either way, the prospect of multiple equilibria opens up. . . . It should, however, be noted that multiple equilibria of this type are rarely looked for, and never found, in any empirical investigation. For an extensive search, see Carruth and Oswald 1988.

Equilibrium in economics is often associated (indeed often synonymous with) market clearing, and as such each individual is also in equilibrium in the sense that (s)he is buying or selling what (s)he wishes to buy or sell at the prevailing (equilibrium) price. For the NRU, the equilibrium does indeed correspond to (labour) market clearing with realized expectations (on inflation). But the NAIRU relies on a rather different equilibrium concept. It is based on a macroeconomic requirement (that is one which has no individual counterpart and cannot be derived by summation from the individual level) that real wages rise in line with labour productivity, that is, that labour's share in national income is constant. In the nature of these models any other outcome would be unsustainable since it would involve a continually rising or falling labour share (and hence one which would eventually exceed the feasible limits of zero and one). There is no market identified within which the NAIRU is determined (whereas the NRU is set within the labour market), and this is further discussed below. This means that the adjustment process has to be further considered since the market mechanism of prices adjusting in the face of excess demand cannot be invoked.

The route through which equilibrium may be attained has not received much attention, and it is argued here that it is far from clear that, within the context of the models proposed, there would be a movement towards, rather than away from, the NAIRU. Stability appears to have two aspects. The first concerns the adjustment of demand to the supply-side determined levels of output and unemployment, and the second the stability of the interaction of wages and prices. Here the second of those issues is examined, leaving until later a full consideration of the adjustment of aggregate demand. In a fully integrated model it would not be possible to make this separation between supply and demand sides of the economy but in the context of the models underlying the NAIRU it is possible since some form of the classical dichotomy is deemed to operate. In effect, two separate questions are being asked: first, on the supply side. does the real wage move towards the rate which would apply in equilibrium? And second, does aggregate demand (which is assumed to set the level of unemployment in the short run) adjust towards a level consistent with the NAIRU?[16]

In the perfectly competitive model, the postulated adjustment process towards the NRU is clear: prices rise (fall) in the face of excess demand (supply). There are some well-known difficulties with this concerning the question of who is the price adjuster is a model with only price takers (Arrow, 1959). In the competitive case, it is then assumed that the aggregate behaviour of the (average) real wage can be derived from a consideration of individual labour markets, and specifically that the real wage (relative to productivity) falls (rises) in the face of high (low) unemployment (as a proxy for excess supply of labour). It should also be noted that for consistency (and from the application of Walras' Law) excess supply (demand) in the labour market is matched by excess demand (supply) in the product market and hence that prices rise (fall) relative to wages in the product market when wages fall (rise) relative to prices in the labour market.[17] It should be noted here that this approach is based on the excess supply of labour (high unemployment) being matched by an excess demand for output (high capacity utilization). It is rather counterintuitive to think that high unemployment is associated with high capacity utilization. Indeed, the assumption which runs through most discussions of inflation and unemployment is the reverse, namely that unemployment and capacity utilization are negatively related, often expressed in terms of Okun's Law.

The nature of the adjustment process is rather different when the imperfectly competitive case is taken. The NAIRU is intended to represent an equilibrium position from the interaction of wage and price setting. But the wage- and price-setting behaviour are drawn from rather different considerations. Although the corresponding curves (for example, the *p*- and *w*-curves in Figure 7.1) are placed together on the same diagram, the question is whether there is any 'market place' where they interact such that the NAIRU (and the corresponding real wage) can be determined. The familiar analysis is of the interaction of the demand schedule for and supply schedule of a particular product where they meet in the market for that product, and the adjustment of price takes place in that market at a speed which depends on the extent of excess supply or demand. But that is not the case with the wage and price behaviour. In this regard the *p*- and *w*-curves in Figure 7.1 are on a par with the IS-LM lines: they relate to the aggregate level, drawn from different considerations and await a specification of the disequilibrium behaviour. In the case of the IS-LM model, though, it is usually assumed that *Y* rises (falls) when *Y* is below (above) the IS curve, and *r* falls (rises) when *r* is above (below) the LM curve. For the NAIRU, the real wage adjusts on both the price side and the wage side, and the adjustment of the level of economic activity is left unspecified. The general notion is that when unemployment is below the NAIRU, wages rise faster than (expected) prices from wage determination considerations,[18] but prices rise faster than (expected) wages from price determination considerations, giving rise to accelerating inflation. The overall effect on realized real wages clearly depends on the relative size of the wage inflation and price inflation (and could depend on the responsiveness of wages and prices to unemployment and capacity utilization respectively and on the accuracy of wage and price expectation formation). But it is also the case in the LNJ type model that, when unemployment is, say, below the NAIRU, the real wage may be higher or lower than the equilibrium real wage. The additional of an error correction mechanism for both wage and price equations could diminish the problem raised here though it does not eliminate it, in part because the value of the wage–price ratios towards which adjustments are made are different from each other and from the 'equilibrium' wage–price ratio.

In the model of LNJ (1991), from their equations (44) and (45) in Chapter 8, the NAIRU can be solved for (their equation 47) under the assumption of $D^2p = 0$, $Du = 0$ (hence constant inflation and unemployment). It is also possible to solve out for the equilibrium real wage. Now suppose unemployment is below the NAIRU, then their equation (48) clearly indicates that price inflation would rise. Whilst expectations and misperceptions will play a role, in the price adjustment equation, $p - w$ will be higher from lower unemployment by a factor β_1 times U and β_{11} times DU, and from the wage equation $w - p$ will be higher from lower unemployment by a factor β_1 times U and β_{11} times DU. The real wage may be rising or falling, and depending on its initial level moving towards or away from the equilibrium real wage.[19]

7.6. THE ROLE OF DEMAND AND SAY'S LAW

Although the NAIRU is derived from supply-side considerations, it is still necessary to ask the question as to whether there is reason to think that the aggregate demand will move to a level which is consistent with the NAIRU. In other words, are there reasons to think that the wages and profits which would be generated from output at the NAIRU would lead to a level of expenditure which would willingly buy that level of output? The issues which arise here are by no means new, and indeed were a key element in the development of the neoclassical synthesis (following, for example, Modigliani, 1944; Patinkin, 1951, 1965). It was generally considered then that there was a sense in which the real balance effect did permit the eventual restoration of full employment through higher levels of aggregate demand, but with the recognition that any such restoration would take a long time. The argument is well known, namely that a lower price level raises the real value of stock of money, which through a wealth effect on consumer demand, stimulates a higher level of demand.

There were always two important reservations to be made to this argument. First, the argument concerns the effects of a *lower* price level – it is a comparative static argument on the effects of one price level lower than another. But, of course, to actually move from one price level to another requires that prices *fall*, and the effects of a *falling* price level may be quite different from the effects of a *lower* price level. The effects of falling prices on expectations, confidence and the stability of the financial system all suggest that the achievement of a higher level of demand through the real balance effect was not without danger. Second, the effect of a lower price level comes through its effect on the value of 'outside' money, that is money which has been created outside of the private economy and which constitutes net worth (for which there is no counterpart liability) for the private sector (Kalecki, 1944). Since credit money involves matching assets and liabilities, it does not constitute net worth for the private sector, and in industrialized economies 'outside' money is, at most, to be identified with government-issued money.

The central question concerning aggregate demand can be readily exposed by reference to the LNJ (1991) model. When their model has been extended to encompass open economy and demand aspects, there are five basic equations (price equation, wage equation, link between output/capacity and unemployment, aggregate demand equation and competitiveness equation), from the equilibrium levels of the wage–price ratio, output, unemployment and competitiveness and demand can be solved. The aggregate demand equation is:

$$y_d = \sigma_{11} x + \sigma_{12} r^* + \sigma_{13} (m - p) + \sigma_{14} Dpe + \sigma_{15} c^* \qquad (7.6)$$

where x includes fiscal stance, world economic activity and world relative price of imports, the foreign real rate of interest is $r^* = I^* - Dp^*e$ (nominal rate of interest minus expected foreign inflation), $m - p$ is (log) real money supply, Dpe expected inflation and c^* expected long-run competitiveness. It can be readily seen that if the level of demand (y_d) is to adjust to the level of output as set on the supply side, one or more of the variables on the right-hand side of equation (7.6) have to adjust. In the formulation of LNJ (1991), this would involve some combination of the fiscal stance, the real money supply and the expected rate of inflation. These are clearly rather different routes and involve quite different possible adjustment mechanisms. The first of those would involve adjustment by the government through either the fiscal stance or through monetary policy (assuming that the government can change the money supply). This is perhaps the more likely route especially if governments have some belief in the NAIRU and adjust fiscal stance and monetary policy to guide unemployment towards the NAIRU. The second possibility would be the adjustment of the price level, and we cast doubt on the empirical relevance of this below. The third would be some adjustment to price expectations.

It may be interesting to note the following in the LNJ approach: suppose that the fiscal stance is changed such that there would be a 1 per cent decrease in demand. Then prices have to fall to increase the real balance effect by a comparable amount. Further, suppose that the size of the real balance effect on demand is 0.05. The real balance effect only arises from changing prices in respect of exogenous money, and this is taken to be equivalent to M0 (cash and reserves with Central Bank). The ratio of M0 to income is around 0.06 (for the United States). and hence prices would have to be 67 per cent lower to offset the 1 per cent decrease in demand from a change in the fiscal stance.[20] With an approximate coefficient on unemployment in the inflation change equation of 1.4 in the estimates of LNJ (1991) for the United States, in year one inflation would be 1.4 per cent lower, 2.8 per cent in year 2 and so on. Prices will be 67 per cent lower than otherwise after around 9½ years (which would involve not only inflation being lower, but also becoming negative). Assuming that during those 9½ years, the stock of money grew as it would have done otherwise, then after nearly a decade with prices falling (assuming that the initial rate of inflation was in single figures), the real value of the outstanding money stock would have tripled. This puts the real balance in its most favourable light, and takes no account of the dynamic effects of such a deflation nor the effects on the financial system. Other estimates of the effect of unemployment on the rate of inflation are lower than those of LNJ (cf. figures from Gordon, 1997 cited above), and the use of those figures would serve to reinforce the point being made here.

An alternative to an appeal to the real balance effect is one to Say's Law to the effect that supply creates its own demand, and hence there would then be no problem with aggregate demand sustaining full employment. This could apply in the case of the NRU. But the NAIRU is rather different in the sense that it does not correspond (in general) to a position of market clearing and there is involuntary unemployment. At the prevailing wages (where the real wage is presumed to be higher than that which would appertain in a comparable perfectly competitive case), the sum of notional (in Clower's terminology) demands will equal the sum of notional supplies. For individuals unable to effect their notional supplies, their actual supplies will be below the notional ones, and hence their actual demands below their notional ones. If Say's Law is taken to be that potential supply would create an equivalent amount of aggregate demand, and that potential supply corresponds to full employment, then when actual supply of labour is below the potential, we can speculate on how supply compares with demand. If their marginal propensity to spend is equal to unity, Say's Law continues to hold, and there is no problem: but note the assumption is required that the marginal propensity to consume equals unity.

The conclusion which can be drawn from this discussion is that there is no convincing mechanism given by which aggregate demand would adjust to undermine a level of unemployment equal to any supply-side determined NAIRU.

7.7.   THE ROLE OF AGGREGATE DEMAND

The discussion above makes clear that aggregate demand plays no role in the determination of a NAIRU (indeed that has been part of our definition of a NAIRU). To reinforce the point on the neglected role of aggregate demand and its significance, a simple model is presented below which reflects some features viewed as significant in thinking about a NAIRU but generally absent from other models. The purpose of this model is not to claim that this is the right one, and others wrong (for all these models should be regarded as figments of the imagination), but rather to reflect these influences so that others can judge their relevance. Variables have conventional definitions and are in logs (unless otherwise indicated), D is the difference operator.

The wage equation repeats equation (7.1) above:

$$Dw = a_0 + a_1 Dp + a_2 U + a_3 (w - p - T) \tag{7.7}$$

From this bargaining approach, under the equilibrium condition of $Dw = Dp^e = Dp$, it can be derived that:

$$-a_3 (w - p) = a_0 + (a_1 - 1) Dp + a_2 U + + a_3 T \tag{7.8}$$

However, a different specification of the price equation is used and this is given by:

$$p - w = b_0 + b_1 CU + (a - 1)(k - 1) + \log f \tag{7.9}$$

where this is derived from profit maximization with a homothetic production function of the form $Y = f(L^\alpha K^{1-\alpha})$, $f' > 0$, and the second derivative f'' can be positive or negative depending on the returns to scale, CU represents capacity utilization, k is the log of a measure of the capital stock and l is the log of employment. In the price equation $\log f'$ can be positive or negative. The mark-up of price over marginal cost depends on the elasticity of demand, and variations in the elasticity of demand over the business cycle are reflected in term involving CU, and b_1 can be positive or negative. Capacity utilization can be thought of as measured against some convention of full capacity. The terms $k - l$ and $\log f'$ arise from the marginal productivity of labour term, and hence can be treated as reflecting marginal costs. As an approximation $k - l$ is equal to $k - n + U$ (where n is log of full employment) and U is the rate of unemployment by approximating $\log (1 - U)$ by $- U$. The link between CU and U is written as $CU = -cU - e(k - n)$ (c, e positive) to reflect that CU can shift relative to U, depending on the level of investment.

Combining these equations (which at this stage appear to omit any reference to aggregate demand) yields:

$$0 = a_0 + (a_1 - 1) Dp + a_2 U + a_3 T - a_3 b_0 - \alpha_3 b_1 (-cU - ek + en)$$
$$- a_3 (a - 1)(k - n + U) - a_3 \log f \tag{7.10}$$

and rearranging gives:

$$[-a_2 - a_3 b_1 c + a_3 (\alpha - 1]U = a_0 - a_3 b_0 + (\alpha_1 - 1) Dp + a_3 T - a_3$$
$$(eb_1 + (a - 1)(n - k) - a_3 \log f \tag{7.11}$$

In this equation, α_2 is negative, hence $-\alpha_2$ positive, $\alpha_4 b_1 c$ can be of either sign, and $\alpha_3 (\alpha - 1)$ is expected to be positive.

The effects of higher inflation is negative if $\alpha_1 - 1$ is negative (unless $\alpha_1 = 1$) and so higher inflation lowers unemployment at the cost of lower real wage. The effect of a higher k depends on the sign of $\alpha_3 b_1 e + (\alpha - 1)$ which we see as likely to be negative so that a higher k lowers U. The effect of n is the opposite of the effect of k (and hence is thought likely to raise the rate of unemployment). Finally, a higher value of f' is associated with higher unemployment.

Equation (7.11) clearly suggests that the level of unemployment (which could be described as a supply-side equilibrium level of unemployment based on the mutual consistency of wage and price behaviour) depends on the rate of inflation, the target real wage, the log of the capital stock (k), the level of full employment and f'. A solution for the equilibrium real wage can also be derived from this model.

The significance of all of the variables included (other than the rate of inflation which would in any case drop out if $\alpha_1 = 1$) is that they are likely to be both path dependent and to be influenced by the level of aggregate demand through its effects on investment and the capital stock. There is though in this model a minimum level of unemployment which is set by the extent to which the capital-output ratio can be raised (and hence the real wage).

This model would still involve an 'equilibrium' rate of unemployment which reconciles wage and profit claims, and has some of the attributes of a NAIRU. However, it hopefully serves to illustrate the dependence of that 'equilibrium' rate of unemployment on the path of aggregate demand. Further, whether this 'equilibrium' rate of unemployment involves a significant degree of unemployment depends on the degree to which the real wage aspirations of workers can be fulfilled by a higher capital stock (which would serve to create a higher level of capacity and a higher capital–output ratio).

7.8.   HOW ARE REAL WAGES SETTLED?

The derivation of the NAIRU which has been outlined above depends on
the interaction of price determination and wage determination in circumstances where those determinations are undertaken separately. This is
reflected in, for example, Figure 7.1 where prices and wages are viewed as
being set independently, even though enterprises and (sometimes) households are involved in both sets of decisions. This separation and interaction
is a general feature of NAIRU models. There are real wage implications of
both price and wage determination, and in effect it is variations in the level
of economic activity (measured by the level of employment in Figure 7.1)
which reconciles the conflicting real wage implications.

   This general approach clearly assumes that the predominant force which
influence real wages and the level of economic activity is the interaction of
price and wage formation undertaken on a decentralized basis. The essential decentralization involved here is the separation between wage and price
determination. The question to be raised here is whether this captures the
essence of the ways in which wages and the level of economic activity are
settled in an economy.

   It can readily be acknowledged that in most (perhaps all) market economies the determination of nominal prices and of nominal wages take place
in different arenas. But the question is whether both of them generate relationships between real wages and some measure of the level of economic
activity (akin to that envisaged in Figure 7.1). There are (at least) three
alternative mechanisms.

   The first alternative would be where wage and price determination is
undertaken in a centralized manner, and specifically that there is central
agreement over the ratio of wages to prices, that is, the real product wage.
In general, the real wage which would result would depend on many factors
such as the bargaining strengths and skills of the two parties, but would not
necessarily include any reference to variables linked to the level of economic activity such as unemployment and capacity utilization. Specifically,
real wage claims could be reconciled around the bargaining table, and in
effect the level of economic activity does not need to be invoked to secure
that reconciliation. The levels of (un)employment and of capacity utilization could then be determined by the level of aggregate demand forthcoming at the agreed real wage.

   The second alternative would arise where the process of decentralized
enterprise level bargaining is effectively over the real product wage at the
level of the enterprise. The more usual formulation is to view nominal
wages being set in the process of wage negotiations. and then the enterprise
through its pricing decision set the real product wage (and the nominal

wage translates into a real wage for the workers, depending on the general price level).

The third alternative arises where wage determination is not only in terms of money wages but also where there are no direct implications for real wages arising from the determination of wages. For example, efficiency wage considerations can be seen to lead to a relationship between the ratio of money wages to unemployment benefits and the level of unemployment, with no immediate implications for real wages. Such implications would arise from the way in which unemployment benefits are set: for example if those benefits are adjusted to maintain their value in real terms, then real wages are eventually influenced by the real value of unemployment benefits. However, if unemployment benefits can be treated as the numeraire of the economy with no adjustment (by government) of benefits to the level of wages or prices, then there are no implications for real wages. It would then be the case that the interaction of the pricing decisions of firms (the p-curve in Figure 7.1) and the level of aggregate demand would effectively settle the real product wage and the level of economic activity. In turn the level of economic activity would, via the level of unemployment, settle the ratio of money wages to unemployment benefits.

The purpose of this discussion is to illustrate the point that there are alternative ways in which wage and price determination can be viewed. It has been suggested that where price determination and wage determination take place independently and where wage determination involves real wage implications, then the equilibrium level of unemployment can be seen as akin to a NAIRU and reconciles the claims on national income of enterprises and workers. But in other situations, such as that illustrated in the previous paragraph, price and wage determination need not settle the equilibrium level of unemployment.

7.9. NAIRU AND THE REGIONAL DISTRIBUTION OF UNEMPLOYMENT

There are generally considerable variations in the rate of unemployment across the regions of an industrialized market economy, and the purpose of this section is to consider whether the NAIRU concept is consistent with that observation. There are, of course, other important variations in rate of unemployment, for example between ethnic groups, and some similar issues would also arise. For convenience I will refer to regional variations.

It has been argued above that the NAIRU is a macroeconomic phenomenon, in the sense that it is the rate of unemployment which is deemed to be consistent with a constant rate of inflation. It is (implicitly) assumed that there are little variation in the pace of inflation across regions. But whilst it is a macroeconomic phenomenon, it does have microeconomic underpinnings as should be clear from the previous discussion. In this vein, it is possible to work back from the aggregate level NAIRU to consider how the corresponding equilibrium rate of unemployment would vary across regions.

Following LJN (and simplifying as before), their equation (20) (p. 107) could be replicated on (say) a regional basis as $u_i^* = \beta_i(1 - \alpha_i\kappa_i)/\alpha_i\kappa_i(1 - b_i)\varphi$ where i indexes the regions. The b_i term represents the ratio of benefits to wages which is likely to vary across regions whether through variations in the level of unemployment benefits or in the level of wages. This equation then reads that the rate of unemployment will be higher in those regions with higher benefits to wages ratio (and hence when there is a national level of benefits with relatively low wages), with lower market power (κ) (and hence lower prices relative to wages, and higher real product wages) and a higher mark-up of wages over alternative income (which may reflect higher union power or it may reflect that higher wages have to be offered to ensure a high level of work effort).

This formula for equilibrium regional unemployment highlights the general feature of the NAIRU, namely that there is no explicit role for productive capacity or for demand. Clearly this formula rules out that the cause of high unemployment in a region could be lack of demand for the products of the region or through a lack of productive capacity.

On a regional basis, the regional NAIRUs would differ because either the regional p-curves or the regional w-curves differ. In so far as the differences come from the p-curve, that is from a difference in productive capacity or in the degree of market power, then the observed pattern across regions would be that high wages are associated with high levels of employment (and hence low unemployment). In so far as the differences come from the w-curve, then the observed pattern would be that high wages are associated with low levels of employment (and high unemployment), assuming that the slope of the p-curve is negative (that is, where there are diminishing returns). The generally observed pattern is that wages and levels of employment are correlated across regions, which suggests that it is differences in the level of productive capacity or market power which generates cross-regional differences.

In respect of variations across groups (for example, by skill level or by gender), if we can assume that the availability of productive capacity for different groups is little different, then the major cause of variations would be the equivalent of differences in the position of the w-curve. The groups with less bargaining power, which would be reflected in a w-curve further to the right, would receive lower wages but gain from higher employment levels. Similar groups whose work effort is more easily monitored, and for which efficiency wage considerations are less significant, would also find the corresponding *w*-curve to the right. Although this may warrant further investigation, causal observation may suggest that those groups with low wages tend to suffer from less employment opportunities, counter to the argument just developed.

7.10. NAIRU TRACKING ACTUAL UNEMPLOYMENT

It has been observed (for example, Worswick, 1985) that there is a tendency for the estimates of the NAIRU to move in line with observed unemployment.[21] One response to this would be that movements in the NAIRU are driving movements in the actual level of unemployment, that is the NAIRU is acting as a strong attractor for actual unemployment. This argument runs into two particular difficulties. First, although I am not aware of any formal tests on this, it would seem that at most the change in NAIRU and the change in actual unemployment are contemporaneous rather than the NAIRU leading actual. Second, the point would be more convincing if there was supporting evidence that movements in the factors which are said to determine the NAIRU were consistent with the movements in the NAIRU. I have argued elsewhere (Sawyer, 1998) that the (rather limited) evidence on movements in variables such as level of unionization and unemployment benefits over the past 20 or so years should have reduced the NAIRU whilst most estimates of the NAIRU have risen. These two difficulties do illustrate that the NAIRU is obtained from estimated price and wage equations, and those estimates can only be *ex post*.

There are a number of reasons for thinking that estimates of the NAIRU will trail the actual experience of unemployment. The first arises from the observation that the NAIRU is also the rate of unemployment which maintains a constant labour share. It is generally observed that whilst the share of labour does vary over time (and has tended to decline in recent years) it does not move greatly. Thus an estimate of the rate which maintains a constant labour share is likely to fall within the range of experienced unemployment, and as the experienced rate of unemployment changes (and specifically if, as in most European countries over the past two decades, shifts up) so will the estimated NAIRU.

The second reason has often been placed under the label of hysteresis, whereby the path of unemployment influences the position of any equilibrium end-point. One mechanism which has been much discussed is that the experience of unemployment has persistent effects. For example, there are three main elements to the idea that the duration of unemployment can effect a worker's chance of finding a job:

1. effects on job search;
2. effects on the worker's skill, motivation and morale;
3. job screening and employer perceptions. (LNJ, 1991, p. 258)

Insofar as these factors lead to a combination of reduced effective supply of labour or a greater mismatch between supply and demand, they may lead to rising unemployment. It is in keeping with the NAIRU approach that this is an essentially supply-side explanation.

Another mechanism is the adjustment of the capital stock, which has been discussed above (see also Sawyer, 2000). In terms of Figure 7.1 the *p*-curve will tend to shift inwards as capacity falls.

These considerations lead to a more significant one, namely how useful are the estimates of the NAIRU? Price and wage inflation and unemployment (and other variables which may be of relevance) fluctuate over the business cycle (and generally do not display any pronounced trend). Now suppose that the mechanism generating price inflation was quite separate from the mechanism which generates unemployment. A regression of price inflation on unemployment may or may not be successful (and it is known that there are many ways in which price inflation and unemployment can be measured so that it may be remarked cynically that only the successful regressions are publishable). Suppose it is successful (in the sense that it passes relevant statistical criteria, that the coefficient on lagged price inflation is not significantly different from unity and that on unemployment is negative and statistically significant) and an equilibrium solution for unemployment is derived and given the name of the NAIRU. What does it tell us ? The most it can tell us is that if over the estimation period unemployment had been at a particular level (the calculated NAIRU) then inflation would have been stable.[22] But it cannot tell us what are the determinants of the NAIRU, and in particular cannot tell us what would have happened if the level of aggregate demand had been higher (and we would expect that as a consequence investment and then the capital stock higher).

7.11. CONCLUSIONS

Two issues arise in respect of the NAIRU approach which should be kept distinct. The first is the question of whether inflation (notably wage inflation) is negatively related to the level of unemployment (though other variables may be involved as well). Much empirical effort has been devoted to investigating the answer to that question (and I have participated myself,

Henry et al. 1976). The second is the question of whether there is a level of unemployment for which inflation would be constant and, if so, what are the determinants of that level of unemployment? In particular, is any such level of unemployment to be regarded as capable of being shifted through changes in the capital stock, measures to arrive at a consensus over the distribution of income and so on? There is some link between these questions in that if the answer to the first question is no, then it is not possible to calculate a NAIRU.[23]

The focus of this chapter has been more on the second question than the first. For example, if the NAIRU corresponded to the NRU (in the sense of being a level of unemployment which was accepted as full employment), then the apparent trade-off between wage inflation and unemployment would be observed, but the NRU would not constitute a limit on economic activity in that most people would not wish to push employment past the full employment level. The relevant question would then be how strong an attractor is the NRU and what is the role of aggregate demand in reaching that point.

There is little consideration of aggregate demand in connection with the NAIRU. Aggregate demand has to be considered in deriving relationships between the real wage and employment, and in underpinning any level of employment (equilibrium or not) which could be achieved. Further, aggregate demand enters into the determination of the level of unemployment in two further respects, namely through its effect on capacity and in a range of cases where the relationship between price and wage is settled at the enterprise level.

Stiglitz (1997) elaborates three criteria for evaluating the NAIRU:

> does the derivation of unemployment from some natural rate provide a robust and useful way to predict changes in the inflation rate? . . . The second criterion [is] can economists explain why the NAIRU changes over time? . . . [T]he third criterion asks whether the NAIRU is a useful way to frame policy discussions despite all the uncertainty surrounding its precise level and direction of change. (p. 4)

This chapter has only briefly touched on the first two criteria, and has considered matters which are relevant to the third criterion. With regard to that criterion, the basic arguments pursued in this chapter are that there are a series of theoretical weaknesses with the approach to the NAIRU, and in particular there has been a rather cavalier dismissal of the role of aggregate demand. Specifically, if the notion that for some given set of institutional and other arrangements there is a level of unemployment which would be consistent with constant unemployment, then it is necessary to explore the determinants of that level of unemployment, and the degree to which it can be shifted over time with appropriate aggregate demand, income distributional and supply-side policies.

NOTES

1. I am grateful to Philip Arestis and to participants in the Labour Market Group for comments on an earlier draft.
2   The distinction is maintained in this paper between the 'natural rate of unemployment' (NRU) as defined by Friedman (1968) (see quote later in the text) as the level of unemployment which would correspond to a market clearing competitive labour market and the NAIRU as the level of unemployment at which inflation would be constant which would include the NRU as a special case where markets are competitive.
3. The quote is from *European Economy*, Supplement A, January 1995, p. 2 as reported in UNCTAD (1995, p. 172).
4   It can be noted here (as others such as Cross, 1995 have done) that the NAIRU is a misnomer in that the equilibrium refers to constant inflation (rather than rising or falling inflation), and hence it is the price level which is non-accelerating.
5. Any particular NAIRU is the solution to a particular model with the imposition of certain equilibrium conditions (for example, that expectations are fulfilled). The term equilibrium is used in the limited sense of a solution to the model in question when a range of stationary conditions have been imposed on the model, and it is not intended that the term carries any broader connotation such as market clearing.
6. For a model which leads to this type of conclusion see Sawyer (2000).
7. The figures which LNJ (1991) estimate for the United States are β_1 3.10 γ_1 0.32 β_2 2.10 γ_2 0.37. From their equation (48) it can then be calculated that the implied coefficient on $(u - u^*)$ (actual unemployment minus the NAIRU) in the equation for the acceleration of inflation is then 3.42/2.47 which is approximately 1.4.
8. Thus the NAIRU is macroeconomic in the sense described by Pasinetti when he wrote that 'It must be noticed that the foregoing investigation is not "macro-economic" in the sense of representing a first simplified rough step towards a more detailed and disaggregated analysis. It is macro-economic because it could not be otherwise. Only problems have been discussed which are of a macro-economic nature; an accurate investigation of them has nothing to do with disaggregation. They would remain the same – i.e. they would still arise at a macroeconomic level even if we were to break down the model into a disaggregate analysis' (Pasinetti, 1974, p. 118).
9. In the case of utility, it could be argued that since it is used in the context of an individual maximizing utility, each individual (and hence the users of the concept of utility) would know by introspection whether utility existed. Similar consideration would apply to rational expectations.
10. The four alternative interpretations are: (i) labour market adjustment with expected real wage changes a function of the excess demand for labour, and unemployment is a negative proxy for that excess demand; (ii) a trade-off between inflation and the level of economic activity, (iii) expected real wage changes are a function of unemployment, which operates as the 'industrial reserve army' of the unemployed; and (iv) the 'surprise function' with movements in unemployment as a function of inflation surprises.
11. In the Federal Reserve macroeconomic model, there are two equilibrium relationships between the (log of the) real wage and the unemployment rate, one arising from the equilibrium money wage equation and the other from the equilibrium price equation. Dynamic adjustment equations for wage and price changes in terms of deviations of the actual wage (price) from the equilibrium level are estimated (Table 6, p. 22). The text calculated the NAIRU as 'a bit less than 6 per cent, currently, in terms of the civilian unemployment rate'. Source: A Guide to the FRB/U by Macroeconomic and Quantitative

Studies, Federal Reserve Board, October 1996. See also Bank of England (1999, pp. 13, 27 and 30).

12. There are, in our view, some very considerable differences in approach as between what is said in Chapters 1, 7 and 8 of LNJ (1991) and in Chapter 2. In the former, they present a variety of models in which wages and prices are settled at the firm level and the relationship between wages and unemployment benefits is a crucial one. In the latter 'we do not propose to be too specific' (p. 364), and aggregate price and wage equations interact to set the NAIRU, and there is no explicit mention of unemployment benefits.

13. For example, 'Equation (7) then becomes the marginal productivity condition and is a standard labour demand function' (LNJ, 1991, p. 341).

14. There are also issues of the stability of an equilibrium and movement to equilibrium: (cf. Sawyer, 1992).

15. For example, we estimated the relationship between unemployment and capacity utilization for the USA and found the following:

A regression of unemployment on a measure of capacity utilization (deviations of output from trend) over the period 1967 qtr 4 to 1996 qtr 4 yields
Dependent variable Unemployment U

	D1	D2	U(−1)	CU	CU(−1)	D1*T	D2*T
estimated coefficient	6.624	8.047	0.791	−0.190	0.116	0.00372	0.00902
standard error	1.559	2.067	0.064	0.015	0.024	0.00264	0.00417

rho = 0.396 (s.e. 0.124), R-squared = 0.9875, Adjusted R-squared = 0.9869, Durbin-Watson statistic = 2.0697

D1 = dummy value 1 from 1967(4) to 1980(4), 0 otherwise; D2 = dummy value 1 from 1981(1) to 1996(4), 0 otherwise; CU measure of capacity utilization, T time

These suggest that over some lengthy periods there is a time trend in the relationship and further that the nature of that time trend shifts from period to period.

Gordon (1997, fn.4) reports that the relationship between unemployment and ratio of actual to 'natural real' GDP differed in the first half of the 1990s from most of the postwar period.

16. In models such as those of LNJ (1991), aggregate demand does not depend on the distribution of income or the real wage. This permits some degree of separation between the two aspects of stability considered in the text which would not be present when aggregate demand is dependent on the distribution of income (and hence on the differential movement of prices and wages).

17. The brief description in the text refers to the neoclassical view of the competitive labour market. A perspective based on Keynes (1936) especially chapter 2 would be rather different. Our point here is not that the neo-classical analysis of the labour market is right or wrong, but rather that it does have a clear adjustment process.

18. We seek to avoid the use of the term 'labour market' here since the wage setting processes have little in common with a market in which there are demand and supply schedules based on parametric prices.

19. For the United States, their estimates are such that higher unemployment would raise the real wage since the effect of unemployment in the price equation is much greater than the effect in the wage equation. However, the pattern varies considerably across countries (cf. their Table 2, p. 406).

20. For a constant level of demand, with the change in fiscal stance equivalent to 1 per cent of income (0.01 Y), we have the following σ_{13} $D(M-p) = 0.01$ Y; (not in logs). Putting $\sigma_{13} = 0.05$, $(M-p)/Y = 0.1$, then $D(M-p)/(M-p) = -(0.01/0.05)/0.1 = 2$; hence the real value of the money stock triples, and prices would be required to fall to one-third of their initial level. At the end of 1996 the monetary base was given as just over \$450 billion and GDP in 1996 was around \$7500 billion: hence the ratio of monetary base to GDP was

circa 0.06. Within the monetary base, cash held outside the banks is given as over $395 billion, which implies an average holding of cash of a rather incredible near $1500 for each person in the US. However, figures in *Survey of Current Business*, July 1997 suggest that at the end of 1996 more than half of the cash included in the monetary base is held outside the United States (nearly $210 billion were foreign holdings from a total of $398 billion).

21. This may not have been so pronounced in the United States, where for a considerable length of time there was something of a consensus that the NAIRU was around 6 per cent, and where unemployment did not rise so dramatically after 1973 as in most other countries. Even so, the following figures do indicate some such effect:

	1960–68	1969–79	1980–88
Actual	4.74	5.85	7.38
Equilibrium	5.01	5.97	6.36

Source: LNJ (1991, p 436)

22. Even that need not be the case for the inflationary (and other) implications of a constant level of unemployment of x per cent need not be the same as the inflationary implications of unemployment of x cent when unemployment is changing.

23 However if, say, wage changes (relative to expected inflation) were a positive function of the level of unemployment, one could impose the condition that wage change equals inflation equals expected inflation, and calculate a NAIRU. But such an estimated NAIRU would not have the usual implications for counter-inflation policy.

REFERENCES

Arrow, K.J. (1959), 'Towards a theory of price adjustment', in M. Abramovitz (ed.), *The Allocation of Economic Resources*, Stanford: Stanford University Press.

Bank of England (1999), *Economic Models at the Bank of England*, London: Bank of England.

Blanchard, O. (1995), in R. Cross (ed.), *The Natural Rate of Unemployment*, Cambridge: Cambridge University Press.

Carruth, A.A. and Oswald, A.J. (1988), 'Testing for multiple natural rates of unemployment in the British economy' in R. Cross (ed.), *Unemployment, Hysteresis and The Natural Rate Hypothesis*, Oxford: Basil Blackwell.

Congressional Budget Office (1994), *The Economic and Budget Outlook: Fiscal Years 1996–2000*, Washington: Congressional Budget Office.

Cross, R. (1995), 'Is the natural rate hypothesis consistent with hysteresis?', in R. Cross (ed.), *The Natural Rate of Unemployment*, Cambridge: Cambridge University Press.

de Vroey, M. (1997), 'Accounting for involuntary unemployment in neoclassical theory: some lessons from sixty years of uphill struggle', in R. Backhouse, D. Hausman, U. Mäki and A. Salanti (eds), *Economics and Methodology Crossing Boundaries*, London: Routledge.

Eatwell, J. and Milgate, M. (eds) (1983), *Keynes's Economics and the Theory of Value and Distribution*, London: Duckworth.

ECE (1992), *Economic Survey of Europe in 1990–1991*, United Nations publications, Sales No. E.92.II.E. 1.

Friedman, M. (1968), 'The role of monetary policy', *American Economic Review*, **56**, 1–17.

Giorno, C., Richardson, P., Roseveare, D. and van den Noord, P. (1995), 'Potential output, output gaps and structural budget balances', *OECD Economic Studies*, no. 24 1995/1.

Gordon, R.J. (1982), 'Inflation, flexible exchange rates and the natural rate of unemployment', in M. Baily (ed.), *Workers, Jobs and Inflation*, Washington: Brookings Institute.

Gordon, R.J. (1997), 'The time-varying NAIRU and its implications for economic policy, *Journal of Economic Perspectives*, **11** (1), pp. 11–32.

Greenspan, A. (1997), 'Statement to the Congress', *Federal Reserve Bulletin*, March.

Hahn, F. (1995), 'Theoretical reflections on the "natural rate of unemployment"', in R. Cross (ed.), *The Natural Rate of Unemployment*, Cambridge: Cambridge University Press.

Henry, S.G.B., Sawyer, M. and Smith, P. (1976), 'Models of inflation in the U.K.: an evaluation', *National Institute Economic Review*, no. 76.

Kalecki, M. (1944), 'Professor Pigou on "The classical stationary state": a comment', *Economic Journal*, **54**.

Keynes, J.M. (1936), *The General Theory of Employment, Interest and Money*, London: Macmillan.

Layard, R. and Nickell, S. (1985), 'The causes of British unemployment', *National Institute Economic Review*, 110.

Layard, R. and Nickell, S. (1986), 'Unemployment in Britain', *Economica*, **53** (Supplement).

Layard, R,. Nickell, S. and Jackman, R. (1991), *Unemployment: Macroeconomic Performance and the Labour Market*, Oxford: Oxford University Press.

Lombard, M. (1995), 'A re-examination of the reasons for the failure of Keynesian expansionary policies in France, 1981–1983', *Cambridge Journal of Economics*, **19**, 359–72.

Madsen, J. (1998), 'The NAIRU and classical unemployment in the OECD countries', *International Review of Applied Economics*, **12**.

Manning, A. (1992), 'Multiple equilibria in the British labour market: some empirical evidence', *European Economic Review*, **36**: 1333–66.

Modigliani, F. (1944), 'Liquidity preference and the theory of interest and money, *Econometrica*, **12**.

Nickell, S. (1990), 'Inflation and the UK labour market', *Oxford Review of Economic Policy*, **6** (4).

OECD (1994), *Economic Outlook*, Paris: OECD.

Pasinetti, L.L. (1974), *Growth and Income Distribution: Essays in Economic Theory*, Cambridge: Cambridge University Press.

Patinkin, D. (1951), 'Price flexibility and full employment', in *Readings in Monetary Theory*, selected by a Committee of the American Economic Association, Blakiston, New York.

Patinkin, D. (1965), *Money, Interest and Prices*, 2nd edn, London: Harper & Row.

Pesaran, H. and Smith, R. (1995), 'The natural rate hypothesis and its testable implications', in R. Cross (ed.), *The Natural Rate of Unemployment*, Cambridge: Cambridge University Press.

Phelps, E. (1995), 'The origins and further developments of the natural rate of unemployment', in R. Cross (ed.), *The Natural Rate of Unemployment*, Cambridge: Cambridge University Press.

Sawyer, M. (1982), 'Collective bargaining, oligopoly and macro economics', *Oxford Economic Papers*, **34**.

Sawyer, M. (1983), *Business Pricing and Inflation*, London: Macmillan.

Sawyer, M. (1987), 'The political economy of the Phillips' curve', *Thames Papers in Political Economy*, Summer.

Sawyer, M. (1992), 'On imperfect competition and macroeconomic analysis', in A. del Monte (ed.), *Recent Developments in the Theory of Industrial Organisation*, London: Macmillan, 79–113.

Sawyer, M. (1998), 'New Keynesian macroeconomics and the determination of employment and wages', in R. Rotheim (ed.), *New Keynesian Economics. Post Keynesian Alternatives*, London: Routledge, 118–33.

Sawyer, M. (2000), 'Aggregate demand, investment and the NAIRU', University of Leeds, mimeo.

Setterfield, M., Gordon, D.V. and Osberg, L. (1992), 'Searching for a will o' wisp: an empirical study of the Nairu in Canada', *European Economic Review*, **36**, (1), 119–36.

Stiglitz, J.E. (1997), 'Reflections on the natural rate hypothesis', *Journal of Economic Perspectives*, **11** (1), 3–10.

Treasury (1997), *Pre Budget Report*, Cmnd. 3804, London: HMSO.

UNCTAD (1995), *Trade and Development Report*, 1995, New York and Geneva: UN.

Worswick, D. (1985), 'Jobs for all ?', *Economic Journal*, **95**.

Index